The Changing Public Sector

The Changing Public Sector: A Practical Management Guide

MALCOLM PROWLE

Gower

Published by
Gower Publishing Limited
Gower House
Croft Road
Aldershot
Hampshire GU11 3HR
England

Gower
131 Main Street
Burlington
Vermont 05401–5600
USA

British Library Cataloguing in Publication Data
Prowle, Malcolm
The changing public sector: a practical management guide
1. Public administration – Great Britain
I. Title
352.3´0941

ISBN 0 566 08216 0

Library of Congress Cataloging-in-Publication Data
Prowle, Malcolm
The changing public sector: a practical management guide / Malcolm Prowle.
p. cm.
Includes bibliographical references and index.
ISBN 0-566-08216-0 (hardback)
1. Administrative agencies–Great Britain–Management. 2. Great Britain– Politics and government. I. Title.

JN318.P76 2000
352.3´0941–dc21 00-026417

Typeset in Great Britain by IML Typographers, Birkenhead and printed in Great Britain by MPG Ltd, Bodmin.

Contents

Preface

Twenty-five years of academic and practical experience have led me to conclude that in spite of the complexity and jargon associated with the topic, management is little more than applied common sense. Unfortunately, in many organizations, common sense is not always applied in practice.

This book is about practical aspects of management in the public sector. Thus it is not a book about public policy making or political science. Over the last twenty years or so the public sector has gone through something of a revolution and the pace of change seems likely to continue into the future. Hence the approaches and techniques of management have also had to change and will continue to do so. Many times I have read books on public sector management, often written by sociologists or political scientists, which try to complicate and/or politicize what are essentially simple matters, or try to argue that the public sector is 'different' and therefore conventional managerial methods cannot be applied. I have two main comments to make on this view. Firstly, in my view it is the easiest thing in the world to complicate the essentially simple but it is much more difficult to simplify the complex and identify those key issues that make it easy to understand and apply in practice. Secondly, of course the public sector is different. A lifetime's involvement in many parts of the public sector in the UK and overseas have shown me that only too clearly. However, that does not make the basic managerial task any different and, with some degree of adaptation, most conventional aspects of management can be applied to public sector organizations (PSOs). Much of the written material I have collected over the years can be divided into two types. Those research reports, books and articles which identify the complexities and difficulties connected with various aspects of public sector management, and those which describe the attempts made by various people to put managerial principles into practice. My sympathies are with the latter group.

I have three main aims with this book:

- To set the context of public sector management in the UK by looking at the various changes in policy, configuration, culture and financing which have taken place especially over the last twenty years.
- To describe, in some depth, the various aspects of management practice (for example strategy and finance) and the ways in which they have been or can be applied in the public sector. The aim is to give the non-specialist manager or service professional a working knowledge of each aspect of management as it may be applied in the public sector. In my experience, specialist public sector managers, in areas such as finance, HR or IT, are as bad as service professionals such as doctors and teachers in building a mystique around their practices which makes them unintelligible to the non-specialist. My aim is to pull down that mystique in relation to the various aspects of management.
- To describe the changes which have been taking place recently, and are likely to continue into the future, which will impact on the public sector. I then consider the impact of these changes on the public sector itself and on its managerial practices and skill requirements.

The book is aimed at four classes of reader. Firstly, those non-specialist managers or service professionals in the public sector who require a working knowledge of each aspect of management as it may be applied in the public sector. Secondly, students who may be pursuing MBAs, undergraduate degree or diploma courses in public sector management or professional courses with a public sector dimension. Thirdly, those who sit as non-executive directors or governors, for example, in various PSOs. Although such people are often very experienced in commercial management issues, they may feel the need for a guide to management in the public sector. Fourthly, public sector managers in overseas countries who are in the process of undertaking public sector reform and who wish some practical knowledge of UK experiences.

My thanks are due to a number of people who have read drafts of the various chapters, including: Chris Potter, Tom Jones, Sharon Prowle and Stephen Rea. Also to my wife Alison for improving on my inadequate grammatical and literary skills.

Malcolm J. Prowle

List of figures

List of tables

Glossary

ABC	Activity-Based Costing
BPR	Business Process Re-engineering
BSI	British Standards Institute
CBA	Cost–Benefit Analysis
CCTA	Central Communications and Technology Agency
CUA	Cost Utility Analysis
DCF	Discounted Cash Flow
DSO	Direct Service Organization (of a local authority)
EAZ	Education Action Zone
EPR	Electronic Patent Record
FE	Further Education
FEFC	Further Education Funding Council
FM	Facilities Management
FMI	Financial Management Initiative
GSO	Government Stationery Office
HAS	Health Advisory Service
HAZ	Health Action Zone
HE	Higher Education
HEFCE	Higher Education Funding Council for England
HRM	Human Resource Management
ICT	Information and Communications Technology
IIP	Investors in People
IT	Information Technology
LEA	Local Education Authority
NHS	National Health Service
NICE	National Institute for Clinical Excellence
NPV	Net Present Value
OFSTED	Office for Standards in Education
PAF	Public Audit Forum
PBB	Priority-Based Budgeting
PC	Personal Computer
PCG	Primary Care Group (of the NHS)
PFI	Private Finance Initiative
PI	Performance Indicator
PPP	Public–Private Partnerships
PRB	Pay Review Bodies
PRP	Performance Related Pay
PSA	Public Service Agreement
PSO	Public Sector Organization
QAA	Quality Assurance Agency (for higher education)

QUANGO	Quasi-Autonomous Non-Governmental Organization
T&D	Training and Development
TEC	Training and Enterprise Council
TNA	Training Needs Analysis
TQM	Total Quality Management
VFM	Value for Money
ZBB	Zero-Based Budgeting

PART I

The UK Public Sector: Structure and Trends

CHAPTER ONE

Introduction

This century has seen substantial changes in the composition and size of the public sector of the economy in the UK and other developed countries. Moreover, the policies of successive Conservative governments in the period 1979 to 1997 saw radical changes taking place in the organization and funding of the public sector. As we move into the new millennium, the various political, economic and technological trends in the world suggest that the public sector will continue to undergo substantial change. This book is about the public sector in the United Kingdom, the changes it has undergone in the past, will undergo in the future and the impact of those changes on the practice of management in public sector organizations (PSOs). However, before considering the trends that have taken place in the sector it is first useful to give some consideration to what is meant by the term 'public sector'.

THE PUBLIC SECTOR: PROVISION AND FINANCING

In considering the meaning of the term 'public sector' it is necessary to draw a distinction between the twin issues of service provision and service financing. This is illustrated in Figure 1, using health services in the UK as an example. A similar analysis could be prepared for any other sector, such as the education sector.

SERVICE PROVISION \ SERVICE FINANCING	Public	Private
Public	***Most NHS Services*** **(1)**	***Private patients treated in an NHS hospital*** **(2)**
Private	***NHS funds used to purchase care in private hospitals*** **(3)**	***Private patient treated in a private hospital*** **(4)**

Figure 1 Public sector services: provision and financing

This diagram shows that health services can be delivered either by public sector organizations such as NHS hospitals or by private sector organizations such as private hospitals. On the other hand, the funds necessary to provide health services can come from a combination of private or public sources. Private funding implies people paying out of their own pocket, usually via some form of private health insurance, while public funding suggests governmental sources. Within each of the four boxes are examples of each type.

This analysis leads us to four combinations:

- Services which are publicly financed and publicly provided (1) – these are clearly part of the public sector.
- Services which are privately financed and privately provided (4) – these are clearly ***not*** part of the public sector since they involve a contractual arrangement between a private individual and a private company.
- Services which are privately financed and publicly provided (2) – these could be considered as being part of the public sector since they involve activity by a PSO.
- Services which are publicly financed and privately provided (3) – since these involve public expenditure they can be regarded as part of the public sector.

Thus it is suggested that three of the four combinations described above can be considered as forming part of the public sector and are thus of relevance to this book.

THE UK PUBLIC SECTOR 1900–1979

Let us first consider the growth and development of the public sector in the UK. It is not always appreciated how extensively the public sector has changed during the twentieth century. A hundred years ago the public sector in the UK and most developed countries was vastly different from the way it is today. Consider first the size of the public sector and its relation to the overall size of the economy of the UK. A common way of doing this is to express total public sector expenditure as a percentage of the gross domestic product (GDP) of the country. This shows how large the public sector is compared to the whole of economic activity. Consider the data shown in Table 1.

Table 1 UK public expenditure and gross domestic product

Year	*Public expenditure as a percentage of gross domestic product*
1910	12
1930	22
1950	34
1970	40
1980	45
1984	45
1988	42
1992	44
1996	42

It will be noted that the trend in public expenditure has been consistently upwards, reaching around 40 per cent of GDP at the start of 1970. Since that time it has been in excess of 40 per cent of GDP and seems unlikely ever to drop back to the pre-war levels. This is because since the end of the Second World War the size and composition of the public sector has undergone many changes in functions and organization but has never reverted back to the limited role it had prior to the 1940s. The only exceptions to this trend are the two periods of World War (1914–18 and 1939–45) where public expenditure increased extremely rapidly as a direct result of high levels of military expenditure.

This upward trend in the size of the public sector needs some broad explanation, and identification of the main causal factors. At the start of this century the involvement of government, in the UK and most other developed countries, was largely limited to three areas of activity, namely:

- ***defence of the realm*** – expenditure on armed forces
- ***maintenance of law and order*** – police, courts, prisons and so on
- ***trade*** – regulation and promotion of trade matters.

Given this limited range of activity, the public sector, in all developed countries, was much smaller and restricted in range. Since that time there are three factors which have contributed to the upward trend in public expenditure leading to the public sector being much larger and complex than it was, and having a greater direct impact on the life of the average citizen. These three factors are:

- creeping involvement in social welfare
- increasing need for services
- increased involvement of the state in economic management.

CREEPING INVOLVEMENT IN SOCIAL WELFARE

There is a general recognition that in a modern state, government needs to be actively involved in many aspects of social welfare (for example education, health and pensions). Politicians of the left and right may argue and debate the extent of that involvement but few politicians of the right would suggest that the welfare state be contracted back to pre-First World War levels. This size of welfare spending in developed countries is illustrated by the international comparisons shown in Table 2.

Table 2 Public expenditure on social welfare

Country	*Public expenditure as a % of GDP (1995)*	*Public expenditure on health as a % of GDP (1995)*	*Public expenditure on education as a % of GDP (1997)*
UK	44.4	5.2	4.6
USA	34.9	5.6	5.0
Germany	49.8	5.8	4.5
France	54.3	6.6	5.8

Source: *OECD*

In all four of the countries shown it can be seen that:

- total public expenditure consumes a substantial proportion of the total GDP of the nation
- public expenditure on health and education form a substantial part of GDP and hence total public expenditure.

However, this was not always the case. Within the UK, major welfare reforms took place in the early part of the twentieth century, which resulted in an increase in the degree and scope of government involvement in welfare issues. The main aspects of this were determined by two key pieces of legislation passed by the then Liberal government of the day. These were the Old Age Pensions Act of 1908 which provided for a non-contributory but means tested pension and the National Insurance Act of 1911 which provided a contributory but non-means tested cover against sickness and unemployment for some classes of worker. Between the two World Wars the development of the welfare state was somewhat limited although there were key developments in the fields of social housing, pensions and education.

The Beveridge Report of 1942 paved the way for the foundation of the modern welfare state as it is currently known. Beveridge made recommendations for the development of comprehensive systems of social security and the development of a national structure of health services. Following the end of the Second World War the new Labour government embarked on a huge programme of improvements in social welfare, which basically involved the implementation of the Beveridge recommendations. The social security developments were underpinned by the passing of the National Insurance Act of 1946 and the National Assistance Act of 1948. However, perhaps the flagship policy of this period was the creation of the National Health Service (NHS) in 1948, which brought into public ownership large numbers of what were previously private or voluntary hospitals. Relating back to the comments made above, it is interesting to note that the provision of what are now termed family health services (general practitioners, dentists, community pharmacists and opticians) all remained in the hands of private practitioners. However, even though the services were provided by these private practitioners the funding for the services was public and the practitioners obtained most of their income through the means of contractual arrangements with the NHS. This somewhat strange arrangement was basically the political compromise that had to be made by the government to get the NHS formed.

In the area of education the critical development to be noted was the passing of the 1944 Education Act. This provided for the provision of universal free state secondary education and provided the framework for the education services we have today.

INCREASING NEED FOR SERVICES

Once governments had become involved in various aspects of social welfare they had virtually committed themselves to responding, to a lesser or greater extent, to increases in the need for services. Unfortunately, at the time of initial involvement, it was not always perceived that the needs and hence demands for services would grow substantially. Take, for example, the NHS. At the time the NHS was formed, there was a strong belief that the pool of sickness and thus the need for health services was finite, and that the provision of a certain level of resources to the NHS would meet all the health needs of the population. With the benefit of hindsight, that view now seems naïve, and current conventional wisdom is that the demands for health services are virtually unlimited.

There are probably three specific causes of this increasing need and demand for many public sector services:

- **Ageing population** – it is a well-known demographic phenomenon in developed countries, including the UK, that the average age of the population has increased and continues to increase. In addition to an increase in the normal human biological lifespan, more people are avoiding premature death (defined as less than sixty-five years of age) and surviving into their eighties and nineties. This is illustrated in Table 3.

Table 3 The ageing population

Year	*% population aged 65–79*	*% population aged 80+*
1951	9.5	1.4
1971	10.9	2.3
1991	11.9	3.8

Source: Social trends 1992

The table shows a clear trend of an increase in the proportion of elderly and very elderly people in the population. Older people have a greater need for social services and health care than younger people and thus, as a group, consume substantially more resources. As the population ages, the demand for additional resources in relation to health and social services increases dramatically. Also, the ageing population places increasing demands on pensions, particularly where no earmarked pension fund (funded by contributions) exists as is the case with the UK state pension.

- **Scientific and technological developments** – this is a phenomenon particularly associated with health care. Most people are aware of the continual developments in medical science and technology. Take, for example, artificial joint replacements. Forty years ago these were virtually unheard of, yet today they are commonplace. Consider also transplant surgery. In 1967 the world's first heart transplant took place in South Africa and the patient survived eleven days. Today there are several transplant centres in the UK alone and patients survive many years. In addition, behind these glamorous surgical procedures there are a whole host of smaller-scale medical and surgical developments taking place in many hospitals in the country. These various developments, although usually worthwhile, consume yet more health care resources and the very existence of a new medical service creates its own need, and hence demand for that service, where none previously existed. Furthermore, there seems no limit to the ingenuity of medical science. Just consider, for example, the potential impacts of genetic engineering and multiple organ transplants. Thus, overall, it can be seen that such developments generate new needs and demands on health service resources.
- **Population aspirations** – this is a more nebulous issue but it is often argued that today's population is not prepared to accept readily the standards and types of public services which were tolerated by previous generations. This trend could also be fuelled by developments such as the Patient's charter and, in turn, puts increasing pressure on public sector resources.

STATE INVOLVEMENT IN ECONOMIC MANAGEMENT

During the period 1935–45 there was an increasing international acceptance that governments needed to have a much larger involvement in the management of their economies. This was the period of Keynes, the birth of macroeconomics and the use of large-scale public spending in the USA and Germany to boost flagging economies. Also, in the period immediately following the end of the Second World War, large parts of the UK economy passed into public ownership through the large-scale nationalization of industries such as coal, steel, electricity and gas. These policies reflected the view of the then Labour government that public ownership of such strategically important industries was essential for economic management purposes. As will be discussed later in the book, all of these industries were de-nationalized through the privatization policies of Conservative governments in the 1980s and 1990s.

It is now generally accepted that government should have a strong role in economic management. However, the extent and nature of that involvement is open to disagreement, as the debate between monetarism and Keynesianism in the 1980s illustrated. In the modern world, governments are involved in economic management in a number of ways, and the following are current examples of PSOs in the UK which are involved in and have a role in economic management:

- **government departments** – several departments are concerned with aspects of economic management and economic development including, for example, the Treasury, Department of Trade and Industry, and Department for Education and Employment
- **Regional Development Agencies** – these have responsibilities concerning social and economic development within UK regions

- **Export Credit Guarantees Department** – facilitates exports of goods and services
- **Office for National Statistics** – collects and collates a wide range of economic information
- **local authority economic development departments** – have substantial roles concerning the economic development of their areas.

THE UK PUBLIC SECTOR: 1979–97

Table 1 above showed the overall trend in public expenditure since the start of the century. However, these bald statistics cannot disguise the fact that in the 1980s and 1990s, although total public expenditure as a proportion of GDP did not change substantially, the public sector in the UK underwent something of a revolution. Of particular note were those government polices which:

- resulted in the privatization of large parts of the public sector
- forced PSOs to compete with other PSOs and private sector organizations.

It has been argued that these changes which took place in the UK have had worldwide impact and consequently, for better or worse, many other countries have followed the UK in adopting policies of privatization and competition. These policies will be discussed in greater depth in Chapter 3.

WHAT THIS BOOK IS ABOUT

The main themes of this book are illustrated in Figure 2.

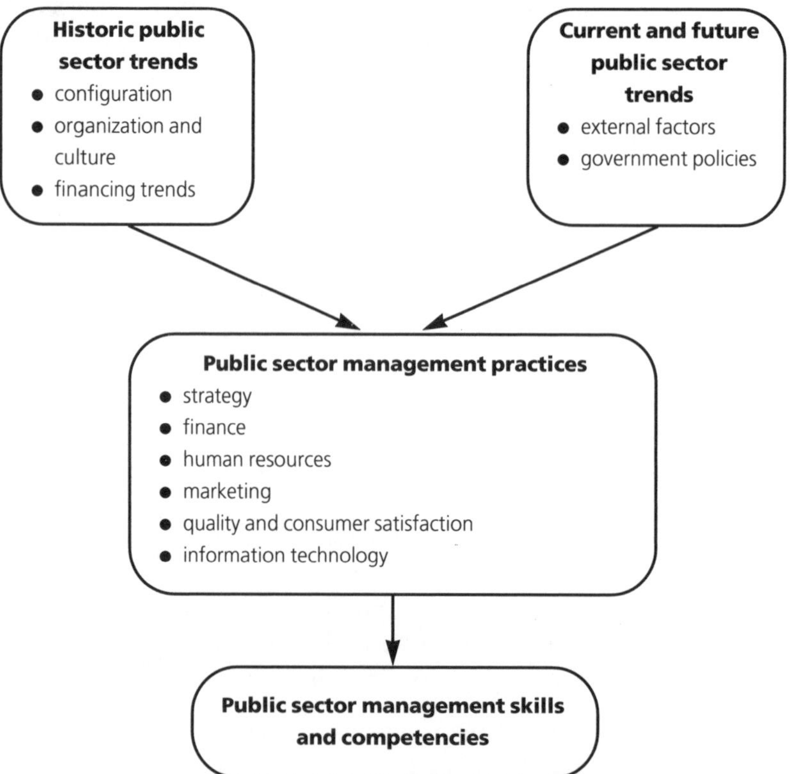

Figure 2 Structure of the book

Thus there are three parts to this book, as described below.

PART I: THE UK PUBLIC SECTOR: STRUCTURE AND TRENDS

Chapter 2 is basically descriptive in that it looks at the composition of the UK public sector as it currently stands. Chapter 3 examines, in some depth, the various changes and trends which have taken place across the public sector over the last twenty years. It is important to emphasize that government policy had a fair degree of consistency across large parts of the public sector even though the details of that policy varied from sector to sector.

PART II: PUBLIC SECTOR MANAGEMENT APPROACHES

To a very large extent the public sector and its managerial practices had a fair degree of stability from the end of the Second World War to the late 1970s. Since 1979 the changes which have taken place in the structure, organization and financing of the public sector have had a profound impact on public sector managerial practices and public sector managers themselves. Thus, Part II of the book examines each aspect of managerial practice (for example finance and human resource management) and considers, in some detail, the radical changes which have taken place in managerial practices in each case as a result of policies and trends over the last twenty years. These changes in managerial practice have, in turn, changed the methods of working and the skill requirements of public sector managers. Thus the aim will be to give public sector managers a good practical overview of each area of managerial practice.

PART III: PUBLIC SECTOR MANAGEMENT IN THE FUTURE

In 1997, the Labour Party was returned to government office after an absence of some eighteen years and this election potentially heralded a further sea change in attitudes and practices towards the public sector. Part III of the book looks at external trends, and trends in government policy towards the public sector, and the potential impact of these on public sector managerial practices. In turn, it considers the impact this will have on public sector managers and service professionals themselves.

CHAPTER TWO

Organization of the Public Sector

This short chapter is designed to give the reader an overview of the organization and structure of the UK public sector at the time of writing. This will provide a background and context to the later sections of the book. However, in reading this chapter caution must be exercised since the organization of the public sector is subject to continual change.

There are three distinct ways of looking at the configuration of the public sector in the United Kingdom. This is summarized in Figure 3.

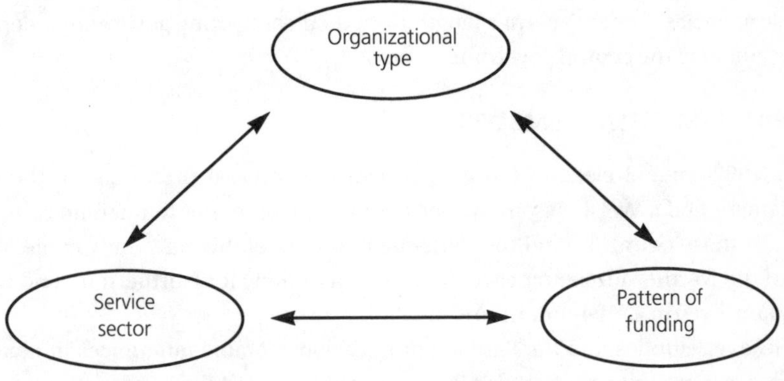

Figure 3 Structure of the public sector

ORGANIZATIONAL TYPE

Most PSOs can be classified as belonging to one of the following organizational types:

CENTRAL GOVERNMENT DEPARTMENTS

These are the government departments which undertake the work of central government and support the policies of the various Secretaries of State. The main departments are as follows:

- Cabinet Office
- HM Treasury
- Foreign Office
- Home Office
- Department of Health
- Department for Education and Employment
- Department of the Environment and the Regions
- Department for International Development
- Department of Defence
- Department of Social Security
- Department of Trade and Industry

- Department of Agriculture
- Department of National Heritage
- Lord Chancellor's Department.

In addition, associated with these departments will be a series of executive agencies which undertake various operational activities on behalf of the relevant department. Some examples of such executive agencies are:

- Benefits Agency – Department of Social Security
- Medical Devices Agency – Department of Health
- Highways Agency – Department of Environment
- Passport Agency – Home Office
- Prisons Agency – Home Office.

Although these agencies operate at arm's length from their sponsoring government department they are still a component of the central government sector.

REGIONAL PARLIAMENTS/ASSEMBLIES

Following the 1997 general election the government put forward proposals for the creation of a Scottish Parliament and a Welsh Assembly. These proposals were put to referenda and approved by the electorate of those countries and the Parliament and Assembly have now come into existence. Also, as part of the Northern Ireland peace process an Assembly for Northern Ireland was proposed, subsequently approved in a referendum, and created.

Clearly, these Assemblies and the Parliament have considerable differences in organization and constitution and, in particular, the Scottish Parliament has tax-raising powers.

LOCAL GOVERNMENT

The pattern of local government varies across the country but basically there are three types of local authority:

- **county councils** – which run services such as education, social services and consumer protection
- **district councils** – which run services such as housing, waste collection and street cleaning
- **parish or town councils** – which have a limited range of services such as allotments, street lighting and playing fields.

Traditionally, the UK had a uniform structure of local government across the country. However, following the recommendations of the Local Government Commission, this uniform pattern began to break down. In many parts of the country the county and district local authorities have been merged to give a unitary local authority. However, in other parts both district and county authorities continue to exist.

NATIONAL HEALTH SERVICE

The National Health Service comprises the following types of organization:

- **health authorities** – concerned with health policy and the specification of services required. Also within each health authority there will exist a series of primary care groups (PCG) with responsibility for the commissioning of services

- **NHS Trusts** – concerned with the provision of hospital, community and ambulance services to a wide range of patients
- **special health authorities** – these have specific functions such as, for example:
  - NHS Supplies Authority – supplies to the NHS
  - NHS Information Authority – information and IT development.
- **community health councils** – their role is to act as the voice of consumers of health services.

NON-DEPARTMENTAL PUBLIC BODIES (QUANGOS)

These organizations are neither central government departments nor are they executive agencies. They are formally referred to as non-departmental public bodies (NDPB) but the popular term QUANGO (or quasi non-governmental organization) was developed to describe them. They are too numerous to provide a complete list and so some examples of these bodies are given below:

- Regional Development Agencies
- Further and Higher Education Funding Councils
- Countryside Commissions
- English Heritage
- Housing Corporations.

FURTHER OR HIGHER EDUCATION INSTITUTIONS

Under this heading is included the following organizations which are corporate bodies in their own right, formed under the relevant Education Act of Parliament:

- higher education institutions – universities, colleges of higher education
- further education institutions – FE colleges, technical colleges, agricultural colleges.

Universities are sometimes referred to as being private sector organizations since some of them obtain only a small part of their total funding from government sources. However, in the view of the author, this is misleading and in terms of funding, governance and public perceptions universities should be regarded as being PSOs.

GRANT MAINTAINED SCHOOLS

One of the policies of the previous Conservative government was that of permitting schools to opt out of local education authority control. Such a step required the approval of the majority of parents in a ballot. Such schools were known as grant maintained schools since they received funding directly from central government (via the Schools Funding Agency) and not their local education authority.

OTHER

A number of other PSOs can be identified which do not fall neatly into either of the above types:

- **Police authorities** – police authorities are responsible for policing services in their area. They have strong local authority representation and they obtain 50 per cent of their funding from the Home Office and 50 per cent via a precept on their constituent local authorities.
- **Fire authorities** – where a single local authority does not manage its own fire service there will be a combined fire authority comprising representatives of constituent local authorities. Funding will be obtained by precept on the local authorities.

- **Probation Committees** – funded by the Home Office with responsibility for probation services in the local area.
- **Magistrates' Clerks Committees** – funded by the Lord Chancellor's Department with responsibility for magistrates' courts in the local area.

MISCELLANEOUS

Beyond the above there will be a large number of other organizations whose precise status is either debatable, or verges on other sectors. Some examples of this would include the following:

- private companies owned by universities, colleges or local authorities
- housing associations – these are voluntary bodies largely financed by the Housing Corporation
- general medical practitioners – these are private sector partnerships but receive the majority of their funding through contracts with the NHS.

SERVICE SECTOR

As an alternative to the above, PSOs could be classified according to the service sector to which they belong. Frequently, service provision cuts across organizational type and there will be established relationships between the various organizations within a particular sector. A complete sectoral analysis is difficult to produce but some examples are shown in Table 4.

Table 4 Public sector organizations by service sector

Sector	*Organizations*
Education	Department for Education and Employment Further and Higher Education Funding Councils Local education authorities Further and high education institutions Grant-maintained schools
Health	Department of Health Health authorities NHS Trusts Local authorities (environmental health)
Economic development	HM Treasury Department of Trade Department of Environment Regional Development Agencies Training and Enterprise Councils Local authorities (Economic Development Units)
Law and order	Lord Chancellor's Department Home Office Police authorities Magistrates' courts Probation services

FUNDING PATTERNS

Another approach to the classification of PSOs could be in accordance with the pattern of funding they receive. PSOs can be funded from two main sources:

- tax revenues
- charges for goods and services.

Each of these approaches will be summarized in turn.

TAX REVENUES

The vast bulk of public expenditure in this country is financed from the proceeds of tax revenues. Such taxes can be levied by central government or locally levied.

Central government raises revenue by a variety of means including direct taxes such as income tax and indirect taxes such as VAT. In this country, by and large, systems of hypothecated or earmarked taxation, whereby the proceeds of one taxation source are attributed to a particular programme of public expenditure, are not employed (that is, road taxes are not earmarked for roads spending). Instead, all of the proceeds of taxation are available to the government Exchequer to finance its various public expenditure programmes.

In the UK the vast majority of taxes are levied and collected by central government. This is not the case in many other developed countries where it is common for a variety of sales taxes or income taxes to be levied at the local level by state or provincial governments or local authorities. This one fact illustrates the extremely centralized nature of public sector management in the UK.

The only two examples of locally levied taxes in the UK are:

- **Council tax** – local authorities can raise revenues through the levying of the council tax on inhabitants within their area. However, even this degree of local discretion is limited through the power of central government to cap council tax increases.
- **Scottish income tax** – the Scottish Parliament will have the power to levy supplementary income tax up to an additional 3 pence over and above national (UK) tax rates. However, it remains to be seen whether this power will actually be used in practice.

CHARGES FOR GOODS AND SERVICES

By definition, taxes are not related to the individual's consumption of goods and services but are either flat rate or are related to the individual's ability to pay the tax. Thus, another source of finance for PSOs are charges directly made to individuals and organizations and based on their actual consumption of the goods and services provided by the PSO. Charges can be based on the full economic cost of providing the goods or services (possibly including a profit element) or there may be some form of subsidy. Charges made by PSOs are extremely varied but include the following examples where the charge is related to the consumption of the particular good or service, with or without a subsidy:

- local authority leisure centre charges
- college fees payable by students
- NHS prescription charges
- sales of the Government Stationery Office publications
- school meal charges
- council housing rents.

In trying to classify PSOs according to their funding pattern one must recognize at the outset that this is an imprecise classification. However, the following analysis is suggested.

PREDOMINANTLY EXCHEQUER-FUNDED

PSOs in this category obtains the vast majority (over 90 per cent) of their funds direct from the central government Exchequer. Some examples of organizations falling into this category would be:

- central government departments
- Welsh Assembly
- health authorities and NHS Trusts
- regional development agencies
- education funding agencies.

LOCALLY LEVIED TAXES

PSOs in this category have powers to raise a substantial proportion of their funding through locally levied taxes. These locally levied taxes are in addition to large amounts of Exchequer-based funding and other income sources. The only two UK examples of this which have already been quoted are:

- **local authorities** – council tax on inhabitants within their area
- **Scottish Parliament** – power to levy supplementary income tax.

REVENUE FROM CHARGES

PSOs in this category obtain significant levels of funding by means of charges levied on their consumers. Some examples of this are as follows:

- **Universities** – as from October 1999 universities will levy a fee on students attending the institution, thus raising substantial sources of income. This is in addition to Exchequer funds provided by HEFCE.
- **District councils** – these councils raise significant amounts of income from housing rents, leisure centre charges and so on in addition to Exchequer grants and council tax.
- **TECs** – raise significant amounts of funding from the provision of courses, advice and so on in addition to Exchequer-based funding.

CHAPTER THREE

Public Sector Trends

The last twenty years have seen immense changes in the UK public sector. Although the detail of such changes are specific to the individual PSO and the sector to which it belongs, many of the changes show clear trends across all parts of the public sector. Differences in language and details of application and, it has to be said, an inability by some managers to accept that they could learn something from other sectors have often disguised this fact.

These trends are important since they have, to a very large degree, influenced the types of managerial practices employed in PSOs and the skills needed by public sector managers. Just by way of example, thirty years ago very few civil servants would have seen a need to develop skills in financial management since it was just not relevant to the job they were doing at the time. Similarly, thirty years ago, one would have been unlikely to find an NHS manager or a head teacher who had skills and knowledge in performance indicators. These and other techniques are now part of the standard toolkit of public sector managers everywhere.

These policy trends can be considered in the three main groups shown in Figure 4.

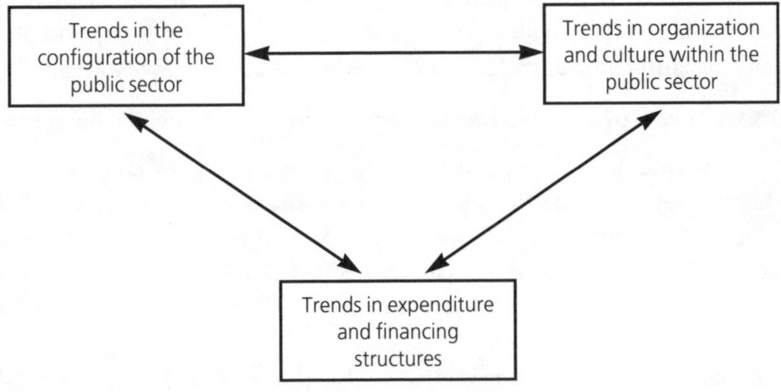

Figure 4 Public sector policy trends

TRENDS IN THE CONFIGURATION OF THE PUBLIC SECTOR

In a later section, those internal organizational changes and developments that have taken place within PSOs in recent years are discussed. In this section, consideration is given to macro-changes in the configuration of the public sector which have taken place in the last twenty years. There are three main types of change which can be identified:

- the dichotomy of service policy and purchasing, and service provision
- the mix of public sector and private sector service provision
- organizational simplification.

DICHOTOMY OF SERVICE POLICY AND PURCHASING, AND SERVICE PROVISION

In many PSOs (for example the NHS, central government and local government) there has been a requirement to separate the policy-making function of the organization from that of actual service delivery. The policy-making function would be responsible for defining what type of services are to be purchased while the actual provision of those services would be undertaken by a separate unit within the PSO.

Some examples of where this approach has been applied in the public sector are as follows:

- **NHS internal market** – within the NHS internal market, it was the health authority which was responsible for deciding which services should be provided, and in what volumes, and for specifying the details of service provision. The health authority would then agree a contract with an NHS Trust (or some other provider) to actually deliver those services. In spite of a change in rhetoric and the dropping of the use of the term 'internal market' this service purchaser–provider dichotomy still exists in the NHS, with the primary care groups (PCG) adopting the role of service purchaser in place of the health authority.
- **Executive agencies** – within central government departments there has been a separation of the policy-making function from that of service delivery through the creation of separate executive agencies with responsibility for service provision. Thus, in the department of Social Security, policy making is retained within the department itself while the actual tasks of assessing and paying benefits to individuals are undertaken by an executive agency entitled the Benefits Agency.
- **Local government** – for certain specific services (leisure services, waste collection and so on) the relevant local authority department (the client department) would define what types, volumes and quality of services should be provided. The actual provision of those services might then be provided by a separate contracting unit of the council known as a direct service organization (DSO).

Two additional points need to be made about this service purchaser–provider dichotomy:

- It is usually the case that the service provider has to operate in a quasi-commercial manner and it must aim to achieve tight financial and operational objectives. For example, NHS Trusts, as well as achieving contract objectives in terms of quantity and quality of services must also achieve financial targets concerning rate of return on assets employed. Similar requirements are placed on the DSOs of local authorities which may be compulsorily wound up if they do not achieve a stated rate of return.
- In some situations the service purchaser must expose the contract for service provision to open competition from other public and/or private sector organizations. Thus, service providers must compete to win contracts and hence funds. In local government and central government the often general nature of the service required (for example cleaning) means that there can be full competition between the in-house provider and the private sector. In the NHS internal market the very specialized nature of health service provision means that there is little private sector competition. Thus the degree of competition is often very limited.

MIX OF PRIVATE AND PUBLIC PROVISION

Over the last twenty years there have been substantial changes in the mix of public and private sector service provision caused by increasing private sector involvement in the provision of what are traditionally public sector services. Such trends undoubtedly reflect changes in political perceptions of the role of the state in service provision, with an increasing emphasis on the state as an enabler rather than a direct provider. Also, it must be noted that although many traditional public services are now delivered by the private sector, they are still financed by public funds.

This enhanced involvement by the private sector has taken several forms:

- **Outright privatization** – most of what were nationalized public utilities (and hence publicly owned) were subject to outright privatization and converted into private companies. Consequently these former public utilities are no longer part of the public sector. Examples of such privatizations include British Gas, electricity boards, British Steel, British Rail and regional water authorities.

  Many but not all of these privatizations have taken a similar format:

  - A private company has been created to provide and manage the infrastructure for service delivery. Thus, for example, there is Railtrack managing tracks and stations of the rail system, Transco managing the gas pipeline network and the National Grid managing the electricity supply network.
  - Several private companies have been formed to actually deliver services using the service infrastructure referred to above. Thus, the electricity supply companies supply electricity, the rail companies provide rail services and the gas companies provide gas supply services. In recent years a trend has been for these companies to encroach into the traditional markets of the other former public utilities. Hence there is the strange phenomenon of electricity companies supplying gas and gas companies supplying electricity.

  Although private companies, these companies are subject to regulation of price and service standards by agencies such as OFGEM for the gas and electricity supply industries and OFWAT for the water industry. Whereas it seems likely that regulation of the service infrastructure companies (for example Railtrack) will need to continue indefinitely, the regulation of service suppliers may wither away as greater competition is introduced into the market. Thus, for example, in the gas industry there is already substantial competition to British Gas in the industrial gas market and so no regulation is needed. Competition is being developed in the domestic gas market and so in due course regulation in this market may cease.
- **Staged privatization** – the Transport Act 1985 required local authorities to convert their transport undertakings to the form of a company owned by the local authority. However, any capital expenditure of this company would be charged against the capital allocation of the parent local authority. Not surprisingly, many local authorities found it impossible to operate a commercial transport company under this constraint and subsequently sold off their transport companies to private owners. Similar arrangements were employed under the Environmental Protection Act 1992, which gave local authorities several options including that of converting their waste disposal functions to the form of a council-owned company. Again, in due course, these local authority companies might be sold off to the private sector. These two examples can be thought of as staged privatization with the initial conversion to a local authority company and a final transfer to the private sector.
- **Contracting-out** – as mentioned above, many parts of the public sector, particularly central government, local government and the NHS, have been required to subject large parts of their in-house operations to market testing. Thus, for example, the Local Government Act 1988 required local authorities to market test services such as street cleaning, waste collection and catering by exposing in-house service provision to competition from private contractors. Frequently, the result of such a market test exercise was for the in-house service to retain the contract (often as a result of internal efficiency improvements). However, a significant amount of service provision was also transferred to private sector contractors via this process.
- **Private finance initiative (PFI)** – the involvement of the private sector has been further extended through the application of the private finance initiative (PFI). The PFI was a logical outcome of the twin policies of the previous government of curbing public expenditure and market testing service

provision. In 1992, the Chancellor of the Exchequer announced a major change in the government's attitude to the use of private finance in the provision of public services, and many of the irksome restrictions on the use of private finance were removed. The Chancellor also created an advisory panel to advise on ways in which the public sector could achieve greater collaboration with the private sector in developing capital investment projects. The work of this panel led to the promotion of the PFI, which has subsequently been applied throughout the public sector. Basically the PFI involves private contractors bidding for a contract to construct a public sector building (for example a hospital) *and* to provide a wide range of services to support that building. In turn, the private contractor would charge the public sector an annual payment for the use of the building and for service provision. The range of services that might be provided by the private sector is quite wide. For example:

- **NHS hospital** – a PFI project might involve the private contractor constructing a new hospital and providing a wide range of services such as maintenance, cleaning, administration, pharmacy and physiotherapy. The only services which, at present, would definitely still be directly provided by the NHS would be medical and nursing staff.
- **Schools** – with a PFI project involving construction of a new school, the only service that would definitely be provided directly by the local education authority would be teaching staff.
- **Information technology** – in a central government department, a PFI project could involve the private contractor financing the cost of new hardware and software and providing ongoing IS/IT services to the department.
- **Roads** – a PFI project might involve a private contractor constructing and maintaining a new road system and levying charges on motorists for the use of that road.

Although the private contractor is involved in financing large-scale capital expenditure, it is important to emphasize the role of the contractor in providing services and not just in constructing a building. Treasury rules inhibit an arrangement whereby the private sector merely finances and constructs a new building and leases that building back to the PSO. Hence, given that the PFI is now seen as the main source of funding for public sector capital projects, the involvement of the private sector in service provision seems likely to continue to increase.

ORGANIZATIONAL SIMPLIFICATION

There are some clear trends within the public sector of simplification of the organizational structure within a particular sector. Some examples of this include:

- **Local government** – in many parts of the country the local government structure has been reduced from a two-tier structure to a unitary structure.
- **NHS** – there have been a number of changes including the merger of health authorities and of NHS Trusts, and the abolition of the regional tier of the NHS and its incorporation into the Department of Health.
- **Further education** – over the last five years there have been a number of mergers of FE colleges, thus reducing the total number of colleges.

As will be noted in Part III of this book, this process of simplification continues apace with further mergers in both the NHS and the education sector.

Central government shows a mixed picture. In some cases two government departments have been merged into one department (Employment and Education) and other cases have involved the effective elimination of some departments (for example Energy). In other cases a department (for example Health and Social Security) has been broken up to give two separate departments (the Health Department and the Social Security Department).

TRENDS IN ORGANIZATION AND CULTURE WITHIN THE PUBLIC SECTOR

In this section consideration is given to those organizational and cultural changes which have taken place within the public sector and individual PSOs to a lesser or greater extent. Such changes have had a profound effect on managerial approaches in PSOs and the managerial skills needed.

These changes have been described under the following headings:

- increasing central government control
- drive for performance improvement
- internal delegation of decision making
- internal organizational change
- tensions between professionalism and managerialism
- increased consumer responsiveness
- increased entrepreneurialism
- increased emphasis on public accountability and probity
- changed employee relations climate
- an environment of continual change.

INCREASING CENTRAL GOVERNMENT CONTROL

Since the end of the Second World War the public sector has, with a few exceptions, seen a significant growth in the level of central government control. Within the last twenty years this has been manifested in a number of ways including:

- The passing of extensive legislation designed to limit the discretion of local authorities over funding levels and methods of service provision.
- The abolition of regional health authorities within the NHS and their absorption into the Department of Health (as the NHS Executive). This implies the involvement of the central government tier in detailed aspects of the NHS.
- The increasing involvement of education funding agencies, as agents of central government, in the activities of further and higher education institutions.

It is beyond the scope of this book to analyse whether such increased central control has been a good thing or a bad thing. The view of the author is that although central government involvement has, in some cases, resulted in improved performance, in other cases it has just involved unwarranted and undesirable interference in local decisions.

DRIVE FOR PERFORMANCE IMPROVEMENT

Over the last two decades both the present government and the previous government have undertaken a sustained drive for performance improvement in all parts of the public sector. Performance improvement means the pursuit of the classic '3E's, defined as being:

- **improved effectiveness** – improvements in the actual quality and/or quantity of service provided compared to planned objectives

- **improved economy** – improvements in the cost of acquiring resources (for example cost of supplies)
- **improved efficiency** – improvements in the amount of service output generated for a particular resource input (for example numbers of staff, use of buildings, equipment).

There is also a fourth 'E' of equity or fairness but it is probably true to say that little attention has been given to this question of equity in considering the distribution of services and resources between different parts of the community. For example, the year 1982 saw the publication of the Black Report on inequalities in health. This report showed that across the country there were huge inequalities in usage of and access to health services among different social classes in the population. The report was given short shrift by the government of the day.

This drive for performance improvement has been manifested in a number of ways including:

- **Performance indicators (PIs)** – the development and publication of sets of performance indicators for different services (for example NHS Trusts, schools and local authorities) designed to identify the potential for and achievement of performance improvement in the delivery of services. Linked to this, many PSOs have now developed performance management systems designed to enable them to monitor their performance (as measured via PIs) and to take appropriate action to improve performance.
- **Value-for-money (VFM) audit** – the creation of the Audit Commission in 1983 with its responsibility for the audit of local authorities (and subsequently for the NHS) led to a considerable emphasis being placed on VFM audit as well as traditional probity audit. Similarly, in other parts of the public sector the National Audit Office (NAO) has been active in promoting improved VFM through its audit activities.
- **Efficiency unit** – within central government an efficiency unit was created under the leadership of Sir Derek Rayner. This unit conducted a number of so-called 'Rayner Studies' into various aspects of efficiency.
- **Financial management initiative (FMI)** – this was a large-scale initiative within central government departments designed to improve various aspects of financial management and performance management. It had a major role in changing the culture of central government departments towards the idea of performance management.

INTERNAL DELEGATION OF DECISION MAKING

Seemingly a corollary to the issue of increasing central control has been a distinct trend, ***within*** many PSOs, towards delegating decision making to lower levels within the organization. Some examples of this include:

- **NHS Trusts** – the delegation of much decision making to clinical directorates within the Trust
- **further and higher education institutions** – the delegation of decision making to deans and heads of departments
- **executive agencies** – the delegation of decision making powers to district managers in executive agencies such as the Benefits Agency.

This trend has been achieved through the use of techniques such as delegated budgeting, performance management and decentralized personnel systems which, in turn, have been facilitated by the IT revolution and the availability of locally-based systems.

The primary reason for such delegation is the drive to improve the access to and quality of service provision. Delegating decision making to lower levels of management enables decisions about service provision and other matters to be taken more quickly, without the delay of referring the matter to higher authority. Also, it can be argued that lower levels of managers are closer to the issue in hand and will probably make better decisions than more remote senior managers.

However, in spite of the above comments, it must not be assumed that decentralization of decision making is good in all cases and that centralization is bad. The merits of decentralization or centralization of decision making must be judged in a local context, and in making such a decision key factors which should be considered are:

- **managerial skills** – the managerial skills of lower-level managers in the organization, since it would be unwise to delegate decision making to managers who were not competent to undertake such actions
- **information systems support** – the capabilities of the organization's management information systems to provide information and support to managers at lower levels in the organization
- **performance management framework** – the existence of a framework and a set of key indicators with which more senior managers can judge the performance of lower-level managers.

Thus, in considering the delegation of decision making, PSOs have to balance the advantages in terms of quicker and better decision making against the risks of loss of control.

INTERNAL ORGANIZATIONAL CHANGE

Most PSOs have undergone significant organizational change in recent years. There are a number of trends in internal organization which have impacted on PSOs in recent years. Although much of the organizational change which has taken place is organization-specific, there are some generic themes which can be identified. These are:

- restructuring of central functions
- de-layering
- growth in managerialism
- process re-engineering
- changes in staffing mix.

All of these matters are discussed further in Chapter 6 which concerns human resource management.

TENSIONS BETWEEN PROFESSIONALISM AND MANAGERIALISM

There are considerable tensions within many PSOs concerning the role and powers of service professionals (for example teachers, doctors and social workers) and the role of managers. Traditionally, PSOs such as hospitals and colleges were seen as being run by service professionals with support provided by a lower echelon of administrators. The growth of managerialism in the public sector saw considerable tension develop between service professionals and the new breed of general managers with the service professionals seeing power flowing from them to a managerial elite. In the NHS there was a distinct shift in power and influence away from doctors and nurses towards managers. In schools, it remains to be seen whether there will be a trend towards appointing non-teacher managers as head teachers rather than serving teachers. In the Civil Service the trend is still the cult of the generalist, with professionals having limited power and influence.

These tensions have considerable implications, particularly for service professionals, regarding such matters as remuneration, career development, professional standards and status. For example, the claim is often made that the only way for a clinical nurse to get promotion and additional remuneration is to move into management. These issues have been taken on board by the Labour government and will be considered further in Part III.

INCREASED CONSUMER RESPONSIVENESS

Traditionally, PSOs were regarded as being unresponsive to the views of the consumers of their services. However, various changes over the last ten years such as the Citizen's Charter and the NHS Patient's Charter have meant that PSOs must now be more responsive to the needs and views of patients, parents, students, taxpayers and so on. This need for consumer responsiveness has had two major implications:

- PSOs must identify and evaluate the views of consumers about the quality and nature of service provision, and take action accordingly to improve matters. The approaches to this are discussed at some length in Chapter 8.
- PSOs must be more open and provide information about their services. This will enable consumers to make judgements about the quality of services being provided. Examples of this are school league tables and hospital death rates.

INCREASED ENTREPRENEURIALISM

The sociologist Max Weber took the view that the most efficient form of organization was the bureaucracy. Such an organization had employees who closely followed established rules and procedures with no element of discretion being given. The traditional image of a PSO and public sector managers conformed to this bureaucratic model.

Much has changed. Developments such as market testing, PFI and income generation and the need for PSOs to be more publicly responsive have meant that public sector managers have needed to be more flexible, commercially-minded and entrepreneurial than has traditionally been the case. This has had major implications for matters such as staff recruitment and staff training.

INCREASED EMPHASIS ON PUBLIC ACCOUNTABILITY AND PROBITY

In recent years there have been a number of high-profile financial 'scandals' in the public sector. These 'scandals' have resulted in much adverse publicity and many critical reports from bodies such as the Public Accounts Committee and the National Audit Office. Also, there has been the formation of the Nolan Committee on Standards in Public Life, and the guidance provided by that committee. During the same period there were also a number of high-profile 'scandals' in the private sector (for example Maxwell and BCCI) which have led to developments such as the Cadbury Report on Corporate Governance, and this and other such reports have had, at least, some applicability in the public sector.

The result of these developments are that within all parts of the public sector there is now a very strong emphasis placed on matters such as probity, accountability and avoidance of fraud. Most PSOs are now required to produce documents covering subjects such as guidance on business conduct and fraud prevention strategies. Although these are important issues and one cannot argue against the need to avoid misuse of funds and fraud, it is a debatable point as to whether the public sector has now gone 'over the top' on some of these matters to the detriment of other aspects of management. In particular, the question must be raised as to whether this ongoing emphasis on probity and accountability is inhibiting:

- entrepreneurialism among public sector managers
- the identification of improvements in effectiveness and efficiency of service provision.

CHANGED EMPLOYEE RELATIONS CLIMATE

Few would argue that the employee relations climate in the public sector has substantially altered over the last twenty years or so. In general, this has meant a shift in power away from organized labour and towards management. There are many reasons why such a major change has taken place and it would be difficult to disentangle the effect of each. Some of the most important factors have been:

- the privatization of much of the former public sector
- job insecurity brought about by high levels of unemployment coupled with the threat of competition and outsourcing
- changes in employment legislation
- attempts at decentralizing some aspects of pay bargaining
- the increasing emphasis on management as opposed to administration in the public sector
- the aftermath of the defeat of organized labour in the 1983 miners strike.

AN ENVIRONMENT OF CONTINUAL CHANGE

Until some twenty years ago the public sector and its employees had a fair degree of stability. It was usual for there to be some form of organizational restructuring every 10–15 years but in between there was considerable stability and job security. Since the early1970s most parts of the public sector have undergone continual organizational and cultural change. The key point is that global developments in economics, politics and technology mean that such change is likely to continue for the foreseeable future. Many public sector managers still yearn for, and often lobby for, a return to organizational stability but the reality is that such stability has probably gone for ever. Thus, public sector managers and staff have to learn to live with and cope with an environment of continual change and, however difficult, this should be seen as an opportunity to be grasped and not something to be avoided and inhibited at all costs.

TRENDS IN EXPENDITURE AND FINANCING STRUCTURES

This section concerns the expenditure patterns and financing structures of the public sector. There have been a number of trends concerning the expenditure and financing of PSOs which are described below:

- targeted funding
- efficiency improvements
- cost structure
- service charging.

TARGETED FUNDING

In simple terms, the traditional approach to funding in many parts of the public sector was for central government to provide funds and guidance as to how those funds should be used to meet government priorities. However, it was for PSOs to make detailed decisions about the use of those funds. Government would monitor the funds but, by and large, funds were not earmarked for specific purposes. To some extent, there has been a recent trend for governments to provide funds which are earmarked for particular purposes, thus providing central government with a greater degree of control. On the basis of recent government budgets, this trend is set to continue and will be discussed further in Part III.

EFFICIENCY IMPROVEMENTS

For a number of years many PSOs have received funding from central government which has incorporated some requirement or assumption that the PSO will generate efficiency improvements. For example, the NHS as a whole might receive 2 per cent real growth in resources in a particular year but the government would publicly assume that it would generate a further 1 per cent growth through the achievement of efficiency gains. This requirement for efficiency gains would then percolate down to all parts of the NHS – the health authorities and the NHS Trusts. It is a debatable point as to whether what was achieved were really true efficiency gains or represented crude cuts in service levels. In all probability it was a bit of both. However, apart from efficiency gains achieved through investment in technology (the substitution of capital for labour) it is self-evident that no organization can continue to achieve true efficiency gains in perpetuity.

Nevertheless, this policy of achieving efficiency gains seems set to continue in many parts of the public sector and has implications for managerial practices and cultures. Ironically, it is not often appreciated that one impact of the PFI could be to inhibit this search for efficiency improvements. Where local authorities, NHS Trusts or central government departments have entered into PFI contracts, where the contractor is responsible for large elements of service provision, then (unless the PFI contract says differently) any operational efficiency gains achieved by the private contractor will accrue largely to the contractor, in terms of enhanced profits, and not to the public purse.

COST STRUCTURE

Until relatively recently most PSOs had a cost structure which was largely fixed in the short to medium term. This was because most PSOs were labour-intensive organizations and employed large numbers of staff on permanent and, largely, full-time employment contracts. The changes in the organization and uncertainties of funding in the public sector have meant that PSOs have needed to be able to respond quickly and adjust their costs in response to changes in funding levels. This has required a change in their cost structure to introduce a greater element of variability. Two examples of this are:

- the use of temporary staff or short-term contracts in place of full-time staff
- the short-term rental of equipment instead of its purchase or lease.

SERVICE CHARGING

It has been an increasing trend for PSOs which are actually delivering services to charge for the services they provide. Such charges may be levied in two ways:

- directly on the consumers of services (for example patients, students)
- on government funding organizations such as education funding agencies or service purchasers such as health authorities.

This trend requires PSOs to be able to identify the costs of providing specific services and to price them accordingly. This has major implications for financial management in the organization, which will be discussed in Chapter 5.

CONCLUSION

Not surprisingly, the variety of changes impacting on the public sector over the last twenty years have substantially changed the sector in organizational and cultural terms. In turn this has had a substantial impact on the practice of management in PSOs, and the term 'New Public Management' is often used to summarize the changes that have taken place. In Part II of the book different aspects of managerial practice and the way they have had to alter to meet the changes within the public sector are considered. These aspects of managerial practice are shown in Figure 5.

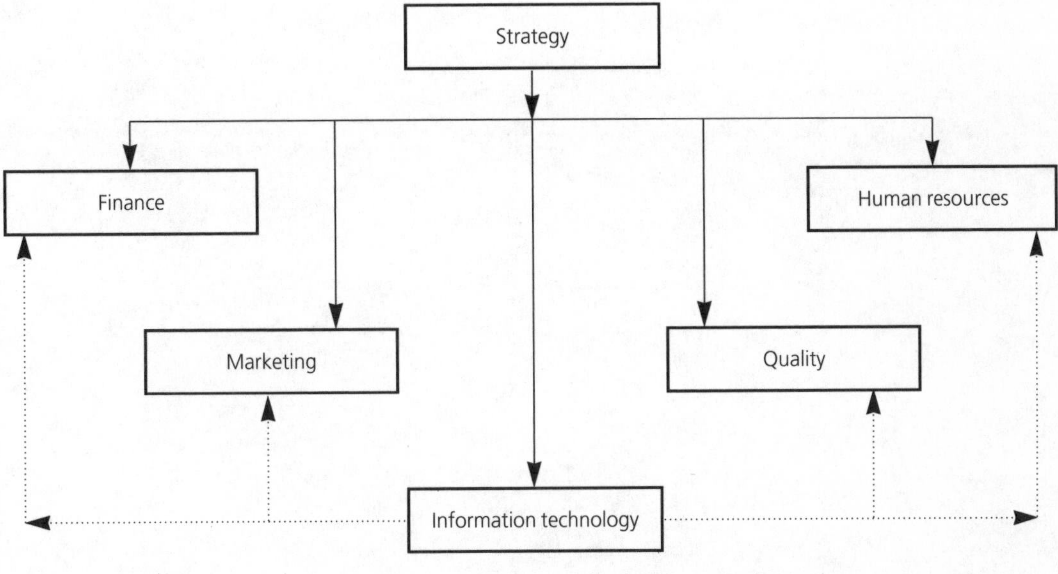

Figure 5 Aspects of public sector management

PART II

Public Sector Management Approaches

CHAPTER FOUR

Strategic Management in the Public Sector

Strategic planning and management has been operated in the public sector, to varying standards, for many years. However, the importance of strategic management is not always appreciated in the public sector and, quite often, there is considerable lip-service and scepticism. There may be a number of reasons why this is the case:

- Strategic management is often taken as synonymous with strategic planning, which it is not. Strategic management is a more all-embracing concept of which strategic planning is an essential part.
- Strategic management is seen as an academic exercise of little relevance to PSOs. This is often because managers in PSOs, although having substantial experience and expertise of operational management in their organization, have little strategic perspective.
- Strategic management is regarded as being impossible to undertake in the public sector, because the political dimension makes it impossible to act in a strategic manner.
- The purpose of strategic planning as having a longer term perspective is often not understood. Some talk about 'short-term strategies' which is really, to a large extent, an oxymoron.

In simple terms, strategic management is to do with establishing where the PSO wishes to be in the longer term (3–5 years) and identifying the means of getting there. The aim of this chapter is to try and outline the purpose of and practical approaches to strategic management and the reason why it is a vitally important management task in PSOs.

STRATEGIC MANAGEMENT: THE IMPACT OF THE CHANGING PUBLIC SECTOR

In Chapter 3 a number of trends were outlined which have taken place in the public sector over the last twenty years, and it was noted that these trends have had major impacts on the practice of public sector management. Although strategic planning and management have always had a role in PSOs, there are three key trends which have had a considerable impact on the conduct and importance of strategic management in the public sector today. These are:

- the purchaser–provider dichotomy
- the drive for performance improvement
- the delegation of decision making.

PURCHASER–PROVIDER DICHOTOMY

Prior to the purchaser–provider dichotomy, strategic management in all PSOs was similar in broad terms but obviously different in detail. The organization would set itself some strategic objectives in relation to service needs, and plan how to marshal its own resources to best achieve those objectives. The separation of policy and purchasing from service provision has radically affected the process of strategic management and there are now considerable differences between service purchasers and service providers. These can be summarized as follows:

- **Service purchasers** – service purchasers will be concerned to ensure that the public services provided will best meet the needs of their clients and potential clients. However, since these purchasers do not, by definition, actually provide services they cannot directly mobilize physical and human resources to provide those services. However, they do have large amounts of funds available and so can facilitate the provision of services through the means of contractual arrangements with service providers. These service providers might be part of the same organization (for example an executive agency or a local government DSO), part of the same sector (an NHS Trust) or a private sector contractor. Hence, strategic management in a purchasing organization could be said to involve the following three tasks:

  - identifying what services should be provided and the main priorities to be applied
  - developing a contractual framework designed to deliver those services
  - facilitating change in the provider market and individual provider organizations to ensure that the required services can be delivered.

  An approach to strategic management in purchaser organizations will be outlined later in this chapter.
- **Service providers** – it has been already noted that many provider organizations are effectively quasi-commercial in nature. As such they may have a wide range of business-type objectives which might be classified as being:

  - contractual objectives (for example volumes and standards of service)
  - financial objectives (for example rates of return)
  - strategic objectives.

  Furthermore, as already noted, some service providers may operate in an environment where they must meet their financial objectives in order to remain in existence.

  In these circumstances, the approach to strategic management in such service provider organizations is more akin to that undertaken in commercial organizations rather than a traditional PSO. Commercial organizations tend to refer to their strategic planning process as 'business planning' and this is the term which came to be applied in the service provider arm of PSOs during the 1980s and 1990s. Prior to the mid-1980s the term 'business planning' was virtually unused within the public sector. However, the separation of purchaser and provider and the introduction of competition between providers meant that the business planning approach is now widespread throughout the public sector. The election of a new government in 1997 has meant, to some degree, that the term 'business planning' has become politically incorrect and other terms may now be used. However, the principles of business planning still remain in force. Some examples of organizations undertaking business planning in the public sector are shown in Table 5.

Table 5 Business planning in the public sector

Sector	*Service provider*
Local government	Local authority DSOs/transport companies/waste disposal companies
Health	NHS Trusts
Education	Universities/colleges
Central government	Executive agencies

THE DRIVE FOR PERFORMANCE IMPROVEMENT

The very strong emphasis on performance improvement in the public sector was noted in Chapter 3. More and more, the performance of PSOs is being judged by the use of published performance indicators or the result of formal inspections, such as OFSTED inspections in schools. In some cases the continued existence of a PSO or the jobs of its senior managers may rest on achievement of performance improvement. Such improvements often require substantial organizational change and usually take several years to achieve. Hence PSOs require a robust strategic management process to assist in the achievement of performance improvement.

THE DELEGATION OF DECISION MAKING

Also noted in Chapter 3 was the trend towards delegation of decision making in some PSOs. In some provider units this may be extended to the point where individual departments become almost mini-business units operating under a framework of corporate objectives and guidance. Since, by definition, these mini-business units are subject to limited day-to-day control by the corporate centre, there must be mechanisms for ensuring that they conform to corporate objectives and do not just do their own thing. Thus it is common for each mini-business unit to prepare its own strategic business plan and for these plans to be evaluated by the corporate centre and, ultimately, amalgamated into a business plan for the whole organization. An example of such an approach might be the development of business plans for each clinical directorate (for example orthopaedics and cardiology) within an NHS Trust.

KEY ELEMENTS OF STRATEGIC MANAGEMENT

As already mentioned above, strategic management is often thought of as being synonymous with strategic planning. Possibly, this explains to some extent the failure by some PSOs to achieve what is set out in their strategic plans. Consider the approaches illustrated in Figures 6 and 7.

In Model A it is recognized that the shorter-term operational plans of an organization should be derived from the longer-term strategic plans. It is also recognized that there needs to be a process of implementing and monitoring the operational plans. However, the unwritten assumption is that by implementing a series of sequential operational plans, one will automatically implement the organization's strategic plan. Thus, there is no concept of strategic implementation. This is an example of a theoretical model which does not fit the real world since there will be many real-life barriers to implementing the strategy. These will particularly concern the failure to address issues of cultural and organizational change.

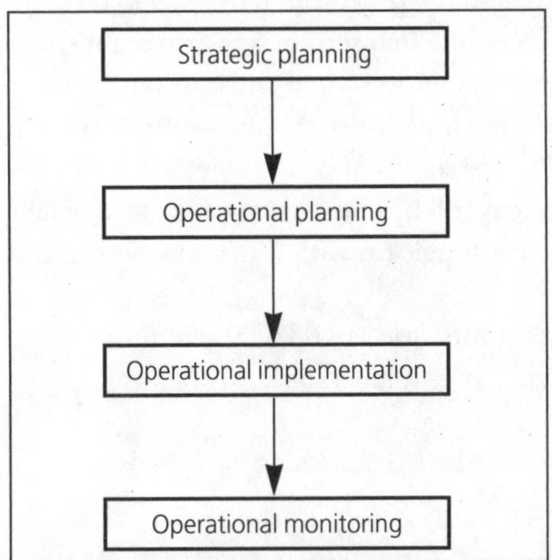

Figure 6 Strategic management approach: Model A

Model B, like Model A, recognizes that operational plans should be derived from strategic plans. However, it also recognizes the underlying reality that strategic plans do not implement themselves, and too often there is a tendency to assume that once a strategic plan has been created then little more needs to be

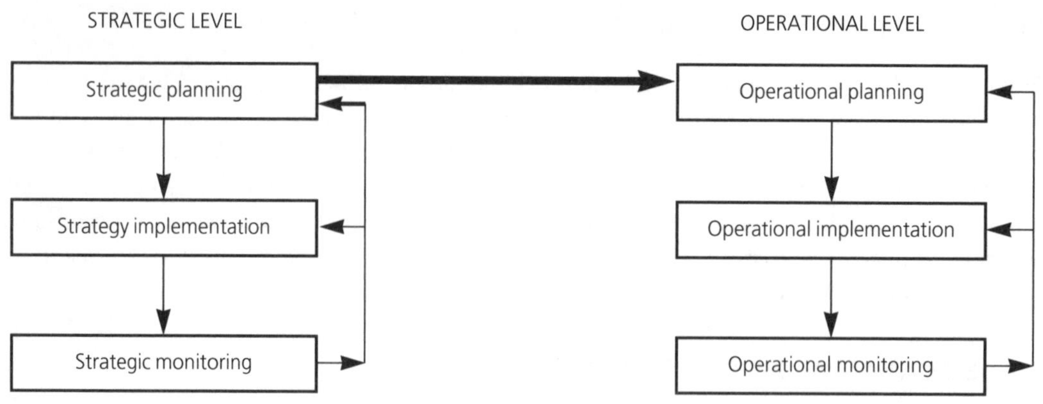

Figure 7 Strategic management approach: Model B

done other than to implement the operational plans. This is a huge mistake, for the implementation of strategic plans is an important and difficult task. The implementation of operational, or short-term plans, is not usually that difficult since they often require little change in the operational practices of organization from those currently undertaken. However, the implementation of a strategic plan often raises issues such as resistance to organizational change, imperfect markets for services and inability to obtain resources, and these issues must be addressed as part of a process of strategy implementation. These matters will be further discussed later.

STRATEGIC MANAGEMENT IN SERVICE PURCHASER ORGANIZATIONS

In general terms, purchasers are concerned with identifying the needs of the general public for service provision, and with shaping future service provision in accordance with that need and the resources available. This is done through the mechanism of letting contracts with providers. From the standpoint of the purchaser, these contractual arrangements should not be developed in isolation, but should be based on some longer-term strategic plan for meeting client needs for services. It is possible that the current range of services provided are not optimum, and the purchaser may wish to reshape the pattern of service over a period of years. Thus, at the same time that purchasers are establishing annual contracting arrangements, it is important that they also address questions of longer-term strategy. In the absence of strategy, contracting decisions lack focus or direction and are more open to short-term pressures and medium-term drift. Whilst daily pressures make the development of a strategic vision difficult to achieve, without it they are likely to result in a purchasing approach which does little more than reinforce the existing pattern of service provision with a few changes at the margin.

As already noted, strategic management in a purchasing function is considerably different to strategic management in a service provider. This section covers three main issues:

- the development of purchaser strategies
- the implementation of purchaser strategies
- strategic monitoring.

THE DEVELOPMENT OF PURCHASER STRATEGIES: STRATEGIC PLANNING

First and foremost, strategic planning is not about predicting the future. Put simply, strategic planning is concerned with where the organization wishes to be in the longer term, its vision for the future, and the means by which it intends to realize that vision. Strategic planning is a vital tool for shaping the future destiny of the organization, and in many ways it is concerned with achieving what can realistically be achieved. This statement recognizes that PSOs operate in a politically sensitive environment, and that short-term political factors will always impact on the strategic plans of PSOs. However, these short-term political factors should be seen as a constraint on strategic planning requiring, possibly, a small deviation from plan, rather than, as some suggest, a reason for not undertaking strategic planning at all.

The process of strategic planning will obviously vary in detail between PSOs, but all strategic planning processes will have some common elements. Figure 8 illustrates the main elements of a strategic planning process which should be found in most purchaser organization.

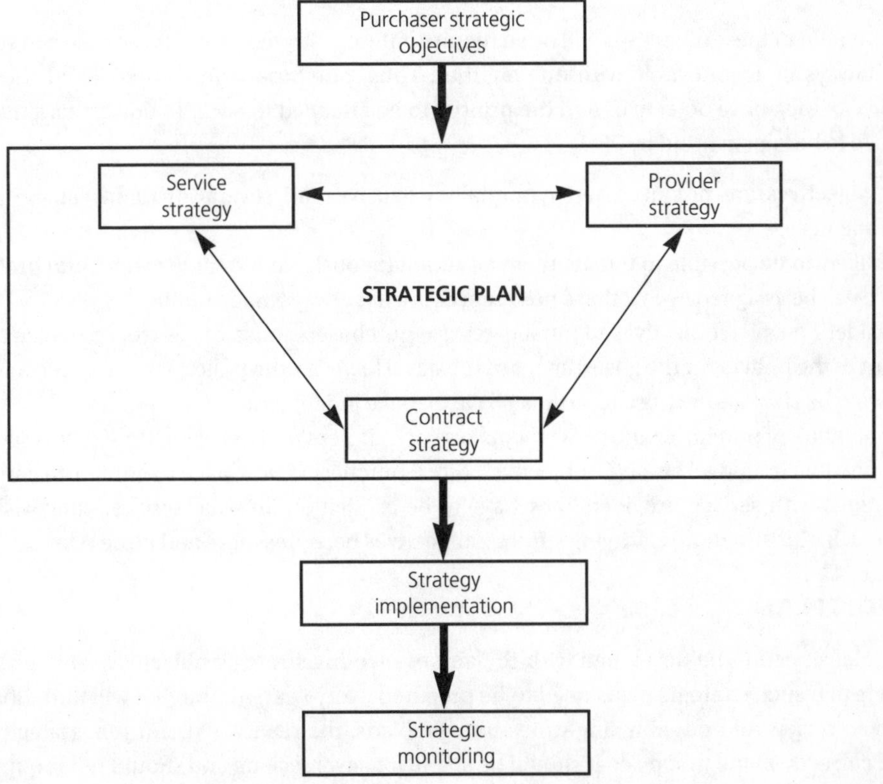

Figure 8 Main elements of a strategic planning process

Let us now look at each of these elements of purchaser strategy in turn.

PURCHASER STRATEGIC OBJECTIVES

Purchaser organizations have limited resources and cannot meet all the needs and demands placed on them. This is obviously a truism and hence as part of strategic planning, priorities need to be identified and choices made. The problem is that in making choices there are often several different strategic objectives that could be pursued by the PSO, and depending on the importance accorded to each of these objectives it would be possible to come up with different (desired) strategies for service provision. Consider the examples of some possible strategic objectives for schools and health services as shown in Table 6.

Table 6 Purchaser strategic objectives

Schools	*Health services*
Improve the academic standards of all pupils	Prolong the life of patients
Improve the academic standards of the most able pupils	Reduce the incidence of premature (under 65) death
Meet the educational needs of prospective employers	Improve the quality of life of patients
Promote greater social and moral well-being among pupils	Promote economic development through a reduction in occupational sickness
Contribute towards educational opportunity in society at large	Improve equality of access to services

Achievement of these objectives will often require different strategies and these different strategies may not always be reconcilable with one another. Thus, purchasers need to consider the relative importance of the above objectives and the priority to be attached to each. In doing this a number of points need to be kept in mind by PSOs:

- These objectives are not necessarily mutually exclusive and several of them can be pursued simultaneously.
- It is unlikely to be possible to pursue them all simultaneously, to the same extent, and preferences may have to be assigned even if these preferences are not always made public.
- In considering which objectives to pursue, service purchasers must, of course, recognize and take account of the policies of the government of the day. However, the policies of the government may not always be clear and so purchasers may have to make judgements.
- The separation of purchaser and provider makes such choices more explicit. Prior to this separation it was possible to 'fudge' strategic objectives. Since purchasers now have to enter into contractual agreements with service providers they have to be explicit about what services they wish to see provided. In this situation, clarifying strategic objectives becomes more and more relevant.

STRATEGIC PLAN

Strategic plans need to be developed with the aim of meeting strategic objectives. One myth to be dispelled is that such strategic plans need to be prepared every year. Although it will undoubtedly be necessary to review and possibly fine-tune strategic plans, the reality is that if the strategic plan is prepared correctly in the first place it should be stable for several years and should not require major revision. This is for the simple reason that the underlying social, economic and physical environment on which the plan is based should itself be largely stable for a period of years. For example, subject to the absence of a major new disease such as HIV/AIDS or a major environmental change, the social and economic characteristics of an area are unlikely to alter significantly over a period of several years and thus the health strategy for the area should not need significant change over that period.

Many believe that a strategic plan for a service purchaser need only be concerned with identifying and defining the types and services to be provided. This is an oversimplification, and purchaser strategic plans should have three elements:

- **service strategies** – the desired type and range of services to be provided
- **provider strategies** – the desired numbers and types of providers used to deliver those services
- **contract strategy** – the desired contractual arrangements with those providers.

Each of these different aspects of the strategic plan will be discussed in turn.

DEVELOP SERVICE STRATEGIES

This aspect of strategy is concerned with identifying the optimum pattern of services to be purchased in the longer term, irrespective of how and from whom they are purchased. This requires a systematic process comprising the following five stages:

- **Assess intrinsic service needs** – few would argue that the provision of public services should be driven by need. However, 'need' is a difficult concept to work with. Firstly, there are difficulties in agreeing what is meant by need and there is voluminous academic literature which suggests need can be defined in several different ways, such as professional assessment of need or perceived need of the individual. Secondly, even if agreement can be reached about what is meant by need there could be difficulties in measuring that need due to the lack of suitable data. However, in practice, even allowing for these difficulties the issue of need cannot just be ignored in strategic planning. Hence, purchasers need to give some consideration to the factors which influence the intrinsic need for public services. For most public services the focus should be on a number of key factors which influence the need for those services. These key factors include:

  - demographic trends
  - social trends
  - economic trends
  - income trends
  - lifestyle trends
  - physical environment trends.

  Use should be made of the best available data. Much of this data will be publicly available, but sometimes it may be necessary to mount special exercises to collect additional data. Although this might seem laborious, such data is needed if the strategy is to be robust and meaningful.
- **Project future service demands** – whatever the outcomes of the needs assessment exercise, the reality is that purchasers will not be starting with a blank sheet of paper. There will already be a current range of services based on traditional patterns in the area and there will be existing gaps in services and delays in accessing services. By taking account of changes in a variety of factors such as demographic, social, economic, technological and environmental trends, the purchaser can project the impact of these changes on the future demands for the current range of services. However, it must be noted that this approach to projecting service demand is based on the extrapolation of existing service patterns, which is a different concept to the intrinsic need for services.
- **Forecast resource availability** – strategies must be prepared in the context of the resources available. Thus, purchasers will need to make projections of the resources they are likely to receive in the strategic period. Factors to be considered include:

  - resource trends available to the public sector
  - resource trends applicable to a particular sector
  - resource trends applicable to the individual purchaser PSO.

Making such projections is an inexact science and purchasers will probably need to consider different bands of resource availability and prepare different strategies within those bands. This is a key aspect of strategic financial planning which is discussed in the next chapter.

- **Identify and agree decision criteria** – formulating a service strategy requires criteria against which to judge the merits of the various alternative service patterns which can be identified. It is essential that such strategic decision criteria are developed prior to a decision being taken and not retrospectively to justify a decision already made. In the absence of such criteria it will be very difficult to make rational choices between competing activities, and choices will be more open to influence by political and professional lobbying. The key issue is the contribution that the various service components will make towards the achievement of strategic objectives. However, some other factors which can be taken into account are the:

  - resource cost of each strategy
  - risk factors associated with each strategy
  - robustness to change in external circumstances
  - controllability of actions.

  Decisions cannot be taken purely by addressing the largest problem first, and a number of criteria need to be weighed against each other in formulating a decision. There are many ways in which these decision criteria might be utilized, ranging from some form of computerized decision support model to merely making subjective assessments of the impact of strategic themes against each of the criteria.

- **Identify alternative service patterns** – in the light of its assessment of needs, demands and strategic priorities, the purchaser will need to identify the various patterns of service that could be provided in the future and how this might differ from the current pattern of services. This is a creative task and needs to be addressed in an open and constructive manner. Every attempt should be made to avoid restricting the discussion to the current service patterns and all options should be considered at this stage. A number of different approaches could be applied:

  - obtain information on different approaches employed by other similar organizations both in the UK and overseas
  - consult service delivery professionals about their views
  - conduct brainstorming sessions within the organization
  - obtain the views of consumers of services.

- **Conduct analysis and identify desired service strategy** – out of the above, a long list of possible approaches will probably emerge which may need some initial filtering to reduce it to a feasible number. Each of these alternative patterns of service should now be assessed against the decision criteria referred to above and from this the desired pattern of service provision should emerge, which will constitute the service strategy of the organization. The analysis of these options is a cumbersome and detailed task and recourse will have to be made to a number of sources of information:

  - published literature on the effectiveness of different approaches to service provision
  - contacts with other similar organizations about their experiences
  - scenario analysis using simulation models designed to project the impact of changes in service patterns
  - professional judgements.

Having done this analysis and identified the preferred strategy, two significant points must be recognized:

- that the desired pattern of services may be substantially different from the current pattern of services provided
- that the shift from the current pattern to the desired pattern cannot be achieved overnight and may take several years to achieve.

Thus, the mechanisms by which the desired pattern of service provision could be achieved are now considered.

DEVELOP SERVICE PROVIDER STRATEGY

Identifying the desired pattern of service provision is only the first stage in strategic planning. The existing range of service providers is not necessarily optimal and the service purchaser must deliberate the means by which those future services are to be delivered. They must consider the desired configuration, in terms of numbers and types, of service providers to be used to deliver those services. In some circumstances, such as executive agencies, this consideration is largely irrelevant since the executive agency is the deemed provider of services on behalf of the relevant government department. For example, the Benefits Agency is the deemed provider of services on behalf of the Department of Social Security. However, in other cases the situation is not so clear-cut and service purchasers need to address the following issues:

- ***options available***
  - which services are open to alternative service provision from a range of providers?
  - who are the alternative service providers now and in the future?
- ***analysis of options***
  - what are the capabilities of those alternative providers?
  - what is the potential for achieving better service integration through purchasing from alternative providers?
  - what are the merits of rationalizing the numbers of providers of a particular service?
  - what are the costs and benefits of extending the geographic range of service provision beyond local providers?
  - what are the costs of changing the existing pattern of service providers?
- ***risks***
  - what are the risks involved in changing the existing purchasing arrangements?
  - what exit strategies are available?

Perhaps one of the best examples of this arrangement was the internal market of the NHS. Health authorities and PCGs, as purchasers, as well as considering which services were to be provided should also consider how those services might best be provided in terms of the range of NHS Trusts, voluntary organizations and private providers.

DEVELOPING CONTRACTING STRATEGY

The third strategic planning issue concerns the configuration of contracts that the purchaser will have with service providers. Purchasers should consider, in strategic terms, why they are adopting a particular form of contract configuration and whether a different configuration is desirable. The important point is that each of these issues has a strategic dimension and should be dealt with strategically and not on an annual ad hoc basis. The key issues to consider are:

- **Length of contracts** – should they be short-term (1–2 years), medium-term (3–5 years) or long-term (over 5 years)? There are advantages and disadvantages to each approach. For example, with the longer contract term less time and effort will need to be devoted to contract negotiation, but the opportunity for changing the contract specification will be less. On the other hand, it has been argued that the longer the contract term then the more confident service providers will be about making large-scale investments in new equipment to deliver better services.
- **Degree of service specification** – should the specification of services be detailed or broad-based? Detailed contract specifications provide greater control but places a greater burden of monitoring on the purchaser. However, broad-based contracts leave the provider with a greater degree of discretion about what services to provide.
- **Basis for reimbursing providers** – what should be the basis for reimbursing providers for the volume and quality of services delivered? The main options are:
  - a block sum for a defined quantum of service being delivered
  - an amount per item of service delivered
  - some combination of the above two approaches.

Most contract reimbursement regimes will fall into one of the above three classes and the relative risks and benefits of each method needs to be analysed in detail. Consideration will need to be given to the detailed aspects of the contract such as disputes procedures and payment schedules.

PUTTING PURCHASER STRATEGIES INTO ACTION

It has been already emphasized that strategic plans do not implement themselves and certain actions need to be undertaken. From the point of view of purchasers it is suggested that there are three strategic actions which need to be undertaken as described below.

MARKET DEVELOPMENT

Where purchasers have a choice of provider, they may be dissatisfied with the current market for service provision and may wish to attempt to manipulate the market and the level of competition. Consider the situation where a purchaser is faced with a monopolistic service provider. Although the purchaser could attempt to regulate the quality and price of the services being provided, in reality the fact that the service provider is a monopolist may well make such regulation extremely difficult to enforce. In such a situation, where it is feasible, it seems almost incumbent on the purchaser to encourage alternative service providers to come into the market as a means of escaping from the monopolistic position. There are already some examples of this taking place in the health sector, where purchasers are encouraging the provision of long-term residential care by the private sector as an alternative means of provision.

EFFECTIVE IMPLEMENTATION PLANNING

A comprehensive implementation plan needs to be prepared to ensure that the planned events actually occur. Such an action plan will have a number of key elements including:

- tasks that need to be performed

- individual responsibilities for ensuring they are performed
- timetable for completing tasks
- resources needed.

In addition, the plan may identify critical success factors and possible bottlenecks to implementation and possible ways around them. The approach to these issues could adopt project management techniques.

FACILITATION OF PROVIDERS

There are many situations where purchasers have little choice but to use the existing range of service providers. Hence it will be incumbent on them to work closely with those providers to ensure that the providers take on board the necessary changes in service provision outlined in the purchaser's strategic plan. This requires a considerable effort at communication with providers and the facilitation of organizational change within those providers. Indeed, in some cases, purchasers may need to make additional resources available to providers to facilitate such organizational change.

PURCHASER STRATEGIC MONITORING

It is also important that purchasers undertake some strategic monitoring. Purchasers undertake substantial in-year monitoring of provider contracts but this form of monitoring says nothing about the success or otherwise of the purchaser's overall strategy. As part of strategic monitoring, purchasers need to assess the impact of their purchasing strategy *in relation to the strategic objectives they have set*. Thus at the time the strategic objectives are being set, purchasers need to think about how, in future years, they are going to collect the information needed to assess whether those objectives have been met. This may require the setting in train of various data collection or survey exercises to ensure such information will be available when it is needed.

The results of this strategic monitoring exercise will then inform future strategic plans. While such strategic monitoring is difficult to undertake in practice, since there may be problems of data collection and evaluation methodology, these difficulties should not constitute a reason for inaction as some strategic monitoring is better than none.

BUSINESS PLANNING AND SERVICE PROVIDERS

Prior to the mid-1980s business planning was virtually unknown within the public sector. It was noted in Chapter 3 that one impact of the purchaser–provider separation was that provider organizations became quasi-commercial in nature and had to achieve certain financial objectives. In addition, some types of service providers often had to compete with one another which meant their very existence was in doubt if they failed to achieve these targets. Hence, their approach to strategic planning is much more akin to that of commercial organizations.

Thus in service providers the approach to developing a strategy is somewhat different from the purchaser approach of identifying needs and deciding priorities. All service providers must prepare strategies on the basis that they are business units which must provide services that meet purchaser needs, must attract income and be financially viable in order to survive. They must prepare longer- and shorter-term plans which are business-oriented. These are business plans.

This section will discuss:

- the need for business planning

- the approach to business planning in the public sector
- how public sector business planning is undertaken in practice.

WHY THE NEED FOR BUSINESS PLANNING

There are a number of reasons why service providers need to prepare business plans and these are discussed below:

- **Statutory requirements** – in some cases it may be a statutory requirement to prepare a business plan. For example, in the NHS, each year all NHS Trusts were required to submit to the Department of Health a three-year business plan. If meeting this statutory requirement were the only reason for business planning it is unlikely that there would be much commitment to the process at local level and the quality of the business plans would suffer accordingly. Hence, other more important reasons must be considered.
- **Avoiding failure** – although no organization would plan to fail such failure can result from a number of causes including:

  - failure to meet contract obligations
  - errors in the costing of services resulting in underpricing
  - failure to control costs
  - income falling faster than costs
  - failure to keep abreast of the latest service developments resulting in contracts being lost to other providers.

  Although there is no guarantee against failure, sound business planning minimizes the risk of failure.
- **Achieving success** – avoiding failure is not synonymous with success. This is more to do with improving service standards, enhancing quality, improving productivity and improving efficiency. The precise indicator of success will be identified by the mission statement and strategic objectives of the organization which are discussed later in this chapter. Again, business planning can assist in achieving success.
- **Organizational co-ordination** – although business planning can take place for the organization as a whole, it is also appropriate and now quite common for individual departments to prepare their own individual business plans. Firstly, it is important for each department to ensure that it is a viable business unit with a viable strategy. Secondly, where the organization has decentralized a large amount of authority to individual departments there is a strong possibility that each will pursue its own agenda thus leading to confusion, duplication and disfunctionality. Thus, the business planning process can be used as a channel for co-ordination and as a means of ironing out any potential disfunctionality.
- **Gaining internal commitment** – a vital ingredient of effective service delivery is to gain commitment from the staff to the mission and objectives of the organization in which they work. Too often, business plans are written by senior managers to be read by other senior managers, becoming little more than a paperchase. In some PSOs, many middle and junior managers, and service professional staff, have little or no involvement in business planning thereby losing a key feature. It is important that all staff are involved in the business planning to help to internalize and work towards the organization's overall objectives.
- **Raising finance** – in any commercial organization, a request to a bank for a large loan is likely to be

met with a counter-request for a business plan in justification. Many PSOs are often in a similar position and have to argue to a higher authority the business case for capital expenditure. Also, in the case of PFI projects, a good business case is essential. The business plan must underpin the content of the business case for undertaking particular capital projects.

THE NATURE OF BUSINESS PLANNING

The classical approach to business planning has a number of interrelated stages which are shown in Figure 9.

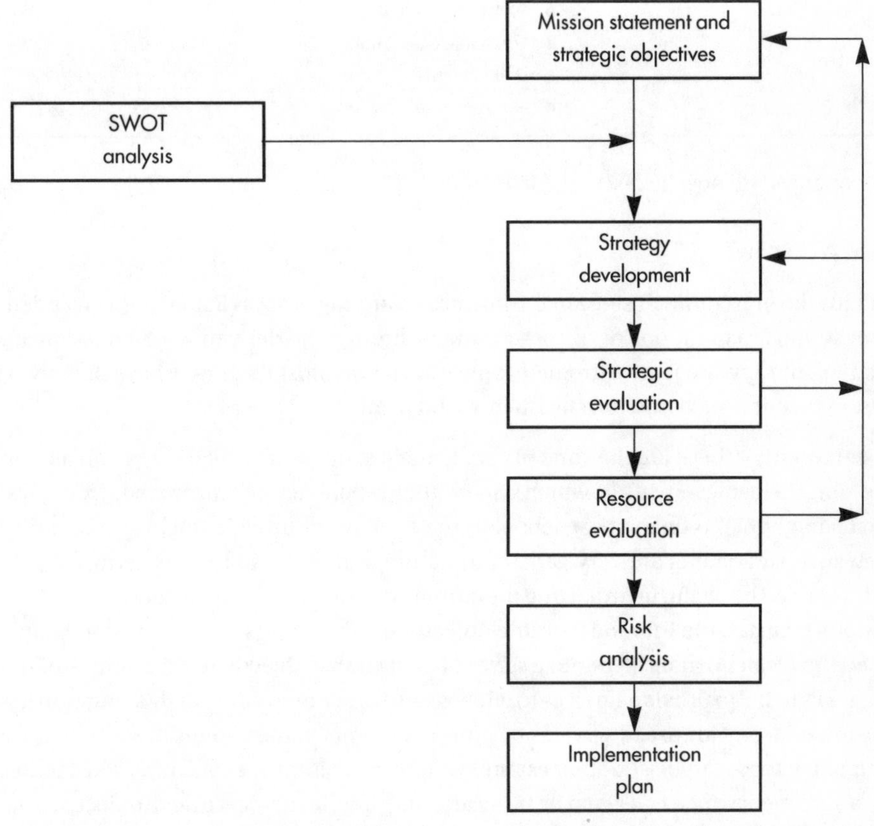

Figure 9 Stages of business planning

These various stages can be linked and summarized in terms of three key questions:

Question	*Stages of business planning*
1. Where do we wish to go to?	• mission statement • strategic objectives
2. Where are we now?	• SWOT analysis including an internal appraisal of the organization and an external appraisal of its business environment
3. How do we get there?	• strategy development • strategic evaluation • resource evaluation • risk analysis • implementation plan

Each of these stages will now be discussed in turn.

MISSION STATEMENT

This is perhaps the most difficult stage in the business planning process in that it involves defining the longer-term strategic aspirations of the organization through the derivation of a mission statement. Mission statements have become extremely topical such that most PSOs now have their own mission statements. In practice, such mission statements tend to fall into two types:

- **Vision statements** – these are the sorts of very general statements which can mean all things to all persons, and the achievement of which can neither be proved nor disproved. Examples of such statements might be 'to be the best school in the area' or 'to provide the best standards of care'. Although such statements are very general in nature and of limited use in terms of longer-term planning they can be useful in projecting the corporate vision of the organization.
- **Expressions translatable into measurable objectives** – these sorts of mission statements contain elements which can be translated into a series of measurable objectives. An example of this type of statement might be 'to provide services to all sectors of the community'. In this situation it would be possible to set targets for use of services by different sectors of the community and to measure the achievement of those targets. Another example might be 'to improve consumer satisfaction continuously', a statement which can again be translated into a series of measurable objectives monitored by the conduct of surveys.

STRATEGIC OBJECTIVES

These outline in more concrete terms what the organization wishes to try and achieve in the longer term. Such objectives should be derived from the mission statement but should be more precise and preferably quantifiable. For example, PSO strategic objectives could cover any of the following:

- to increase the share of the local market (for example numbers of school pupils)
- to diversify into other areas of service activity not currently undertaken
- to rationalize the range of service provision
- to provide a more comprehensive local service
- to make continual improvements in the quality of service delivery.

SWOT ANALYSIS

Business planning must be undertaken in the real world with a full understanding of where one is coming from and what the future may hold. A key element of business planning is SWOT (strengths, weaknesses, opportunities, threats) analysis which comprises two distinct but related elements. Firstly, there is a need to review the organization itself and its internal structure and operations. All individuals and organizations have strengths and weaknesses and in preparing a business plan it is essential to review the internal working of the organization to establish what is done well and what is done badly. It would be pointless to base an entire business strategy around a set of activities in which the provider is known to be weak. It would be sensible to base such a strategy around activities where it is known to be strong. While this may seem obvious, it is not always carried out.

Undertaking just an internal review of the organization would be rather introspective. In any business environment changes in the outside world must be considered to assess their potential impact on the business. The second part of the SWOT analysis concerns the external environment in which the provider organization must operate. The aim is to identify opportunities to seize and threats to avoid or negate. This will be further discussed when considering the actual formulation of business strategies. Arguably, this failure to look externally has been one of the historic weaknesses of the public sector but it is one which will have to be remedied in a quasi-commercial environment.

Each of these aspects of the SWOT analysis is now considered in more detail:

- **Internal appraisal of strengths and weaknesses** – it is essential that an internal assessment be carried out systematically, honestly and preferably by someone who is independently-minded. Experience has shown that many organizations overstate their strengths and understate their weaknesses because they find it uncomfortable to face up to reality. Some of the main areas to be addressed in this internal review are shown below and in an appendix to this chapter a checklist of some of the specific points to be considered is provided:

  - existing range of services and markets
  - human resources
  - management capabilities
  - service delivery capabilities
  - financial performance and position.

  Undertaking an assessment of internal strengths and weaknesses is not always straightforward and simple. For example, an older workforce might be a strength or a weakness depending upon circumstances. On the one hand it might be a repository of great experience while on the other hand it may be resistant to change and new ideas. Similarly, the capability to undertake very specialized clinical procedures might be a strength but might also be a weakness if purchasers do not wish to purchase these services. It is important to identify the underlying strength or weakness in a business context.

- **External appraisal of opportunities and threats** – the following are matters that might need to be considered when undertaking an external review. It is important to realize that these factors can represent an opportunity or a threat depending on circumstances:

  - **Demographic trends** – changes in the size of the population served and its structure in terms of age, sex and social class will impact on the demand for services within the area.
  - **Purchaser trends** – clearly, trends with regard to their purchasers are of great significance to service providers in undertaking business planning and can represent opportunities or threats. It is

important to bear in mind the changing priorities of purchasers and the resources they have available.

- **Competitor trends** – where a provider is operating in a competitive environment, the identification of competitors is a key component of the SWOT analysis. Current or potential competitors may be found in the particular markets in which the provider operates. Depending on the type of service being considered, competitors could come from the local area, regionally, nationally and sometimes internationally. For example, a university might see local further education colleges as competitors for part-time courses and other local and national universities as competitors for full-time courses.
- **Technological trends** – developments in technology are likely to come on stream during the period of the business plan and these can provide both opportunities and threats.
- **Professional practice trends** – in many areas of public service there are frequent changes in professional practice and legal requirements. Changes on the horizon would need to be considered as part of the business planning process.
- **Physical environment trends** – trends in the physical environment can provide both opportunities and threats and need to be considered. Some examples of trends which could have impacts on public service provision could be new road developments, factory developments and housing developments.

The depth of the external analysis review really depends on two factors:

- how much time and resources are available to conduct the exercise
- the nature of the organization's mission statement.

For example, if the mission statement is merely concerned with the provision of local services then the external review does not need to go much wider. On the other hand, if the mission statement and strategic objectives suggests a much wider brief then the review will have to be extensive. The key point with such an external review is that it is methodical. People often glibly claim to have addressed all the relevant issues only to find on further questioning that they have only looked at them superficially.

DEVELOPING BUSINESS STRATEGIES

The next stage is developing a business strategy capable of attaining the mission statement and strategic objectives that the organization has set itself. In reality, a number of different strategies might be developed, recognizing that there are usually several different routes to any destination. Identifying business strategies is a creative task, the importance of which cannot be overestimated, and the aim will be to identify the various types of activities the organization might undertake. This must always be considered in the context of the mission statement and strategic objectives developed earlier. Several approaches can be used including combinations of:

- Brainstorming, involving staff at all levels in the organization, to generate ideas and gain staff commitment.
- Reflecting on the question of 'what business are we in?'. This is used frequently by organizations in the private sector to establish the longer-term business objectives. A community NHS Trust might regard its business as providing clinical care in a community setting. However, perhaps it should think of itself as providing total care in a community setting, thus raising the possibility of winning contracts from social services agencies to provide integrated social and clinical care.

- Identifying the successful strategy of similar organizations with the aim of copying that strategy.
- Obtaining opinions from various external parties about alternative business strategies. For example, one major manufacturer in the electronics field began its strategy development process by asking its customers how they thought it should develop. It would seem eminently sensible for PSOs to get the views of their main purchasers about how they should develop.

EVALUATING BUSINESS STRATEGIES

Having identified and developed possible business strategies, the next stage is to evaluate the options available to establish the best way forward. There are two essential matters to consider:

- is the strategy feasible, in that it will enable the mission to be pursued and strategic objectives achieved?
- is the strategy resource feasible in terms of the availability to the organization of key resources?

Both of the above are important and necessary conditions. It is possible to develop strategies which although feasible in terms of strategic objectives are not feasible in resource terms, and equally, it is possible to develop strategies which although feasible in resource terms will not be feasible in achieving strategic objectives. Many commercial organizations have divested themselves of certain activities and resources for the simple reason that continuation of these activities, even though profitable and resource sound, did not fit in with the mission statement and strategic objectives of the organization. Equally with PSOs, even though a particular strategy is resource sound this does not mean it is a course of action that should be pursued.

Effective strategies must reconcile these conditions of being strategically feasible and resource feasible. The issues of strategic feasibility and resource feasibility will now be considered, separately, in more depth.

STRATEGIC FEASIBILITY

This involves evaluating the various strategies identified to decide which, if any, is the best approach. Clearly, there is no certainty involved here and all strategies must involve some element of risk of failure. Hence the evaluation process is concerned with trying to identify that strategy which has the best chance of success in terms of attaining the organization's mission and strategic objectives. Three different evaluation approaches are described below:

- **Identify competitive advantage** – this approach is suitable in certain specific circumstances such as where an organization is in competition with others to provide some or all of its range of services, and it wishes to preserve or expand its share of the market. As the title suggests, the possible business strategies will be evaluated in terms of whether they can give the organization a competitive advantage over the other providers. Such a competitive advantage could be achieved in a number of ways such as by having lower costs, by product differentiation (for example better quality) or by specialization. This approach may be of use to those PSOs who are operating in competitive environments for some of their service provision.
- **Undertake a strategic appraisal** – this approach could be applied irrespective of whether or not a PSO was in a competitive market. It involves the SWOT analysis and evaluating the various strategies proposed against the results of that analysis. If, for example, a particular strategy involves utilizing one of the existing strengths of the PSO then clearly this would be a plus point for that

strategy. However, if the strategy required an activity in an area where the PSO was weak, such as poorly-skilled staff, then it would be faced with a choice of either not pursuing that particular strategy, or taking action to reduce or eradicate the weakness involved, possibly requiring significant investment to do so. Each of the strategies identified is judged in relationship to whether it involves building on the internal strengths or weaknesses of the PSO, or whether it involves building on areas identified as opportunities for the PSO or areas identified as threats. Thus, for each strategy it will be necessary to build up a scorecard for each of the strategies identified and to come to an informed judgement about which is the best.

- **Portfolio analysis** – this is a somewhat different approach which involves evaluating strategies according to their risk–return profile. In any walk of life the reality is that different sets of activities will generate different rates of return and also will have different risk profiles. Furthermore, in the real world it is always the case that high return is associated with high risk and vice versa. The same concept can be applied with business activities where different activities will have different risk and return profiles. Different business strategies could be evaluated by a consideration of their risk–return profiles, usually referred to as portfolio analysis. Within a PSO there can be various aspects of risk and return which fit into two main groups, those relating to the risk–return profile of service activities and those relating to the risk–return profile of the resources used to undertake those service activities. Dealing first with service issues, it would be important to consider the mix of services, the mix of contract types and the mix of purchasers. Resource issues would need to consider the human resource mix, the fixed asset mix and the mix of capital finance. There is no correct combination of risk and return. It is for each organization to choose a strategy that they judge to be most appropriate for the risk and return they expect to achieve. Clearly, the development of the PFI has major implications for organizations in considering their risk–return profile.

It is important to emphasize that these three approaches to evaluating strategies are not mutually exclusive but can be applied individually or in combination.

RESOURCE FEASIBILITY

As well as being feasible in terms of achieving strategic objectives, strategies must also be feasible in resource terms. 'Resources' in this context means manpower, fixed assets and supplies, and finance, and some of the factors which may result in a strategy not being resource feasible are:

- specialist manpower is unavailable
- fixed assets and supplies are unobtainable
- the whole strategy is financially unsound
- redundant resources cannot be disposed of.

Although finance is not the only resource which must be considered, it is perhaps the most critical. Given the importance of financial viability, it is essential that business strategies are supported by a set of financial projections based on their forecast income and costs. These should incorporate the following financial statements for 3–5 years ahead:

- **Income and expenditure account** – this will show the forecast financial performance for each year in question and will show whether it aims to make a surplus or deficit for those years. It will enable the organization to assess the rate of return it is likely to achieve on its assets.
- **Balance sheet** – this will show the forecast financial position at the end of each financial year in terms of assets and liabilities.

- **Capital programme** – this will indicate the planned pattern of capital expenditure of the organization over the strategic period, and the revenue returns. These figures will influence both the income and expenditure account in terms of depreciation, and the balance sheet in terms of fixed assets.
- **Cash flow statement** – this will show the pattern of cash inflow and outflow over the strategic period, covering both revenue and capital items.

BUSINESS PLANNING AND RISK MANAGEMENT

Any business plan should consider the potential risks faced by the organization and the possible ways in which those risks might be dealt with. Any of the factors listed below will introduce a risk element in the organization which needs to be considered as part of the business planning process:

- **Market and trading position** – including the organization's position in the market-place, its product range and its actual or potential competitors. Where purchasers have considerable choice, providers face considerable risk.
- **Resources and assets** – risk factors surrounding the physical assets and human resources. Some examples here could be the risk of loss of specialist manpower, structural problems in building, unreliable equipment or IT failure.
- **Management skills** – the management skills that the organization possesses and the size of the management agenda facing the management team. Poor-quality management introduces a large element of risk for the organization. However, even the best management team can be overwhelmed by a large and demanding agenda.
- **Information** – inappropriate information, particularly financial information, introduces a considerable risk factor for the organization.

In business planning, issues of uncertainty and risk must be addressed systematically. A possible approach is shown in Figure 10.

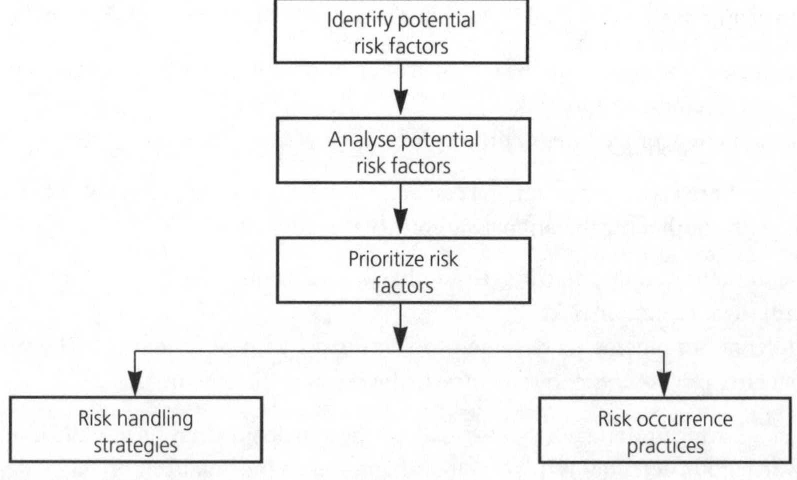

Figure 10 Risk analysis and management

- **Risk identification** – the first stage must be to identify possible sources and causes of risk. This task must be thoroughly undertaken and may require considerable thought, brainstorming and critical evaluation. It is vitally important not to short-circuit this process and to assume that all risks have already been identified. Further analysis often shows that they have not.

- **Risk analysis** – it is essential to analyse the various risks and their likely impact. From a financial perspective such a risk analysis frequently involves the use of a financial model. This will enable managers to see the overall financial impact of changes in basic assumptions by posing 'what if?' questions. For example, it may be desirable to know the impact on financial results if any of the events shown below actually happened:
  - loss of income
  - excessive cost inflation
  - cost overrun on the capital programme
  - capital programme slippage
  - different capital structure
  - technological failure.
- **Risk prioritization** – based on the results of the above analysis, the next stage is to tabulate the various risks identified in terms of order of priority to be addressed.
- **Risk handling strategies** – having undertaken risk analysis and identified the main risk factors, the organization has to decide what to do about it. Broadly, there are only four possible actions in relation to each risk factor:

  - minimize risk
  - transfer or share risk
  - avoid risk
  - retain risk.

  Each of these approaches is discussed below:

  - **Minimize risk** – actions could be taken to minimize the risks faced by the organization. Some examples of approaches that could be applied as a means of minimizing exposure to risk are:

    - an ineffective manager might be replaced or an unreliable machine might be replaced
    - staff training could be undertaken
    - establishment of procedures or protocols.

  - **Transfer or share risk** – organizations can aim to transfer risk or share risk either with the purchaser or with another organization. Examples of this could be:

    - Sub-contracting certain activities to another organization.
    - Insuring against certain risks.
    - Contractual arrangements designed to share risks with other parties. The process of risk transfer to a private company is central to the Private Finance Initiative.

  - **Avoid risk** – having undertaken the risk analysis the conclusion may be that the level of risk associated with certain activities is unacceptably high. Hence the organization might decide to avoid this risk by not undertaking a particular activity or undertaking it in a very different way.
  - **Retain risk** – not all risks can be transferred or eliminated completely and there is sure to be an element of residual risk. Thus, the organization must be clear about which risks it is prepared to retain and accept.

- **Risk occurrence practices** – in view of the residual risks which are bound to be retained within the organization, it is important to have established practices and procedures for dealing with such risks should the risks actually manifest themselves. A number of issues need to be addressed:

  - **Monitor risk factors** – having identified those risk factors which are retained within the organization, it is important that they are monitored effectively. The aim is to minimize potential impact of these risk factors by obtaining an early warning of potential problems. Key aspects of effective risk monitoring include:
    - **effective information systems** – to ensure that there is early warning of problems such as contract overruns which are in the pipeline
    - **clear management arrangements** – to ensure that action is taken in relation to these risks.

  - **Contingency plans** – various forms of contingency plan need to be developed to deal with the impact of retained risk factors which actually manifest themselves. These could involve such matters as:

    - arrangements to hire contract personnel to replace the loss of specialist staff
    - arrangements to lease buildings or equipment to replace any lost through breakdown or sabotage.

  - **Financial provision** – attempts should be made to identify actions that can generate financial provisions to deal with the impact of risks that might occur. Examples include the development of:

    - cost improvement programmes
    - income generation plans
    - programmes of potential fixed asset sales
    - estate retrenchment plans to raise cash through land and building sales.

In summary, the business plan needs to take account of all of the above considerations. The action plan must set out firm measures for risk management.

BUSINESS PLANNING IN PRACTICE

There is no single correct approach to business planning and it is up to PSOs to decide what is best for them. The key point is that they undertake some form of business planning and do it well. The approach to business planning described above is very much the standard model and in practice different organizations will apply this standard model in different ways to meet their own specific needs. Although there will be many variations on a theme, it is suggested that business planning in PSO provider organizations might fall broadly into one of the two following approaches. These two approaches map on to the two types of public sector service provider:

- Those service providers which operate in a competitive environment. An example might be a local authority DSO.
- Those service providers who do not operate in a competitive environment. Examples of this might be an executive agency or rural hospital which is effectively a monopolistic provider.

COMPETITION-BASED PROVIDERS

Those service providers which operate in a competitive environment will probably undertake business planning in a similar manner to that described above, whereby they undertake a SWOT analysis and prepare business plans to meet their strategic objectives in the light of this analysis. Such organizations will look at their existing capabilities and capacities and may well plan to expand their business base by a combination of, for example:

- gaining contracts from a wider range of purchasers
- providing a broader range of services
- focusing on higher-value services.

Such an approach to business planning is akin to that undertaken in the private sector, whereby the organization is trying to influence its own destiny in an active manner.

NON-COMPETITIVE PROVIDERS

These types of provider may undertake business planning in a much more restrictive manner than described above. They will recognize that as in reality they have only one main purchaser, and that purchaser has a finite level of resources and specific priorities, then their business plan must be built around the needs of that purchaser. Thus, business planning becomes a matter of estimating income levels to be derived from the purchaser, and of preparing a business plan within the framework of these income projections and of the declared priorities of the purchaser. In these circumstances, such organizations may regard processes such as SWOT analysis as being time-consuming and of little value. Hence they may not undertake such an analysis every year, if at all. Such an approach is more passive in manner but, in reality, the organization may have little freedom to do otherwise.

IMPLEMENTATION OF BUSINESS PLANS

It has already been noted that purchaser strategic plans do not implement themselves, and the same comment applies to provider business plans. Certain actions need to be undertaken, the key ones of which are described below.

EFFECTIVE IMPLEMENTATION PLANNING

Business plans do not implement themselves. A comprehensive action plan needs to be prepared to ensure that the planned events actually occur. In reality, the large size of many action plans is frequently due to the need to describe the large number of tasks that need to be undertaken to put the business plan into action. Such an action plan will have a number of key elements including:

- tasks that need to be performed
- individual responsibilities for ensuring they are performed
- timetable for completing tasks
- resources needed.

In addition, the plan may identify critical success factors and possible bottlenecks in implementation and possible ways around them. The approach to these issues could adopt project management techniques.

CHANGE MANAGEMENT ARRANGEMENTS

It has already been emphasized that the implementation of a strategic plan will probably require substantial changes in the organization arrangements and operational practices within the organization. Such changes are often so radical that they may generate fierce opposition and resistance to change from many parts of the organization, and the successful implementation of the strategic plan rests on overcoming such resistance to change. Hence the organization needs to develop a suitable change management programme and commit sufficient resources to that programme. This issue of change management is discussed in more detail in Chapter 6.

MONITORING OF BUSINESS PLANS

Few implementations go completely according to plan. Hence it is important that the implementation of a plan is monitored robustly. In practice this means the following:

- **Project management** – having suitable project management arrangements to ensure that the progress of implementing a business plan is constantly reviewed and updated, and that immediate action is taken where the implementation deviates seriously from plan. Hence it is important to have, on the steering group, managers of sufficient seniority that they can initiate the actions required.
- **Information** – clearly, the project management group will require adequate information about the progress being made in implementing the business plan, and the impacts of that implementation.

WEAKNESSES OF PUBLIC SECTOR STRATEGIC PLANNING

A number of general weaknesses with strategic planning in the public sector can be identified. Some of these are discussed below:

- **Paper process** – many public sector strategic plans are weighty documents comprising a voluminous description and analysis of the current organization and pattern of services. As such, they often contain little consideration of alternative approaches to service provision other than 'wish lists' of service developments to be undertaken should funds be made available. It is almost as if the quality of the plan is seen as being synonymous with its thickness.
- **Lack of explicitness** – because of the political nature of many public services, PSOs often try to avoid being explicit about issues of strategic objectives, pattern of services and so on. One example of this concerns obsolete activities. Strategic management must look at ways of improving public sector services and since PSOs have limited resources, the improvement of services may have to result in the discontinuation of services which are obsolete or of limited value. However, this is often a sensitive issue and PSOs sometimes prefer to avoid dealing with this issue.
- **Involvement of service professionals** – service professionals such as teachers, doctors and social workers are the actual deliverers of public sector services in provider organizations. One common weakness is a failure to engage fully those service professionals in the strategic planning process. Consequently, it is sometimes the case that service professionals are neither aware of nor committed to the content of the strategic plan and may obstruct its implementation. It has to be said, however, that this is often the fault of the professionals themselves rather than the strategic planners. Many service professionals are so resistant to change that they still insist on referring to strategic planning as an 'administrative' function and, therefore, one of no relevance to them. Strategic planning should be concerned with improving the quality and quantity of services delivered to the public, but often it appears that service professionals are more committed to retention of existing professional practices than improving services.

- **Organizational change** – very few strategic plans can be implemented without some form of organizational change. As has already been stated, in many ways, strategic planning can be seen as synonymous with the planning of organizational change. However, in many PSOs the production of a strategic planning document is seen as the end of the line and little or no consideration is given to issues of organizational change.

APPENDIX: ASSESSING STRENGTHS AND WEAKNESSES: SUGGESTED FACTORS FOR EXAMINATION

- **Existing services and markets**
  - service range
  - risk of obsolescence
  - stage in the life cycle of the service
  - degree of market penetration
  - quality standards
  - service flexibility
  - market research capability
  - service marketing approaches
  - new service development capability.
- **Human resources**
  - cost of employment
  - mix of staff
  - sickness absence rates
  - age profile
  - skill level or skill shortages
  - industrial relations
  - flexibility of deployment
  - conditions of service
  - turnover
  - morale.
- **Management capabilities**
  - numbers
  - skills
  - shortage areas
  - age profile
  - adaptability
  - recruitment and retention packages
  - performance appraisal approaches
  - hierarchical levels
  - management information systems
  - level of delegation.
- **Service delivery capabilities**
  - unit labour costs
  - access to supplies
  - cost of supplies
  - access to information
  - physical location
  - condition of fixed asset base
  - capacity of fixed asset base
  - overheads.

- **Financial performance and position**
  - unit cost level
  - income and expenditure performance
  - rate of return
  - access to capital finance
  - cash flow.

CHAPTER FIVE

Financial Management in the Public Sector

Money is a key resource for all PSOs and the various trends in the public sector, referred to in Chapter 3, have impacted significantly on the status, role and practice of financial management in the public sector. In particular, the following points should be kept in mind as having had a major impact on the practice of financial management and control in PSOs:

- the emphasis on PSOs achieving strategic objectives
- the continued drive for improved performance including improved resource efficiency
- increased managerial delegation within PSOs including budgetary delegation
- increased emphasis on public accountability and probity
- the trend towards charging for services and hence the need to cost those services.

These factors have had two main implications:

- the need for more sophisticated and higher-calibre financial systems and specialist finance staff in PSOs
- the need for general managers and service professionals in PSOs to have a good grasp of financial issues.

This chapter will consider the main financial management activities in PSOs. The aim will be to give the reader an understanding of the main features of each activity, its purpose and the way in which it has evolved in recent years.

CLASSIFYING TECHNIQUES OF FINANCIAL MANAGEMENT

Many of the techniques of financial management in PSOs have similar names and have similar approaches to those employed in commercial organizations. The key point to note is that all the financial management techniques described below should assist management decision making in the organization, and thus the appropriateness of the various aspects of financial management need to be judged according to the contribution they can make to such decision making.

While good financial management is critical, its importance should not be overstated. In a commercial organization it would be folly to suggest that decisions that affect the future of the organization should be taken on purely financial grounds, and with commercial decisions it is quite often the case that other matters such as quality, human resources or marketing are at least as important, if not more important, than financial matters. Equally, it is the case that the financial dimension of managerial decisions cannot be ignored. Throughout this chapter the way in which various financial management techniques can assist in decision making in PSOs will be emphasized.

One way of classifying financial management techniques is by decision type and timescale. This is illustrated in Table 7.

These various techniques are then discussed in the sections below.

Table 7 Financial management techniques

Organizational decision	*Financial technique*	*Timescale*
Strategic	Capital investment appraisal	over 3 years
	Strategic financial planning	over 3 years
Strategic/managerial	Resource allocation	1–3 years
	Costing	1–3 years
	Pricing	1–3 years
	Budgeting	1–3 years
Managerial/operational	Financial accounting	up to 1 year
	Financial control	up to 1 year

CAPITAL INVESTMENT APPRAISAL

Like most organizations in the private sector, many PSOs undertake a wide range of capital investment in new buildings, refurbishments and new equipment and vehicles. Such capital investment usually requires careful consideration and evaluation for a number of reasons, including the following:

- **Large-scale expenditure** – frequently capital projects involve the expenditure of large sums of money. For example, a new district general hospital can cost in excess of £100 million while even the purchase of a fairly routine piece of equipment can exceed £100 000.
- **Longer-term service implications** – capital investment usually has long-term service implications. The construction of a new school may have implications for education provision in an area for many decades.
- **Irreversibility** – many capital projects, once undertaken, cannot be reversed without significant additional cost. For example, if a new hospital is built in the wrong place there is little that can be done since there is not much of a market for second-hand hospitals.
- **Incremental revenue costs** – some forms of capital investment can lead to lower overall revenue costs, the best example of this being investment in energy conservation where a capital investment can lead to lower annual energy costs. However, the reality is that many forms of capital investment in the public sector often lead to higher revenue costs.

Given the great emphasis placed by PSOs on the achievement of strategic objectives, it will be clear that effective decisions about capital investment will be critical to achieving those objectives. Errors in capital investment decisions can make it very difficult for those strategic objectives to be achieved. Hence, for all these reasons, it is important that decisions about capital investment are rigorously appraised both in service terms and financial terms.

In this chapter some techniques of financial and economic evaluation are outlined which can be used to appraise and evaluate public sector capital projects. Firstly, the basis of the technique will be described, and then its applicability in the public sector will be considered. The techniques of financial and economic appraisal discussed are:

- discounted cash flow (DCF)
- cost–benefit analysis (CBA)
- cost utility analysis (CUA).

DISCOUNTED CASH FLOW AND THE TIME VALUE OF MONEY

As discussed above, capital projects (such as buildings) often take several years to complete and once complete usually have a working life of many years. Any approach to appraising capital projects must therefore adopt a multi-year approach, looking over the complete life of the capital project. Traditional commercial approaches to capital investment appraisal, such as payback and accountant's rate of return, compare the cost of a project with the additional revenue streams the project might generate in the future. For example, using these techniques, a company may compare the cost of building a new factory with the net revenue streams generated by sales of products produced by that factory. The main weakness of such traditional approaches is that they ignore the time factor. They assume that the only issue to be considered is the size of the various cash flows involved and that the timing of those cash flows is irrelevant. Thus they assume that £100 received or paid in year 1 is equivalent to £100 received in year 2 and so on. However, economics teaches that money has a time value as well as a magnitude and argues that £100 in year 1 has a greater value than £100 in year 2, which has greater value than £100 in year 3, and so on. There are two reasons why this is the case:

- **Time preference** – £100 today is intrinsically more valuable than £100 in a year's time because the future is uncertain and in a year's time one may no longer be around to enjoy the benefit of that £100.
- **Opportunity cost** – £100 today can be invested to produce a return which will be in excess of £100 in a year's time. Assuming an interest rate of 10 per cent, £100 today will be worth £110 in a year's time and £121 in two years' time. Consequently, £100 today has more value than £100 in a year's time.

This basic principle of time value of money leads to the DCF approach which takes account of both the magnitude and the timing of the cash flows involved when evaluating capital projects. It is not possible here to give a full explanation of the DCF approach and the interested reader is referred to the many excellent books on the subject, but an attempt is made here to give a brief explanation of the rationale of the method.

With DCF, cash flows, whether they are inflows or outflows, in whatever time period they occur are converted to a common point of reference, namely a present value. Present value is essentially the converse of compound interest. Assuming an interest rate of 10 per cent, then if £100 has a future value of £110 in a year's time the converse is that £110 receivable in a year's time has a present value of £100. Similarly, £121 receivable in two years' time has a present value of £100. Thus, all cash flows can be converted to a present value. When inflows and outflows are combined, the present value becomes a net present value (NPV).

Let us look at a simple example to see how this might work in practice. An organization is considering two possible projects involving investment in new equipment, both of which have a capital cost of £100,000. The organization can borrow money at 10 per cent to purchase the equipment. Both types of equipment have a four-year life and will be used to manufacture different products. There will be production costs associated with the manufacture of the products and revenues from the sales of the products. The financial implications are shown below:

Year	Project X Production costs £	Project X Sales revenue generated £	Project X Net cash flow £	Project Y Production costs £	Project Y Sales revenue generated £	Project Y Net cash flow £
1	–20 000	+60 000	+40 000	–20 000	+38 000	+18 000
2	–30 000	+65 000	+35 000	–30 000	+65 000	+35 000
3	–30 000	+65 000	+35 000	–30 000	+65 000	+35 000
4	–20 000	+36 000	+16 000	–20 000	+60 000	+40 000

Using DCF one obtains the following picture:

Project X

Year	Net cash flow £	Discount factor = present value of £1 in the year (10%)		Present value of cash flow £
0	–100 000	1.00		–100 000
1	+ 40 000	0.91		+ 36 400
2	+ 35 000	0.83		+ 29 050
3	+ 35 000	0.75		+ 26 250
4	+ 16 000	0.68		+ 10 880
Total	+ 26 000		NPV =	+ 2580

Project Y

Year	Net cash flow £	Discount factor = present value of £1 in the year (10%)		Present value of cash flow £
0	–100 000	1.00		–100 000
1	+ 18 000	0.91		+ 16 380
2	+ 35 000	0.83		+ 29 050
3	+ 35 000	0.75		+ 26 250
4	+ 40 000	0.68		+ 27 200
Total	+ 28 000		NPV =	– 1120

Three points should be noted about these results:

- In terms of total cash flow, project Y has a larger positive net cash flow than project X.
- Project X has a larger net present value of cash flows than project Y. This is because the larger positive cash flows in project X occur earlier in the lifespan of the project and thus generate higher present values than cash flows occurring later in the project.
- Project X has a positive NPV whereas project Y has a negative NPV.

DCF techniques provide two decision rules for the financial appraisal of potential capital projects:

- In purely financial terms, projects which show a positive NPV should be undertaken while those which have negative NPVs should not be undertaken. In this case, project X should be undertaken but project Y should not.
- Where several competing projects have positive NPVs but only one can be undertaken (for example because of limited investment funds available), the project with the highest positive NPV should be chosen.

The results of a DCF analysis will be significantly affected by the discount rate used in the analysis. In the above example, for simplicity, a discount rate of 10 per cent was used. However, in the public sector PSOs are usually required to use a discount rate of 6 per cent, as laid down by HM Treasury. The validity of this 6 per cent discount rate may be questioned but it is supposed to represent the marginal rate of return, in real terms, being achieved by the private sector of the economy.

It must be remembered that DCF is only concerned with the *financial* appraisal of potential capital projects and, as such, it does not deal with non-financial costs and benefits. Given the nature of many public sector projects, which involve investment for service provision purposes rather than income generation purposes, it might be thought that DCF techniques have limited applicability. To some extent this is the case, but DCF can be used in the public sector in a number of specific ways:

- **Commercial-type projects** – PSOs may need to assess potential capital projects in a similar manner to a private company. For example, as already noted, some PSOs which are concerned with the provision of services have strict financial targets to be achieved. Thus undertaking capital investment projects which are not financially viable can make it difficult for PSOs to achieve their financial targets. Hence, DCF can assist in the financial appraisal of such projects. Alternatively, a PSO may be considering undertaking a capital project which has a strong income generation or cost reduction element and is akin to a private sector project. Again, DCF is relevant to the appraisal of the project.
- **Decision simplification** – where there are several projects under consideration, with differing costs and differing profiles of benefits, occurring over a period of years, then assessing the financial consequences of each project can be confusing. DCF can be used to present the costs of the project as a single figure (NPV) instead of a profile of costs occurring over several years. This single cost figure can then be compared against the non-financial costs and benefits.
- **Cost–benefit analysis** – as an input into the process of cost-benefit analysis (see the following section).

COST–BENEFIT ANALYSIS

DCF is purely a technique of financial evaluation and several criticisms can be levelled at its use as a technique of investment appraisal:

- DCF techniques use a narrow definition of cost. They consider only financial costs and ignore social costs. Social costs go beyond the financial costs to the organization concerned and cover costs to society at large of matters such as pollution, traffic congestion and noise.
- DCF techniques do not consider the benefits of a project other than those manifested through positive cash inflows. Most public sector capital projects are not undertaken with the aim of generating additional revenues and profits but are concerned with the benefits arising from increasing the range and quality of service provision.

- DCF techniques do not take a long-term view. They only consider projects during the period when cash flows are taking place, and not the complete lifespan of the project which may be many decades.

Cost-benefit analysis (CBA) is a technique of economic evaluation designed to overcome these limitations, although within CBA the principles of discounting are utilized. CBA has been used in many parts of the public sector to assist with decisions about major capital projects, but is fraught with difficulties and has many critics.

The basic methodology of CBA can be summarized as shown in Figure 11.

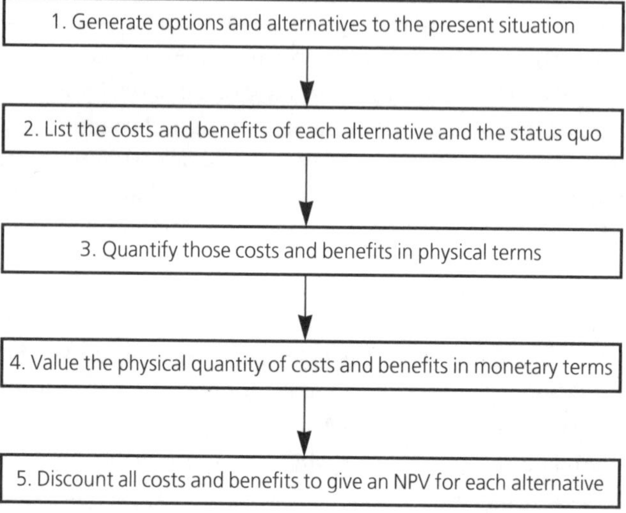

Figure 11 Cost–benefit analysis

Each of these stages is discussed below.

- **Generate options** – it is important in project appraisal that one does not just consider a single approach to the perceived problems. Several different options and solutions must be developed in order that comparisons can be made. One of these options should be the maintenance of the status quo. The identification of options is perhaps the most difficult and creative part of CBA. It requires considerable imagination and creativity and full use should be made of techniques such as brainstorming and assessment of staff opinions.
- **List costs and benefits** – this should not prove too difficult a task. All that is required is that, for each option, a full list of the potential costs and benefits are identified. It must be emphasized that the term 'costs of an option' means more than just the financial costs. It is intended to cover any social costs.
- **Quantify costs and benefits** – given that a list of costs and benefits has been drawn up, the next stage is to try and quantify those benefits and costs in physical terms. Some public sector examples of this would be:

  Benefits
  - reductions in patient mortality rates through investment in new surgical equipment
  - reductions in response times from investment in new police communications equipment

- reductions in supervisory staff numbers resulting from investment in new prisons with improved layout
- reductions in break-ins due to investment in school security equipment
- reductions in journey times resulting from investment in public transport
- reductions in breakdown rates resulting from investment in new ambulances.

Costs

- increases in traffic noise levels resulting from investment in new roads
- increases in the stress levels of staff resulting from investment in new computerized equipment to replace manual procedures.

- **Value costs and benefits** – this is perhaps the most difficult and contentious part of the CBA approach. An attempt must be made to place monetary values on all of the cost and benefits described above. In some cases (for example valuing any staff savings) this is relatively easy to achieve. However, in other areas it is fraught with difficulties of methodology and objectivity. How, for example, does one place monetary values on benefits such as reductions in mortality, reductions in response times and increases in traffic noise levels? In practice, CBA analysts have in the past attempted to place values on benefits such as these, but the approaches adopted have generated considerable controversy and often undermined the whole of the CBA approach.
- **Discount costs and benefits** – having valued the projected costs and benefits of each option over a period of years these costs and benefits can then be discounted at the test discount rate to give an NPV of costs and benefits.

This NPV of costs and benefits combined can then be used in decision making. In terms of economic theory, every project which shows a positive NPV should be undertaken but in practice, limitations on resources available means that choices usually have to be made. Thus, a choice between competing projects can be made on the basis of the highest NPV of costs and benefits.

CBA in the pure form has, in the past, been used in many parts of the public sector to appraise potential large-scale capital developments, such as the Jubilee underground line and the various proposals for the siting of a third London airport. With such projects there have been substantial problems and criticisms relating, particularly, to the valuation in monetary terms of such benefits as reduced traffic congestion, numbers of lives saved, increased travel comfort and so on. Attempts were made, but these had dubious objectivity. However, there are more pragmatic approaches to CBA which can be adopted without destroying the overall philosophy of trying to compare benefits with costs. For example, the approach to capital investment shown in Figure 12 applies a more practical form of CBA, which involves scoring and weighting social benefits and social costs rather than quantifying and expressing them in monetary terms:

- **Identify investment objectives** – objectives must be defined which are specific, measurable, achievable, relevant and time-linked. It is important that these objectives concentrate on the end results of the proposed investment and not the means of achieving them.
- **Generate options** – it is important that as many options as possible are generated as a means of meeting the objectives. In addition, a do-nothing option will also be needed as a basis for comparison.
- **Measure the benefits** – an analysis needs to be undertaken of the benefits likely to be derived from each of the options. In summary the approach to be adopted is as follows:

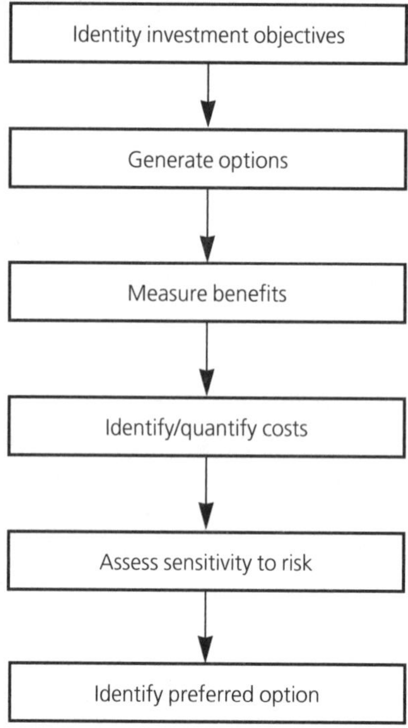

Figure 12 Practical approach to capital investment appraisal

- Those benefits which can be expressed in financial terms, such as cost savings, are to be netted-off against the costs of the option.
- A series of benefit criteria needs to be identified at the outset. These criteria could include quality of service, accessibility to services and physical environment, but should be derived from the investment objectives referred to above.
- A weighting factor needs to be derived for each of these benefit criteria which will indicate their relative importance in evaluating options.
- Each of the possible investment options needs to be scored against each of the benefit criteria identified above and the individual scores weighted by the relevant weighting factor. Thus, it will be possible to derive a total weighted score for each option which will indicate the overall level of benefits to be derived.

- **Identify and quantify the costs** – a thorough analysis of the costs associated with each of the options is required. For each option, an estimate of the magnitude and timing must be made for:

  - capital expenditure
  - running costs
  - any cost savings
  - any residual values such as scrap values.

  All of these cash flows must then be discounted to a present value in line with the approach described earlier, to give a net present cost for each option.
- **Assess sensitivity to risk** – in analysing the costs and benefits of the various options under review, certain assumptions will have been made. It is important to test the impact of these assumptions on

the costs and benefits of the various options, and thus their ultimate ranking. This is usually referred to as sensitivity analysis, and it may involve analysing the impact on each option of changes in benefit scores, changes in the weightings given to the benefit criterion and changes in the cost assumptions. Sensitivity analysis will provide an analysis of how robust each of the options is to changes in the basic assumptions.

- **Identify the preferred option** – the approach suggested is to display the various options in order of benefits with the net present costs displayed alongside. The preferred option will be the one which offers the greatest ratio of benefits to costs, although making such a decision may not be easy and may require some subjective judgement.

The essence of CBA, even in this pragmatic form, is still to look at the costs and benefits impacting on all parts of society, not just the organization itself.

COST UTILITY ANALYSIS

CUA is a tool of economic evaluation which is more limited than CBA. Whereas CBA attempts to identify, quantify and possibly value all of the costs and benefits associated with an option, CUA only considers the costs of each project alongside some measure of the overall impact of the project. As with CBA, several options are identified. For each of the options, the costs are easily assessed, but what is also prepared is an assessment of the impact of each option. It should be noted that CUA only helps in making a choice between competing projects with the same overall objective. It does not assist with any decision about whether or not a project is justified in its own right.

CAPITAL INVESTMENT APPRAISAL: PURCHASER–PROVIDER PERSPECTIVES

The policy of separating the purchaser and provider arms of a PSO has had implications for the process of capital investment appraisal. Basically, since provider organizations are quasi-commercial in nature and have business-type objectives to achieve, then they are more likely to find the financial appraisal technique of DCF as being of relevance to them. For example, a provider organization needs to assess whether investment in a new piece of equipment will generate savings and/or additional income streams that will outweigh the costs of investment and, therefore, improve its financial performance. On the other hand, purchasers are more concerned with the need for service and whether a piece of equipment will improve the quantity or quality of service provision. Hence they are likely to find the economic techniques of CBA and CUA of greatest relevance.

CAPITAL INVESTMENT APPRAISAL AND THE PRIVATE FINANCE INITIATIVE

Chapter 3 noted the increasing role of the PFI as a means of financing capital developments in the public sector. Consequently, there is a process which PSOs must go through to obtain approval for a capital project to be financed via the PFI. The precise details of the PFI will vary between government departments and sectors but in broad terms the process is as outlined below:

- **Outline business case (OBC)** – an OBC must be prepared for the project. This OBC will outline the background and rationale for the project. It will identify possible options for undertaking the project and these options will be evaluated using the various techniques discussed above. A preferred option will be identified using this process. The OBC will also need to incorporate a preliminary evaluation of the preferred option, using a private finance route through the use of PFI and a public finance route. In undertaking this evaluation a comparison of the privately financed route (PFI) and the publicly financed route will need to be made against the following criteria:

- for the public and privately financed routes the value for money provided in the use of public funds
- the potential, under the privately financed route, for transferring risk to the private sector
- for the public and privately financed routes, the affordability of the project to the PSO, in terms of the annual financial impact.

The PSO will need the approval of the relevant government department before proceeding to the next stage.

- **Preparation for procurement** – There are a number of tasks which need to be undertaken following completion of the OBC but prior to commencement of the procurement process. These are:

  - to prepare a specification of the outputs, performance standards and quality standards of the project as opposed to the physical inputs of buildings, equipment and staffing. It is this specification of service outputs that will form the basis for the tendering process.
  - The possible appointment of professional advisors.
  - The preparation of an information memorandum for possible private contractors.
  - The development of an initial contract framework for the project under a PFI arrangement.

- **Procurement process** – this is extremely complex and only an overview can be given here. In the likely event that the proposed contract is above the EU procurement threshold then the contract will have to be advertised in the *Official Journal of the European Community (OJEC)*. The advertisement must not be too prescriptive and must give the private sector the flexibility to come up with novel solutions based on the service outputs already specified. The next steps in this stage would be to:

  - issue the information memorandum to interested parties
  - shortlist a small number of tenderers from those who responded to the advert
  - invite the shortlisted firms to tender or negotiate for the provision of services
  - evaluate tenders or negotiate with tenderers
  - select the best solution.

- **Full business case (FBC)** – an FBC will now need to be prepared which will update the details contained in the OBC in the light of the procurement process. Approval of the relevant department will be needed before contracts can be signed.
- **Contract award** – following approval of the FBC, if the best PFI solution is approved, there might be some further negotiations with the successful private contractor. Contracts can then be awarded and the project can go ahead.

STRATEGIC FINANCIAL PLANNING

In any PSO the finance department has important roles to play in terms of processing financial transactions (for example invoice payments and payroll) on a day-to-day basis, and the operation of medium-term control systems such as budgetary control. However, the finance department and operational managers and service professionals in the PSO should also be involved in strategic financial planning over the longer term. The following issues are important:

RESOURCE FORECASTING

This essentially involves forecasting the likely level of resources available to the organization over a strategic period of several years. Such an analysis will need to assess:

- the impact of the government's public expenditure plans on overall public sector funding
- the impact of public policy trends which will impact on different parts of the public sector and individual PSOs
- the impact of possible changes in the mechanisms of resource allocation
- the impact of inflation on the level of purchasing power available to the organization.

Given the level of uncertainty and risk involved it will be necessary to prepare several different resource scenarios based on differing sets of assumptions and upon which different strategic planning scenarios can be built. Financial modelling is an essential tool and will be discussed further below.

FINANCIAL EVALUATION OF STRATEGIC OPTIONS

In preparing strategic plans, PSOs must develop and evaluate a number of strategic options in relation to the provision of services. This was discussed in more detail in Chapter 4. In considering these different strategies it will be necessary to undertake an evaluation of the expenditure implications of these options. Some options which might need to be evaluated include the following:

- reconfiguration of the range and/or volume of service provision
- rationalization or amendment of methods of delivering services
- the impact of major capital investment.

None of these changes can be achieved in one year and thus there must be a multi-year strategy. Longer-term financial plans will be needed to support strategic planning and it is completely inadequate to rely on an annual financial plan. PSOs need to develop a multi-year financial plan covering at least a three-year period and, in some cases, a five-year time horizon will be needed.

Again, in all of the above situations, it would be beneficial if PSOs could develop a financial planning model (or models). Financial modelling is discussed in greater detail below.

FINANCIAL MODELLING

In undertaking financial planning it would be beneficial if PSOs could develop a financial planning model (or models). Today, quite sophisticated financial models can be prepared using available software applications. The model will represent a simplified approximation of the situation in the real world and will be constructed from the essential and significant features of that real world. Some features of the real world are so important that they must be included in the model, while other features can safely be ignored since they will have no significant impact on the model's validity. It must be emphasized that in undertaking strategic financial planning one is not looking for precision. The aim is to evaluate and compare broad strategic options and thus one is looking for the broad-brush financial implications of these options and the degree of significance, in financial terms, between them.

Financial modelling has been used for many years to answer 'What if?' questions, thus allowing for a large number of different scenarios to be financially evaluated. With regard to strategic planning, such models can take account of various factors and can evaluate the financial implications of different planning scenarios. Thus, for example, such a model could be used to simulate the financial impact of changes in the following factors:

- Resources
  - changes in overall growth rates in resources
  - alternative scenarios for resource allocation.
- Services
  - different levels of service activity
  - different types of service mix
  - alternative approaches to service delivery
  - different levels of capital investment and so on.

Such financial models can be used to simulate the financial impact of changes in a variety of different planning scenarios and can indicate where there are major shortfalls between the resources available and the resources needed to put a particular strategic option into effect.

RESOURCE ALLOCATION

Resource allocation means the process of allocating or distributing funds among competing organizations, competing geographic areas or even competing activities. Although such a task is not the sole responsibility of the finance function, the reality is that since the task involves money then the finance function will have a strong involvement. The increasing pressure on funding for public services has meant that the issue of resource allocation has become of increasing importance. In this section consideration will be given to:

- general principles of resource allocation
- approaches to resource allocation
- trends in resource allocation.

GENERAL PRINCIPLES OF RESOURCE ALLOCATION

Before considering different approaches to resource allocation, it is important to assess these against some general principles. Five criteria are important:

- **Equity** – most people would accept that an approach to resource allocation should be fair or equitable. However, equity is not an empirical concept but a moral one, and it is another matter to define equity precisely. Many would argue that equity implies that equality should be achieved by resource allocation, but this creates practical problems. For example, equality of what? This could be, for example:
  - equal share of the money available
  - fair share of the money available
  - evenly spread services provided across the country
  - equality of access to services.

  Equality for whom? adds a further dimension to this discussion. Approaches to resource allocation could be concerned with equality between different:
  - geographic areas

  - organizational types
  - social groups in the community.

  Equity is an extremely complex and important concept which needs careful consideration when evaluating approaches to resource allocation.
- **Objectivity** – it should be possible for any number of people, after studying the proposed method of resource allocation, to agree the basis for allocating resources. It is not necessary for them to agree that the proposed method is the best approach possible, but only for them to be able to agree the results of a particular chosen method.
- **Simplicity** – the chosen approach to resource allocation should be simple to understand, especially by the people most affected by it. Unfortunately, simplicity of approach often implies a lack of statistical sophistication, and there seems to be a drive towards making resource allocation more sensitive and hence more complex. In practice, resource allocation in the public sector has tended to become increasingly complex and consequently it is only understood by a relatively small number of people.
- **Economy** – resource allocation is not a free good and in itself consumes resources in terms of staff time, computer processing, report writing and decision taking. Clearly, it is not desirable to spend a large proportion of scarce resources on the resource allocation task itself. Thus economy in resource allocation is a desirable criteria.
- **Stability** – an approach to resource allocation should result in a reasonable degree of stability from year to year in the funds allocated. Wide variations each year will seriously inhibit medium- and long-term planning and investment.

APPROACHES TO RESOURCE ALLOCATION

Approaches to resource allocation can be divided into three main types:

- **Formula-based approaches** – these are the approaches used where scarce resources are distributed predominantly by use of some form of mechanistic formulae to measure need for resources. Some examples of such approaches in the public sector are:
  - The weighted capitation approach to resource allocation in the NHS. The formula is used to distribute resources between the various health authorities in the country. The formula uses various factors to reflect the need for health services, and hence health service funds, and includes such factors as population size, age and sex structure of the population and death rates in the population.
  - The standard spending assessments (SSA) used in the distribution of central government grants to local government. For each local authority service an SSA is developed by using specific measures of need for specific services. This is then used to assess the government grant due to each local authority.
  - The resource allocation mechanism used by a local education authority (LEA) to distribute funds to individual schools under the local management of schools arrangement (LMS). The bulk of LEA funds are distributed to schools and the main driver is clearly pupil numbers in each school.

  To develop and use a formula-based approach to resource allocation it is necessary for PSOs to undertake two major tasks as illustrated below:

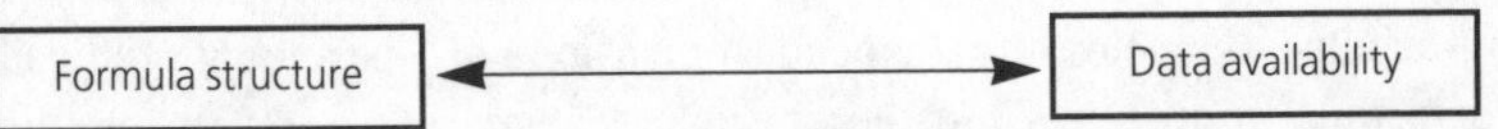

- An acceptable formula will need to be developed which adequately measures the need for resources of the PSOs involved. As already noted it is desirable that this formula is not so complex that few people understand its composition.
- Data must be available for use in the formula. There is no point in including a factor in the formula where no data is available or can be obtained at reasonable cost. In this situation some surrogate data might need to be used. The previous approach to resource allocation in the NHS (termed the RAWP formula) required the use of morbidity (sickness) data within the formula. However, since no reliable data on morbidity was available the formula used mortality data (death rates) as a surrogate.

- **Negotiation** – under this approach scarce funds may be allocated among competing priorities by means of some form of negotiation between the giver of funds and the PSOs needing those funds. Clearly, such an approach can be extremely time-consuming and is open to various forms of influence and pressure.
- **Market mechanisms** – under this approach, scarce resources are allocated by some form of market mechanism. It is well beyond the scope of this book to describe the different market situations such as perfect competition, monopoly and monopsony, but they will all involve the interaction of buyers and sellers reacting to price and cost signals. Thus, buyers of goods and services will allocate their available money by reference to the product range available, the prices of the different products and the usefulness, or utility, of each of the products. Some examples of the use of market mechanisms are:

  - the NHS internal market where funds are allocated, by health authorities, to NHS Trusts on the basis of factors such as the quality and price of services
  - the allocation of funds to universities based on student numbers.

RESOURCE ALLOCATION APPROACHES: MEETING THE CRITERIA

In choosing an approach to resource allocation the various approaches need to be compared against the criteria described earlier. The pattern shown in Table 8 is suggested, although it is recognized that this is a personal and subjective assessment.

Table 8 Resource allocation methods: meeting the criteria

Criteria	*Formula-based approaches*	*Negotiation approaches*	*Market mechanisms*
Equity	Doubtful	Yes	No
Objectivity	Yes	No	Yes
Simplicity	No	No	No
Economy	Yes	No	No
Stability	Yes	Yes	No

TRENDS IN RESOURCE ALLOCATION

The last twenty years have seen a considerable decline in the use of negotiation mechanisms as a means of resource allocation. Resource allocation decisions are extremely politically sensitive and hence the use of formula approaches injected a necessary degree of objectivity into the process.

The development of quasi-markets in parts of the public sector has also resulted in an increase in the use of market mechanisms as a means of allocating funds to service providers.

COST INFORMATION AND DECISION MAKING IN PSOs

In any organization the reason for producing cost information should be for the purpose of decision making regarding the planning, operation or control of the various activities in the organization. So it should be with PSOs.

In recent years PSOs have become far more elaborate and sophisticated in their use of cost information. There are a number of reasons for this:

- **Pricing** – in Chapter 3 mention was made of the increasing emphasis on PSOs charging for services provided. Thus, they will need to set prices for their services and cost information is needed to set such prices.
- **Competition** – the requirements of competition mean that PSOs require a better understanding of their costs if they are to compete with the private sector.
- **Performance improvement** – the need to improve continually the efficiency and effectiveness of their activities means that PSOs have had to examine, closely, their cost base in assessing performance.
- **Investment appraisal** – in undertaking an appraisal of capital investment projects a PSO will need cost information on the total running costs of each project.
- **Responsiveness** – to be responsive to client needs, PSOs may need to amend the mix of and approach to service provision. Thus, the PSO may wish to consider altering its volume and mix of activities such as, for example, expanding one set of activities and contracting another. In this context it will need information on the marginal costs associated with each of the planned changes, and thus information on the fixed, variable or semi-fixed nature of each of the costs involved will be vital.
- **Budgetary control** – discussed below is the development of budgetary control in PSOs. Cost information will need to be produced in a manner that will enable the organization to provide feedback to budget holders about the expenditure they have incurred.

Costing in PSOs can be exceedingly complex. The various systems needed to produce cost information may themselves cost a considerable amount of money to operate and it is important to ensure that the organization is achieving value for money in its use of these resources. Thus, before looking at costing and costing systems in some depth it is important to consider why organizations such as PSOs need such cost information. In developing costing systems full consideration must be given to what are the needs, of the organization for cost information, and how such information would be used, before any investment is made in such systems.

ASPECTS OF COST INFORMATION

Before considering the design and use of costing systems in PSOs it is important to be aware of a number of key aspects of costing and the distinction between different types of cost. These key aspects are as follows:

- product costs and period costs
- direct costs and indirect costs
- fixed costs and variable costs
- total costs and marginal costs.

PRODUCT COSTS AND PERIOD COSTS

Product costing must be distinguished from period costing. Product costing is concerned with the total costs of the organization's products, while period costs are concerned with the costs incurred by different parts of the organization during a discrete time period. In a car factory, product cost information would be available on the costs of manufacturing the different models of car, while period cost information would be concerned with the costs incurred by different sections in the factory over a monthly period. Similarly, in a service organization such as a bank, product cost information would be available on each of the bank's product lines such as house mortgages, commercial loans, insurance and current accounts.

Twenty years ago there was little in the way of product costing in PSOs. However, the separation of the purchaser and provider and the development of competition has meant that provider PSOs must now obtain information about the costs of their products. In a PSO it is not always easy to define products, but with the separation of the purchaser and provider it is essential that this be done. Thus, for example, the following might be regarded as public sector products:

- **FE college** – various types of courses delivered
- **NHS Trust** – various clinical procedures undertaken
- **local authority buildings DSO** – various types of buildings work undertaken (for example plumbing and roofing)
- **executive agency** – various types of service delivered.

Hence PSOs must undertake the following tasks:

- Identify their main product lines.
- Identify the main elements of cost associated with the delivery of each of those products.
- Develop suitable approaches for the attribution of each element of cost to each product. In doing this they need to take account of the content of the next two sections.

DIRECT COSTS AND INDIRECT COSTS

There is a commonly-held view that the cost of a particular product or activity is a unique figure. This is not the case. Cost data is derived by means of a series of costing approaches and assumptions, and differing approaches and assumptions will give different costs for the same activity or product. Thus, when examining the costs associated with a particular product or activity it is vital to understand the costing approaches applied to establish that cost, and the assumptions underlying the approach adopted. It is therefore essential to understand the concepts of cost centres, and direct and indirect costs associated with those cost centres.

The differentiation between direct costs and indirect costs is fundamental to cost accounting practice, but frequently the distinction is misunderstood, even by some accountants. Often, it is the case that the direct–indirect distinction is confused with the variable–fixed distinction (see below), with direct costs being seen as synonymous with variable costs and indirect costs being seen as synonymous with fixed costs. This is a complete misunderstanding since the two types of cost classification are based on completely different principles.

To understand the direct–indirect distinction it is first necessary to appreciate the role of the cost centre in cost accounting. A cost centre is essentially just a component part of the organization against which costs can be collected. Some examples of cost centres in a factory, a hospital and a school are:

Organization	**Types of cost centre**
A factory	• a department • a machine • a product line
A hospital	• a department • a ward • a clinical specialty • a diagnostic group • a consultant
A school	• a department • a curriculum area • a class • an individual teacher.

The distinction between direct and indirect costs is concerned with the different ways in which costs are recorded against cost centres. Consider the factory-based example in Figure 13.

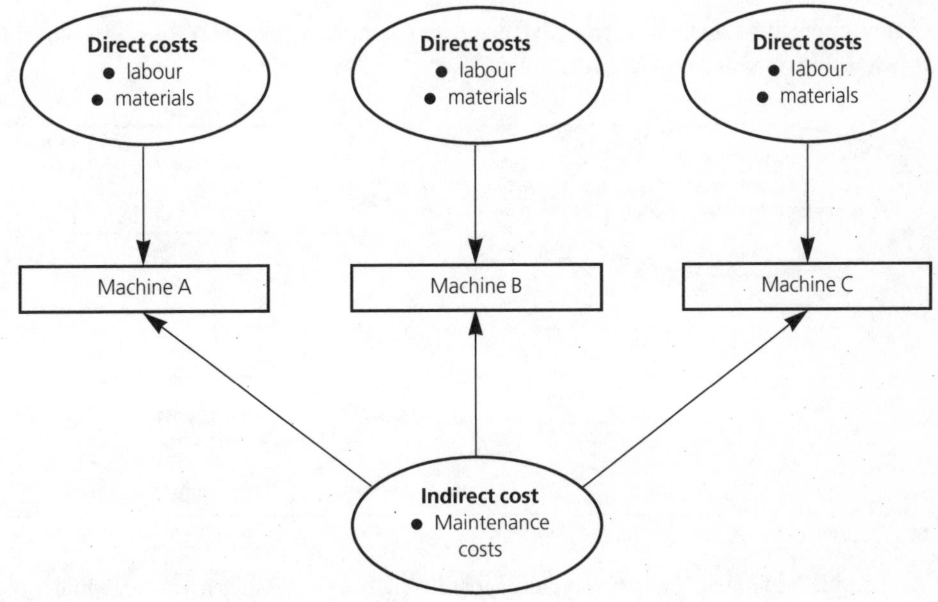

Figure 13 Direct and indirect costs

In this factory there are three machines which represent our cost centres, and there is a need to know the total costs of running each of the machines. Certain costs such as labour and materials are referred to as direct costs, since the information systems in the factory will give us full information about where each of these types of cost have been incurred. Timesheets will indicate the labour costs that have been incurred on each machine and the stores issue system will show the materials costs consumed by each machine. These direct costs are said to be *allocated* to each machine. When looking at the costs of the maintenance department, in this situation, there is no record available of how much maintenance time has been spent on each machine and so it is not possible to allocate maintenance as a direct cost to each machine. To obtain a total running cost for each machine it is necessary to *apportion* or spread the total costs of the maintenance department over each of the machines in a *reasonable* manner. The key phrase here is 'in a reasonable manner' and the basis chosen must be regarded as a proxy for the maintenance requirements of each of the machines. In the case of this example we can state the following:

- **Reasonable basis for apportionment**
  - running hours of each machine
  - age of each machine (in years)
  - product output of each machine
- **Unreasonable basis for apportionment**
  - age (in years) of the machine operator
  - height of each machine
  - original cost of each machine.

Thus, the total costs of running each of the machines will depend on the method of apportionment chosen for maintenance costs, and different methods of apportionment will produce different total cost figures.

Let us now apply this same model to a PSO using, for example, a hospital setting. First consider, in Figure 14, a hospital ward as a cost centre.

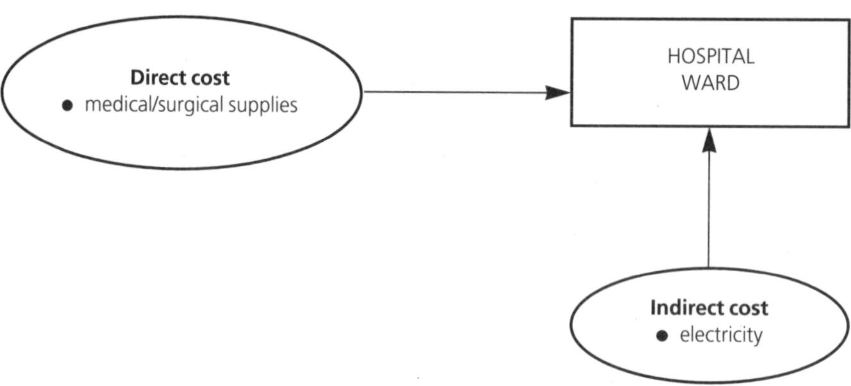

Figure 14 Direct and indirect costs: a hospital ward

In this example we are using just two types of cost to illustrate the issues involved, while recognizing that in reality a hospital ward will incur many different types of cost. Dealing first with direct costs, it is usual in most hospitals for there to be detailed information about the medical and surgical supplies (MSS) costs attributable to each ward and hence these costs can be regarded as direct costs and allocated to the ward. Electricity is also a cost of running the ward but it is usually the case that the only information available concerns the electricity costs of the hospital as a whole. Hence, to obtain the total running costs of the ward it is necessary to apportion the total hospital electricity costs over all wards and departments in some suitable manner. This might be floor area or volume of each building involved. Thus, the figure for the total running costs of the ward will depend on the basis of apportionment chosen for electricity costs.

Let us now consider the individual patient as a cost centre and observe the picture in Figure 15, again using just two types of cost for illustrative purposes.

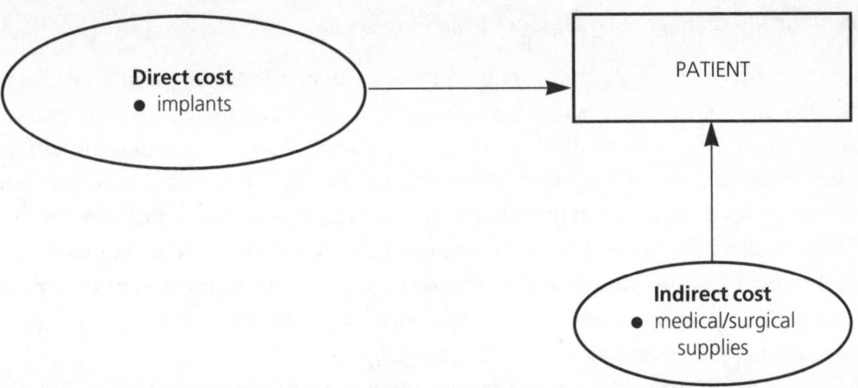

Figure 15 Direct and indirect costs: a hospital patient

In this example we have used patient implants, such as artificial joints, as an example of a cost which is directly identifiable to an individual patient and the cost of which can therefore be allocated to that patient. However, it is unlikely that any hospital ward will keep records of the precise amounts of all the MSS attributable to each patient, and in this situation MSS must be regarded as an indirect cost to the individual patient cost centre. To obtain the total cost of treating a patient then it is necessary to apportion total ward MSS costs over patients in the ward, on some reasonable basis. One way of doing this would be to apportion costs according to a patient's length of stay but other approaches could be used which take account of the patient's diagnosis or treatment profile.

Thus there are a number of points to emphasize regarding the above examples:

- **Mix of allocation and apportionment** – there is no single correct total cost attributable to a particular cost centre. The total costs attributable to a cost centre are derived from a combination of direct costs which are allocated, and indirect costs which are apportioned in some way. Different approaches and assumptions will give different results. Consider the following simple example using the costs of drugs and MSS:

Situation A		**Situation B**	
£		£	
Drugs (allocated)	50	Drugs (allocated)	50
MSS (allocated)	20	MSS (apportioned)	40
Total costs	70	Total costs	90

  In both these situations it is the same patient suffering from the same condition, obtaining the same treatment from the same consultant. The only difference is the accounting method. In situation A directly allocating MSS costs instead of apportioning them produces a different result and hence a different total cost for the patient.

- **Basis of apportionment** – where cost apportionment is applied it is important to realize that there is no single correct basis of cost apportionment. As long as a particular basis of apportionment is 'reasonable' in specific circumstances then it may be used to derive total costs. There is no single 'correct' or 'accurate' cost. The end result of a costing exercise is dependent upon the balance between allocation and apportionment of costs and the method of cost apportionment actually used. Two different costing methods will give two different results, both of which are reasonable.

A number of important managerial issues flow from the above:

- The degree of accuracy of the cost information produced depends on the extent to which costs can be directly allocated rather than being apportioned in some suitable but arbitrary manner. What determines whether a cost can be directly allocated or indirectly apportioned is the sophistication of the organization's information systems. Consider the ward cost example referred to above. If the hospital were prepared to incur cost to place an electricity meter on each ward then electricity costs could be directly allocated to wards and no apportionment would be needed. Similarly, if a system were implemented to record MSS prescribed to patients then MSS costs could be directly allocated to patients and no apportionment would be needed. Clearly, the more sophisticated the information systems, the higher would be the costs of costing.
- The degree of costing accuracy needed by the organization will depend on a range of issues such as: the type of organization, its geographic location, its current efficiency level and the degree of competition it faces in the market. There is no simple answer to this question. For example, a PSO in a rural area facing little competition will probably have less need for accurate cost information than an inner-city PSO facing tough competition.

Thus in designing a costing system there is always a balance to be struck between the need for accuracy of cost information and the cost of obtaining that information. Hence PSOs must take account of the benefits and the costs of costing. Furthermore, it must be recognized that there is ***no*** standard costing system that can be defined for all PSOs, or even all PSOs, of the same type, although some commonality of structure is possible. The dynamic public sector environment resulting from the changes of the last twenty years means that PSOs vary considerably in their needs for financial information, the degree of accuracy required, and the resources they can devote to providing that information. Hence each PSO must make its own judgement on this matter.

FIXED COSTS AND VARIABLE COSTS

The distinction between a fixed cost and a variable cost is simple in principle but difficult to draw in practice. It is essentially concerned with the way in which the magnitude of a particular cost varies in

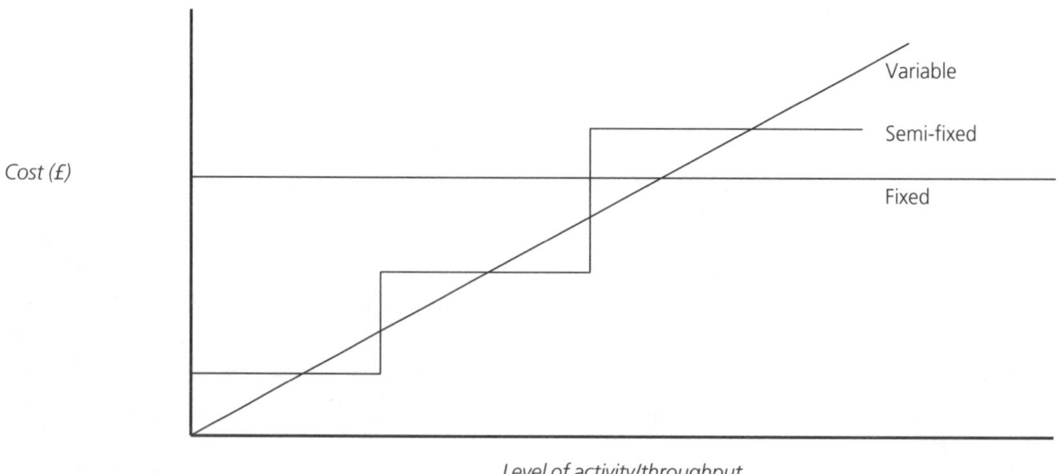

Figure 16 Fixed and variable costs

relation to the activity or throughput level of the organization. Three different types of cost behaviour can be identified. These are illustrated graphically in Figure 16 and discussed below.

- **Variable costs** – this is where the level of cost varies directly with the level of activity in the organization. In a factory setting, direct materials may be regarded as a cost which varies directly with the level of production.
- **Fixed costs** – this is where the magnitude of cost is unaffected by the level of activity in the organization. In a factory setting, the factory rent would usually be fixed and would not vary whatever the level of factory production.
- **Semi-fixed costs** – the above two examples are basically extremes, and in practice most cost types will be neither totally fixed nor completely variable.

The distinction between a variable, fixed and semi-variable cost is not precise and judgements often have to be made. However, Table 9 gives some examples of cost behaviour in the various parts of the public sector.

Table 9 Types of cost behaviour in the public sector

Organization	*Type of cost*	*Activity measure*	*Variable*	*Fixed*	*Semi-fixed*
Hospital	Drugs	Number of patients	√		
School	Teachers' pay	Number of pupils			√
University	Buildings maintenance	Numbers of students		√	
College	Catering	Numbers of students			√
Ambulance service	Fuel costs	Numbers of miles run	√		
Hospital	Nurses' pay	Numbers of patients			√
Fire authority	Equipment maintenance	Number of fire incidents		√	

However, a word of warning is necessary here. The type of cost behaviour encountered may not always be clear and may depend on the way in which the PSO is obtaining goods and services. For example, in the table above it has been shown that nursing pay is a semi-fixed cost in relation to patient numbers. This is because small changes in patient numbers will not result in changes to the nursing staff numbers (and hence pay) although larger changes will take place for larger movements in patient numbers. However, where the hospital employs large numbers of agency nurses then nursing pay may become a variable cost, since increases or decreases in patient numbers may lead to an immediate increase or decrease in the numbers of agency nurses employed.

This distinction between types of cost behaviour becomes important when discussing the issues in the next section.

TOTAL COSTS AND MARGINAL COSTS

Total costs implies all of the costs associated with a particular activity. This will incorporate the direct costs of an activity and a share of the indirect costs apportioned to that activity in the manner described earlier. This is illustrated by the following simple example which is concerned with the costs of manufacturing a product:

Volume of production = 1000 units

Costs of production:

	Total Costs £	*Unit Cost* £p
Materials	2500	2.50
Labour	7500	7.50
Variable Overhead	2000	2.00
Fixed Overhead	1000	1.00
Total	13 000	13.00

Thus the total cost of producing one unit of the product amounts to £13.

The marginal cost is the incremental cost of producing additional units of the product and this will be different from the total cost because of the issues of fixed and variable costs referred to above. If production is increased, then some costs will increase while others will remain unchanged.

Using the above example, consider the impact on cost of increasing production by 50 units (that is, 5 per cent). The following situation is likely to apply:

- **Materials** – producing fifty additional units of product will result in an incremental or marginal cost of £125 being incurred (that is, 50 x £2.50).
- **Variable overhead** – since this overhead is defined as variable it must be assumed that it will vary directly with the level of production. Thus, increasing production by fifty units will result in an incremental or marginal cost of £100 being incurred (50 x £2).
- **Fixed overhead** – by definition this overhead cost is fixed and will not change with increases in production. Thus, the marginal cost in this area is nil.
- **Labour** – this is the most problematic area since it is not clear what impact an increase in production of 5 per cent will have on labour costs. Three scenarios are possible:
  - The increase in production can be absorbed by the existing labour force and thus the marginal cost will be nil.
  - To cope with the increase in production will require employees to work overtime at a premium. Thus the marginal costs of increasing production will depend on the overtime hours required and the overtime premium paid.
  - To cope with the increase in production will require additional employees to be recruited. Thus the marginal costs of increasing production will depend on the numbers and pay of additional employees needed.

For simplicity, in this example we have assumed that the increased production can be met by the existing labour force.

The differences between marginal and total costs can be summarized as follows:

Costs of an additional fifty units of production based on total costs

= increased units x total unit cost

= 50 x £13.00

= £650

Costs of an additional fifty units of production based on marginal costs

= Materials + Labour + Variable Overhead + Fixed Overhead

= £125 + nil + £100 + nil

= £225

This distinction between total costs and marginal costs is of great importance and has relevance to public sector organizations in two main ways:

- **Forecasting** – this involves forecasting the actual changes in costs that are likely to take place in the PSO as a result of activity changes. Consider the following simple example based on a college.

College financial forecasting

A college has 3500 full-time students and has total expenditure of £7.5 million. The college teaches for forty-four weeks per annum.This equates to an average total cost of £49 per student week.

The college is thinking of starting a short course which will comprise 100 students being taught for ten weeks. Using the total average cost described above the costs of this short course would work out as being:

100 students x 10 weeks x £49 per student week = £49 000.

However, this is almost certainly an overestimate since the total average cost of £49 per student week includes a proportion of costs such as buildings maintenance and heat and light which would not vary even if the short course was undertaken. Hence the college needs to look at each item of cost separately and identify those costs which will vary if the additional students are recruited for the ten-week period.

- **Pricing decisions** – the distinction between marginal and total costs is important for pricing purposes. This is discussed in the section on marginal cost pricing.

ACTIVITY-BASED COSTING

Activity-based costing (ABC) is an approach to costing which was developed in the USA, became popular in this country in the 1990s, and is seen as having considerable relevance in the public sector. ABC was developed through a recognition that in manufacturing industry, over a 40–50 year period, the composition of product costs had altered substantially. The main features of this were as follows:

- **Direct labour** – because of the introduction of automation and IT the proportion of product cost represented by direct labour had fallen dramatically.
- **Direct materials** – the proportion of product cost represented by direct materials had remained largely unchanged.

- **Overheads** – in recent years a number of overhead functions such as materials handling, quality assurance and marketing had grown substantially and thus the proportion of product cost represented by overhead had grown by roughly the same extent that direct labour had fallen.

As seen earlier, traditional approaches to costing involved the direct allocation of direct labour and materials costs, while overhead costs were usually apportioned on some suitable broad-brush basis. The advocates of ABC recognized that applying such crude approaches to the treatment of overhead costs, which are now such a high proportion of cost, was severely distorting total product costs. ABC uses more sophisticated approaches to apportion overhead costs, thereby eliminating much of the distortion. The ABC approach involves identifying what activities in the organization actually 'drive' the level of particular types of cost, rather than apportioning a statistical share.

Using material store costs as an example, the traditional crude approach would be to apportion the total amount of material store costs between products pro rata to the volume or value of the different products involved. ABC recognizes that material store costs have three different elements and that a different activity drives the level of cost in each case:

Activity	*Cost driver*
Materials receipt	Numbers of batches received
Materials storage	Volume of store space occupied
Materials issue	Number of batches issued

ABC would look at the numbers of batches of materials received in relation to the different products and apportion materials receipts costs pro rata to the numbers of batches in each case. Similar calculations would be needed for materials storage and issue.

ABC is often seen as having great potential in PSOs. It can be used to identify the activities which drive particular items of cost in service delivery. For example, the ABC approach could be used to determine what are the factors which drive disease treatment costs in a hospital or course costs in a university. This is illustrated in Figure 17 using university course costs as an example:

Figure 17 Activity-based costing in a university

For each of the activities which contribute towards a university course the cost driver will differ from case to case:

- **teaching** – numbers and lengths of classes per course
- **libraries** – number of book issues per course
- **examinations** – number of examination papers set per course and marked
- **student records** – number of students per course.

ABC may assist in getting a better understanding of how costs behave, but there are two common problems with its use in the public sector:

- the lack of suitable data on activities which can be used as the basis of cost attribution
- the relatively high costs associated with setting up an ABC system.

PRICING

There is often confusion in the public sector about the difference between costs and prices. The distinction between costs and prices can be summarized below:

- **Cost** – this a financial expression of the resources committed by an organization to a particular activity or product. Thus, when we say a particular item costs £45.23 this means that the manpower, material and other resources committed to making that item are estimated in monetary terms to be equivalent to £45.23.
- **Price** – a price is the amount of money that a purchaser or consumer is prepared to pay to receive a particular good or service, and the income a provider finds acceptable. The key thing to note is that a price relates to the market and not the supplying organization. It therefore follows that a price of a commodity can be in excess of its cost (implying a surplus), can be equal to cost or can be below cost (implying a deficit).

Pricing is a complicated task and it is beyond the scope of this book to provide a full consideration of the factors involved. Nevertheless three broad approaches can be identified as detailed below.

TOTAL COST PRICING

This approach might be applied where the organization involved is a monopolistic provider of goods and services or, alternatively, the organization is operating in accordance with some formal pricing framework. In these circumstances the price paid might be calculated as being the total cost plus a percentage mark-up. The percentage mark-up would represent the profit element. NHS Trusts operate under this form of pricing framework, in that the prices they charge to purchasers must be based on the total costs of service provision plus a nationally defined rate of return. The former state utilities have a similar form of price regulation.

RULING MARKET PRICE

In these circumstances there is considerable competition and the price of product is largely determined by market forces. Thus the provider organization can do little to influence the ruling market price, and must align their costs of production with it.

This leads us to a consideration of price-based costing or target costing. For several years, certain manufacturing firms, particularly of Japanese origin, have operated systems of target costing. At its simplest, target costing works as follows:

- establish the market price for a particular product
- deduct required profit margin to leave the targeted costs of the product
- establish minimum quality standards for the product
- design and manufacture the product within that target cost limit and minimum quality standards.

Ongoing pressure on public sector resources raises the question of whether some form of target costing, under the heading of price-based costing, would have applicability. Instead of prices for services being driven by the costs of the provider, the costs of the service might be driven by the price that the purchaser was willing and able to pay. The process might operate as follows:

- establish the price for a particular service that a purchaser is able and willing to pay
- deduct required rate of return to leave the targeted costs of the service
- establish *minimum* quality standards for the service
- design and deliver the service within that target cost limit and minimum quality standards.

Example: Marginal cost pricing

Carne PLC is a British company which manufactures canned meals for sale in the UK. Carne manufactures and sells one million cans each year, at a selling price of £1.10 per can. The following cost data is available:

	Total (£)	*Per tin (£p)*
Direct material costs	400 000	0.40
Direct labour costs	200 000	0.20
Variable overhead cost	80 000	0.08
Fixed overhead cost	180 000	0.18
Total costs	860 000	0.86

Carne has received a request from a Mongolian supermarket to supply a once-off order of 20 000 canned meals for sale in Mongolia. They are offering a fixed contract price of £15 000 for this contract. This equates to £0.75 per can. Carne wishes to know whether it should accept this contract and what should be the key factors in making this decision.

Clearly, the offer price offered by the Mongolians is less than the total cost of production and less than the current UK selling price. However, there are three important factors to bear in mind:

- this is a once-off contract that will not be repeated
- it represents a very small increase in production for Carne (2 per cent)
- since the product is being supplied to customers many thousands of miles away, then selling the product at a lower price will not affect UK sales.

In these specific circumstances, Carne would be justified in accepting the contract since the contract price (£0.75) exceeded the marginal costs of production (£0.48). The marginal costs of production per can are calculated as follows:

	Marginal Cost(£)
• Materials – definitely marginal	0.40
• Labour – probably fixed since it is a small production increase	–
• Variable overhead – variable by definition	0.08
• Fixed overhead – fixed by definition	–
• Total marginal cost	0.48

There could be major problems with such an approach in terms of restrictive practices by professional bodies and trade unions that might inhibit the chances of achieving the target cost limit. Nevertheless, it is worthy of consideration.

MARGINAL COST PRICING

In some situations, prices could be based on marginal costs rather than total costs. Consider the simple commercial example shown on the opposite page.

Marginal cost pricing can also be utilized in PSOs. Consider the following example from the NHS.

Example: Marginal costing in the NHS

The orthopaedic department of a Trust hospital currently undertakes 300 artificial hip-joint replacements during the year. The costs of this activity are £750 000, giving an average unit cost of £2500. Another health authority, 100 miles away, has asked the Trust to quote a price to undertake a once-off contract of thirty joint replacements to help in reducing local waiting times. The increase in workload to the orthopaedic department of undertaking this contract is small (10 per cent). Hence, it seems likely that the marginal costs of undertaking this contract should be somewhat less than the total costs, because some elements of cost will remain unchanged as a result of this additional workload. This is illustrated below.

Cost type	*Total cost £000*	*Percentage financial impact of a 10 per cent workload increase (estimated)*	*Marginal costs £000*
Wards	100	+6	6
Theatres	150	+6	9
Drugs	30	+10	3
Diagnostics	80	+3	2
Paramedical	100	+6	6
Implants	150	+10	15
Support services	80	+5	4
Overheads	60	–	–
Total	750	–	45

On the basis of the normal NHS costing and pricing rules the Trust should quote a price based on the total cost and thus the quotation should be 30 x £2500 = £75 000. Using the marginal costs of undertaking the contract the quotation should be £45 000. In this situation the Trust could quote a price based on marginal costs rather than total costs.

However, as with the Mongolian example, certain safeguards are needed in relation to marginal cost pricing:

- The contract must be a once-off and not ongoing. There are examples of NHS purchasers trying to negotiate marginal cost prices for fairly large contracts year after year. This must be avoided since marginal costs do not cover overheads.
- The contract must be for an increase in workload which can be absorbed by existing slack capacity in the Trust without large incremental costs. Slack capacity can occur in physical facilities such as

operating theatres and clinics, or in human resources such as surgical time. If the Trust is working close to full capacity then the additional work can only be done with substantial incremental cost or by displacing some other work.

- The contract price must not disturb the local price.

BUDGETARY MANAGEMENT

In any organization of significant size, a system of budgeting is an essential managerial tool and the public sector is no exception to this rule. It must not just be a narrow instrument of financial control operated by the Finance Director with the aim of constraining overall expenditure within set limits – financial control is but one function of a budget system. Instead, the budget should be a key element of the management process in the organization, which aims to improve overall organizational performance in terms of the quantity, quality and cost of services provided and show how plans for change are to be implemented.

PURPOSE OF A BUDGET SYSTEM

A number of reasons can be put forward as to why organizations operate budgetary systems. These include the role of budgeting systems with regard to:

- **Delegation** – in a small organization comprising 2–3 persons it is easy for one person to make all of the detailed expenditure decisions. However, once organizations get to a certain size they become too large and complex for one individual to manage all aspects of expenditure. Delegating certain decisions to lower levels of management is one way of resolving this problem by means of a system of budgets. Giving a subordinate manager a budget delegates to that manager the power to incur expenditure up to the budget level without the need to refer to higher authority. There is a strong argument for saying that delegation will improve the speed of decision making, since the manager does not need higher authority to implement a decision. It may also lead to better decisions because the manager is closer to the point of action and therefore better informed. How far down the organization budgets should be devolved is a complex question which depends on a number of factors such as the capability of managers to manage budgets, the availability of information and the need for flexibility in the use of resources. This issue will be returned to later when considering budget structures.

  In recent years there have been a number of significant approaches to budgetary delegation in the public sector. Some examples of this are:

  - The development of local management of schools (LMS). Under LMS, responsibility for the majority of school expenditure is delegated to the governors and head teacher of the school. Further delegation to heads of faculty and department may also take place in the school.
  - The delegation of a large proportion of hospital budgets to a series of clinical directors responsible for the activities of the directorates of surgery, medical, paediatrics, pathology and so on.
  - The delegation of a wide range of budgets to divisional managers in a range of executive agencies such as the Benefits Agency.

- **Financial planning** – budgeting must be seen as an important element in the planning process. In Chapter 4 business planning and the development of longer-term strategic objectives was discussed. Prior to the start of each financial year, the organization will also need to prepare an annual plan which outlines the activities to be undertaken and the resources to be used for the year ahead, and this annual plan will need to be derived from the longer-term strategic plan of the organization. The budget will then be the expression of that annual plan in financial terms.

- **Control** – having set a plan and allocated resources accordingly, it is important that the plan is achieved. This is also true in financial terms and one key role of a budgeting system is to exert managerial control over spending to ensure that actual expenditure does not deviate too far from what was planned in the budget, in terms of both individual budgets and the PSO as a whole. This is usually referred to as budgetary control, and involves periodically feeding back information to budget managers about their actual spending in a period, compared to planned expenditure, so that corrective action can be taken where needed.
- **Motivation** – finally and perhaps the most neglected function is that of motivation. Much evidence exists to show that budgetary systems are not behaviourally neutral. The way in which budgets are set and budgetary control is operated can have a considerable impact on the managerial performance of an individual.

STRUCTURE OF A BUDGET SYSTEM

Too often, a budget system is seen as being synonymous with a computer system. This is wrong. Any budget system has three main components, as illustrated in Figure 18.

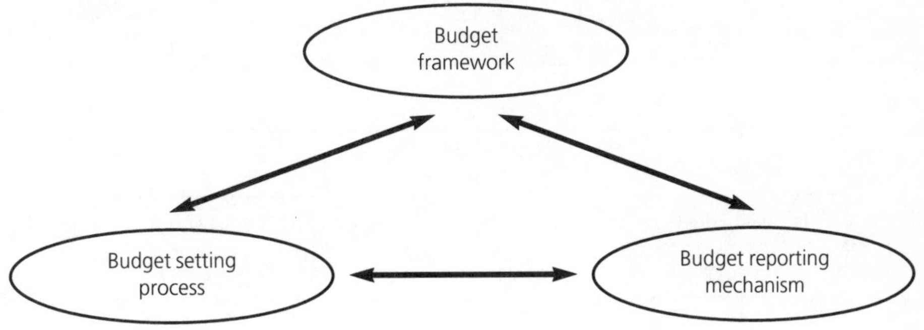

Figure 18 Structure of a budget system

Each of these components of a budgetary system are discussed below in the context of a PSO.

BUDGET FRAMEWORK

The role of the budget system as a means of delegation within the organization has already been discussed. A budget framework must reflect the framework of responsibility and accountability in the PSO, and in designing such a framework the following questions must be addressed:

- Who are to be the budget holders in the organization?
- What specific activities are they responsible for?
- What items of expenditure are to be included in their budgets?
- What items of income are to be included in their budgets?
- What performance standards are required from them?
- What powers of authority do they have in relation to their budgets? For example, are they able to switch funds between different budget categories or do they require higher approval?

Answers to these questions are never clear-cut and will vary. No two PSOs will have the same organizational and managerial arrangements and, consequently, neither will they have the same budgetary framework. For example, in some organizations buildings maintenance might be the responsibility of a central estates manager while in other organizations the same budget might be delegated to individual operational managers. There is no one correct approach and PSOs must implement the organizational arrangements which best meets their local needs. Selecting the most appropriate budget framework is not purely an accounting matter, and budget responsibility is a corporate topic which has financial, operational and managerial implications. The main issues to be considered in designing a budget framework are:

- potential improvements in the speed and quality of decision making achievable through delegation of budgets
- risks of loss of financial control through delegation to staff not competent to manage budgets
- costs of implementing financial systems needed to support delegated budgets
- capability of the finance department to provide support to budget holders
- potential loss of flexibility and efficiency caused by fragmenting budgets over a larger number of persons.

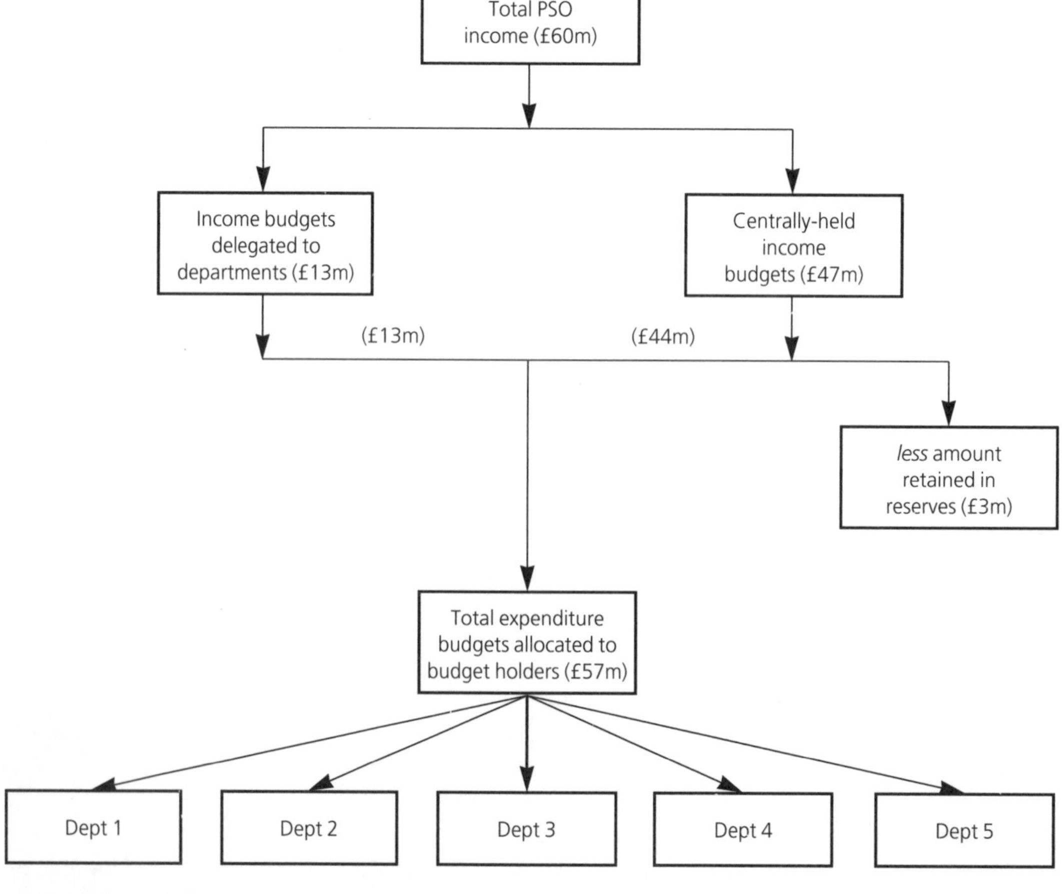

Figure 19 The budget-setting process

BUDGET SETTING PROCESS

Whatever budget framework is adopted, it will be necessary to have some process or mechanism by which the annual budget of the organization is set both globally and in terms of individual budgets. The global budget must be set by reference to the funds made available to the organization from central government, purchasers and so on, and any external income expected to be generated. This is illustrated in Figure 19 shown on the opposite page.

Basically there are two main types of budget:

- income budgets
- expenditure budgets.

Dealing first with income budgets, it is usual for the vast bulk of income budgets in PSOs to be retained centrally within the organization rather than being delegated to individual departments. On the other hand, it may be the case that some income budgets are delegated to an individual department. Thus, for example, if there is an in-year increase in income directly accruing to an individual department then it is likely that this will result in an increase in that department's income budget. Thus, a department which won an additional contract in-year would expect to see both its income and expenditure budgets increased accordingly.

The budget setting process must set expenditure budgets for individual departments such that the total of these budgets plus reserves does not exceed the total funds available. The total funds available to a department are the sum of the income budgets delegated to it and its share of the central income budget. There are three main approaches to setting expenditure budgets and these are outlined below.

WORKLOAD-BASED BUDGETS

With some budgets or parts of some budgets the budgeted level of expenditure can be linked to the planned level of workload in the department. Take, for example, a catering budget of a hospital:

Projected number of meals for the year	=	240 000
Standard cost of provisions per meal	=	£0.75
Consumables budget	=	£180 000

The standard cost of provisions is a target cost which will apply throughout the year but which will clearly vary from meal to meal. Budgets such as these are flexible budgets, since the overall budget level will be flexed in accordance with the numbers of meals actually produced.

However, a prerequisite for setting workload-based budgets in PSOs is the availability of credible measures of workload on which those budgets can be based. In many areas of PSO activity (particularly those related to service professionals) such workload measures do not yet exist and so workload-based budgets cannot be developed.

INCREMENTAL BUDGETING

Under this approach, the main determinant of the budget of a department will be the budget it had in the previous year. Thus, the starting point for the 2000/01 budget will be the budget for 1999/00. Adjustments will be made for the effects of inflation, new developments, changes at the margin or the need to generate an efficiency improvement. However, the budget of the department is not linked to its projected workload nor is any attempt made to justify the historic level of the budget. Consider the following using the simple example of a transport budget:

	£000
Budget (1999/00)	100
deduct cost improvement target on existing service (2%)	2
	98
add cost of pay awards (4%)	4
	102
add costs of extended service	5
Budget 2000/01	107

This example illustrates a typical approach to incremental budget setting which has traditionally been applied in many PSOs. The weakness of this approach is that the base budget is not queried for appropriateness and relevance and there is no link with the workload. Also, these budgets are effectively fixed budgets, since the budget will not usually be changed in-year in response to changing workload demands placed on the department.

ZERO-BASED BUDGETING (ZBB) AND PRIORITY-BASED BUDGETING (PBB)

These approaches were developed to overcome the weaknesses of the incremental approach of failing to look at the base budget of a department. PBB is essentially a simpler and more pragmatic version of ZBB but the thrust is the same in both cases. Under ZBB/PBB, no budget is automatically rolled forward as is the case in the incremental approach. Budgets must be scrutinized and budget managers must indicate:

- the specific and discrete activities they undertake in their departments
- the costs attaching to each of those activities
- the benefits and priority of undertaking each of those activities.

Senior management can then scrutinize all departments in the organization and compare the costs with the benefits and priorities attaching to each activity. They may then make adjustments to base budgets in individual departments in line with overall corporate priorities.

Whatever the merits of ZBB/PBB in principle, there are some clear practical problems:

- The procedures are cumbersome and time-consuming.
- It will probably be difficult to switch resources from one area of activity to another without retraining staff and/or making redundancies.
- Often, within many parts of the public sector, all activities are seen as having value. Emotional factors often prevail and it is difficult to achieve cut-backs in one department in order to expand activity in another department, whatever the logical merit.

Hence, in practice, it is very rare to see a true ZBB/PBB approach applied in PSO.

These three approaches to budget setting are not mutually exclusive. For example, the provisions element of a catering budget might be a flexible or workload-based budget while the catering staffing budget might be a fixed budget established by the incremental or PBB method.

BUDGETARY REPORTING MECHANISM

To manage their budgets effectively, budget managers need to be provided with information which shows their progress against budgets. Thus the provision of budgetary information must be a clear part of the information and IT strategy of the organization. The precise configuration of information systems will vary considerably between organizations but a number of common themes can be identified which are applicable to all budgetary information systems:

- **Relevance** – budget managers want information which is relevant to them. This comes down to issues of responsibility and control. It is important to provide managers with information on those items of expenditure for which they are responsible and over which they can exert control.
- **Frequency and timeliness** – information needs to be provided to managers as frequently as is necessary for them to manage their budgets. It also needs to be provided as quickly as possible after the end of a period.
- **Format** – the precise format of a budget report will vary from system to system. It will usually show the following information:

  - total budget for the year
  - budget for the month, which may be a simple twelfth of the annual budget or may be adjusted to reflect seasonal variations in some type of expenditure such as heating costs
  - expenditure for the month
  - variance for the month
  - cumulative budget for the year to date
  - cumulative expenditure for the year to date
  - variance for the year to date.

  Budget reports might also include non-financial information such as workload and manpower information.
- **Accuracy and content** – the information on actual expenditure included in budget reports can be of three main types:

  - cash payments actually made
  - accruals of creditors, being expenditure on those items of goods and services which have been received but for which payment has not yet been made
  - commitments, being those items of goods and services which have been ordered and for which an expenditure commitment exists, but which have yet to be received.

  Budget reports usually include accruals of creditors but they may not include commitments. Budget managers need to be aware of any additional expenditure commitments not included on their budget reports.
- **Support** – support and advice on the content of budget reports is needed by budget managers. In some cases, departments or directorates might have their own decentralized finance officer while in other cases support will be given by a central finance department. Provision of such support is a key role of the finance function.

BUDGET SETTING AND EFFICIENCY IMPROVEMENT

For many years, some PSOs have been required to make annual efficiency improvements in their operational activities. Such efficiency improvements need to be incorporated into the budget setting process. As seen in the portering example in an earlier section, an efficiency improvement target can be incorporated into the budget setting process. It is not logical to give a blanket target to all managers, since the potential for generating efficiency improvements will vary between departments. However, in practice this tends to happen because PSO budgeting setting procedures are not always sophisticated enough to consider the relative potential of departments to generate efficiency improvements. A shift towards a PBB type of budget setting might engender a more focused approach towards efficiency improvements.

Having been set an efficiency target, PSO managers might address the search for efficiency improvements in two main stages:

- **Benchmarking overview** – this will involve some form of benchmarking exercise which compares the costs of the PSOs activities against other comparable organizations. It is not always easy to obtain fully comparable data and so care has to be exercised in the choice of comparators.
- **In-depth review** – the benchmarking overview may indicate areas where costs seem out of line. This may consequently lead to an in-depth review in certain specific areas.

In the early days of efficiency improvements, generating savings was not that onerous since there was still a fair amount of slack in the system. The task is now far more difficult and managers need to be far more imaginative about the sorts of approaches they can apply. Generally, the search for continuous cost improvements has shaved off many margins and larger-scale solutions are now needed. Being faced with the need to identify cost improvements, there are a finite number of approaches that can be adopted and some of these are briefly discussed below.

CAPITAL INVESTMENT

This involves substituting capital for labour, thereby improving revenue efficiency. An example is the use of equipment which automates tasks and saves on manpower. Unfortunately, the planned revenue savings do not always materialize, especially where staff savings are involved, since the 'surplus' manpower is diverted into other areas of activity. Nevertheless, capital investment is the only long-term sustainable approach to efficiency improvement.

PROCESS IMPROVEMENT

Much of the activity which goes on in PSOs is based on tradition and precedent. A root-and-branch review of the various operational processes in the organization might lead to simplification. This could, in turn, lead to an unchanged service at a lower cost or better services at the same cost. In this context the topic of business process re-engineering (BPR) may have great relevance in PSOs. Much of BPR involves the use of improved information systems and hence BPR needs to be considered in the context of IT investment. BPR is considered further in Chapter 6.

REDUCED PHYSICAL CAPACITY

A specific example of this might be operating theatres, where an NHS Trust which increases the utilization of its existing theatres (through better scheduling or weekend working) is able to take one theatre out of commission, thus avoiding a substantial fixed cost burden. A more broadly-based example might be the rationalization of two hospital sites onto one. Such a merger would save on fixed costs while maintaining operational activity.

IMPROVED STAFF PRODUCTIVITY

Approaches to improving staff productivity such as better management, better remuneration systems or better workflows should be evaluated to seek to undertake the same level of workload with lower staff levels.

REMUNERATION COSTS

In the next chapter the issue of staff remuneration is discussed. Although much of public sector pay bargaining is still conducted on a national basis, there are situations where PSOs have some freedom to negotiate local remuneration arrangements. An alternative remuneration structure, possibly coupled with lower staffing levels, might generate overall efficiency improvements.

MARKET TESTING

This involves exposing in-house services to external competition. Market testing could be applied to administrative services such as payroll, or to some aspects of direct service provision. There are two outcomes from market testing:

- **Outsourcing** – as a result of market testing the decision may be to outsource the activity to an external contractor. Some examples of where this may be desirable are:
  - where a department cannot obtain good-quality staff but the contractor can
  - where a contractor has access to modern equipment not available to the department
  - where the workload of a department is uneven throughout the year. The department may have staffing levels designed to meet maximum workload and thus there is slack capacity throughout the rest of the year. It may be more efficient to buy-in services from a contractor as and when needed
  - where the external contractor can provide the same service at lower cost
  - where risks can be transferred to the external contractor.
- **Retention in-house** – market testing may lead to a decision to retain service provision in-house. However, even in this case there are usually benefits, since the pressure of competition often sharpens the efficiency and management of the in-house unit.

Finally, it must be noted that the issue of market testing is now inextricably bound up with the PFI since private contractors may contract to design, build, finance and operate public sector building activities.

A careful examination of these approaches to cost improvement suggests that with the exception of the capital investment approach there must be finite limits to the level of cost improvement that can be achieved by the other methods. For example, there will be a finite limit to the level of staff productivity which can be achieved without jeopardizing quality and effectiveness of service provision.

BUDGETARY VARIANCE ANALYSIS

Earlier it was noted that a typical budgetary control report would show a manager the variation between his actual expenditure and his planned budget both for the month and the cumulative position for the year. In practice, variations from budget may occur for a large number of reasons such as workload pressures, price increases or poor expenditure management. A simple budget variance does not indicate the reasons why expenditure has deviated from budget. The technique of budget variance analysis was developed in industry many years ago as a means of explaining the reasons why expenditure deviated from budget. It has practical application in PSOs as discussed below.

Let us first continue with the example of the catering function using the budgetary data shown earlier.

	Planned	*Actual*	*Variance*
Number of meals	240 000	260 000	+20 000
Expenditure	£180 000	£182 000	+£2000
Cost per meal	£0.75	£0.70	–£0.05

A standard budgetary control report would merely show that the catering department had exceeded its budgets by £2000, but even a cursory analysis would show that there are two factors at work here, namely:

- the volume of meals produced exceeds the plan
- the unit cost per meal is less than planned.

Variance analysis uses this information to disaggregate the causes of there being an expenditure variance as shown below.

Volume variance = (planned volume – actual volume) x standard cost
= (240 000 – 260 000) x £0.75
= –£15 000 (U = unfavourable)

Cost variance = (standard cost – actual cost) x actual volume
= (£0.75 – £0.70) x 260 000
= +£13000 (F = favourable)

Variance analysis reveals the following:

- An unfavourable expenditure variance of £2000 disguises an unfavourable volume variance of £15 000, partially offset by a favourable cost variance of £13 000.
- Responsibility for these two variances rests with different people. The cost variance is the responsibility of the catering department, the volume variance probably rests with some other manager who can control the volume of activity. Variance analysis focuses responsibility for the different causes of an expenditure variance.

What is shown above is a very simple two-part variance analysis. In practice, more complex variance analyses can be prepared. Consider, for example, the highways maintenance function of a local authority. The total budget variance for the department is £100 000. However, this overspend could be due to a number of causes such as:

- the number of miles of road maintained is different from that contained in the budget
- materials had a higher or lower purchase price than that on which the budget was based
- the hourly rates of labour were higher or lower than those on which the budget was based
- the efficiency of working was higher or lower than that on which the budget was based.

Variance analysis aims to establish the impact of each of the above factors on the total budget variance. Thus the overspend against budget can be analysed into a series of variances, as shown in Figure 20.

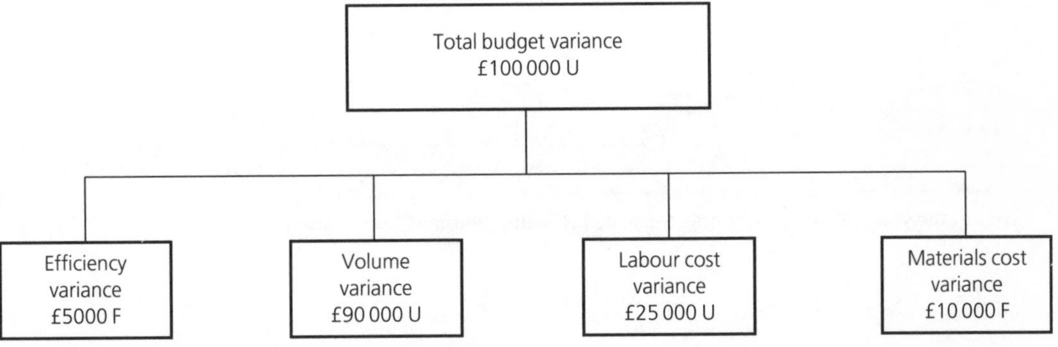

Figure 20 Variance analysis

The four separate contributory variances are as follows:

- A favourable materials cost variance of £10 000. This implies that raw materials have been purchased at a lower unit price than was planned.
- An unfavourable labour cost variance of £25 000. This implies that the hourly rates of pay of employees is greater than planned.
- An unfavourable volume variance of £90 000. This implies that the number of miles of road that have been maintained is greater than planned.
- A favourable efficiency variance of £5000. This implies that the department has worked more efficiently than was planned. In practice this variance can be separated into a labour efficiency variance and a materials efficiency variance.

FINANCIAL ACCOUNTING

All public and private sector organizations have a statutory duty to produce a set of annual financial accounts showing the financial performance of the organization over the previous twelve months. In many parts of the public sector (for example the NHS and local government) the usual period for producing such accounts is for the year ended 31 March but in other PSOs (for example FE colleges) a different accounting period will be used (31 July). The financial accounts of any PSO comprise a number of different and interlocking statements, the key ones being:

- income and expenditure account
- balance sheet
- cash flow statement.

Before looking at PSO financial accounts in a little more detail, it is first necessary to say something about the fundamental nature of the relationship between these different financial statements. This is best illustrated by means of a simple example using a small hypothetical business entitled 'XYZ'. These same principles can then be applied to the financial accounts of a PSO.

PRINCIPLES OF FINANCIAL ACCOUNTING: XYZ: BASIC DATA

XYZ commenced business on 1 April 1999. It purchases widgets, paints them and then sells them on at a higher price. The following information is available about the business:

At the date of commencement of business, XYZ had the following financial position:

	£000
Owner's investment in the business	*35*
Loan from bank	*10*
Cash in the bank	*45*

During the year 1999/00, XYZ undertook the following financial transactions:

	£000
Purchase of widgets	*50*
Sale of widgets	*65*
Payment of wages	*5*
Cost of paint	*3*
Miscellaneous expenses	*2*
Purchase of equipment	*40*
New loan taken out	*5*
Repayment of existing loan	*2*
Payment of bank interest	*1*
Owner's drawings from the business	*2*
Cash received from sales	*61*
Cash paid for purchases of widgets	*48*

At the end of the year, XYZ held stocks of widgets worth £3000.

The financial accounts of XYZ would be as shown opposite:

Income and Expenditure (Profit and Loss) Account for 1999/00:

	£000	£000
Sales of widgets		65
Purchase of widgets	50	
less stocks at year end	3	
Cost of widgets sold		47
Gross surplus (profit)		18
less Running Costs		
Wages	5	
Paint	3	
Miscellaneous	2	
Depreciation of equipment	4	14
Net suplus (profit) before finance charges		4
less Finance charges		
Bank interest		1
Net surplus (profit)		3
less owner's drawings		2
Retained surplus (profit)		1

Balance Sheet as at 31 March 2000

	£000	£000
Assets		
Fixed assets		
Equipment	40	
less depreciation	4	
		36
Current assets		
Stock of widgets	3	
Debtors	4	
Cash	8	
	15	
less current liabilities		
Creditors	2	
Net current assets		13
Total assets		**49**
financed by:		
Owner's investment	35	
add retained profit	1	
Owner's capital		36
Bank loans		13
Total financing sources		**49**

Cash Flow Statement for 1999/00			
	£000	£000	£000
Opening Cash Balance			**45**
Cash inflows			
Sales receipts	61		
New bank loan	5		
Total cash inflows		+66	
Cash outflows			
Purchase payments	48		
Wages	5		
Paint	3		
Miscellaneous expenses	2		
Bank interest	1		
Loan repayment	2		
Purchase of equipment	40		
Owner's drawings	2		
Total cash outflows		–103	
Net cash outflow during 1997/98		–	**–37**
Closing cash balance			**8**

A number of points of clarification need to be made about the structure and content of these statements:

- **Income** – an I&E account differs from a statement of cash flows since it adopts what is termed the accounting accruals concept. Under this concept, income is the amount actually earned by the organization during the year as opposed to the cash actually received. The difference between income and cash received is accounted for by debtors, as the data from the above example illustrates:
  - sales income earned = £65 000 shown in I&E account
  - cash received from sales = £61 000 shown in cash flow statement
  - debtors outstanding at the year end = £4000 shown in the balance sheet.
- **Expenditure** – again under the accruals concept, this is the cost of purchases of widgets made in the year as opposed to the cash actually disbursed. The difference between expenditure and cash spent is accounted for by creditors, as the data from the above example illustrates:
  - purchases made = £45 000 shown in I&E account
  - cash disbursed for purchases = £43 000 shown in cash flow statement
  - creditors outstanding at the year end = £2000 shown in the balance sheet.
- **Stocks** – the business commences the year with no stocks of widgets but at the end of the year stocks of widgets amount to £3000. Hence the amount charged to the income and expenditure account is the cost of the widgets actually sold. This is derived by deducting the remaining stocks from the cost of the widgets purchased.

- **Depreciation** – all organizations make use of fixed assets such as buildings and equipment. The wear and tear involved in using these assets means that inevitably they suffer a reduction in value and this reduction in value is as much a cost to the organization as pay or non-pay expenditure. This cost of wear and tear has therefore to be accounted for in the I&E account under the heading of depreciation. Using the data from the above example, the depreciation charge is computed as follows:

  - Cost of equipment = £40 000
  - Useful life = 10 years
  - Annual depreciation charge = £40 000 / 10 = £4000 per annum

  It should be noted that this depreciation charge does not involve any cash movement to or from the organization. Instead, the surplus (profit) of the organization is reduced by the amount of the depreciation charge and the value of the equipment is reduced in the balance sheet.
- **Bank loans** – the business started the year with an outstanding loan and during the year part of this old loan was repaid while a new loan was taken out. The results of these transactions are reflected as adjustments in the balance sheet and not the I&E account as follows:

  - Loans at start of the year £10 000
  - less repayments £1000
  - add new loan £4000
  - Loans at end of year £13 000

  In addition, an interest payment of £1000 was made during the year and charged to the I&E account.
- **Owner's investment** – at the commencement of the business this amounted to £35 000. The profits earned by XYZ (£3000) accrue to the owner and hence increase his investment but drawings from the business of £2000 reduced his investment by that amount.

PURPOSE OF FINANCIAL STATEMENTS

Each of the three main statements comprising a set of financial accounts serves a specific purpose as described below:

- **Income and expenditure statement** – this is a statement of *financial performance*. It shows the financial performance of the organization (in terms of a surplus or deficit on income and expenditure) that has been achieved over a period of a year.
- **Balance sheet** – this is a statement of *financial position*. It shows the assets owned by the organization and its outstanding liabilities at a point in time, namely the end of the financial year. Thus, the closing balance sheet for one year becomes the opening balance sheet of the next year.
- **Cash flow statement** – this is also a statement of *financial performance* which shows whether the organization has had a net inflow or outflow of cash (as opposed to income and expenditure) over the annual period. Cash flow is important since organizations which are generating a financial surplus on income and expenditure can still experience financial difficulties if their cash flow position is not also positive.

FINANCIAL ACCOUNTING IN PSOs: KEY ISSUES

The principles of financial accounting outlined in the above example, particularly the accruals concept and the accounting for fixed assets, are applied in most PSOs. However, there are some specific points which should be highlighted:

- **Fixed assets** – the traditional way of recording fixed assets in commercial organizations is termed historic cost. By this is meant that, with some exceptions such as land, the figures shown in the balance sheet represent the cost of the asset when it was originally purchased, less depreciation for wear and tear. In the public sector it is more usual for the fixed asset figures to show the current value of the assets rather than their historic cost.
- **Owner's capital** – since there are no private owners of public assets then this section of the balance sheet will differ from that of the private sector. However, this section may show the value of assets which have been financed through charitable donations (for example the NHS).
- **Financial surpluses** – there is a commonly-held view that PSOs should always aim to break even on their income and expenditure position. Although it is clearly the case that PSOs do not aim to make losses or to make large surpluses for distribution to shareholders, it is important that they do aim to make some moderate surplus. Financial surpluses are important as a means of generating resources which can be used to develop new activities and new approaches in the organization. Thus, retained financial surpluses can be used to finance new equipment, staff development and so on.

FINANCIAL ACCOUNTING IN PSOs: THE PRACTICE

Most PSOs will broadly follow the above approach to financial accounting, although the detailed format of financial accounts in the public sector will vary from sector to sector. Summarized below are some examples of the approach to financial accounting in a number of PSOs:

- **NHS Trusts** – all Trusts have to produce financial accounts which include an I&E statement, a balance sheet and a cash flow statement as well as a variety of other statements giving additional information.
- **FE/HE institutions** – all institutions have to produce financial accounts which include an I&E statement, a balance sheet and a cash flow statement.
- **QUANGOs** – the organizations produce financial accounts which include an I&E statement, a balance sheet and a cash flow statement.
- **Local authorities** – the statutory financial accounts of local authorities comprise a complex set of interlocking financial statements. Separate I&E statements are produced for the income collection activity of the authority (the collection fund) and for the service activities of the authority (the general fund). Separate I&E accounts may be maintained for each local authority service (for example education and social services) but there is a statutory requirement to produce a separate I&E statement for DSOs and housing services. These I&E statements will be produced according to the accruals concept. Local authorities also produce balance sheets showing their assets and liabilities.
- **Central government** – traditionally the accounts of central government departments were produced only on a cash flow basis and there was no I&E account or balance sheet. In recent years, central government has adopted the principles of what is termed resource accounting. There are many aspects to resource accounting but two specific ones concern the introduction of accruals accounting and the accounting for fixed assets. This puts central government accounting practice much closer to the approach described in the example above.

FINANCIAL CONTROL

Effective financial control arrangements are essential in any PSO. Given that PSOs are dealing with public funds and operating in a political environment, it is likely that the financial control arrangements in a PSO are likely to be much stricter than in most commercial organizations.

There are three aspects of financial control to consider:

- financial control frameworks
- audit arrangements
- accountability and governance arrangements.

FINANCIAL CONTROL FRAMEWORK

PSOs require a framework of financial control in which to conduct their financial affairs. Usually, this framework has four components, as illustrated in Figure 21.

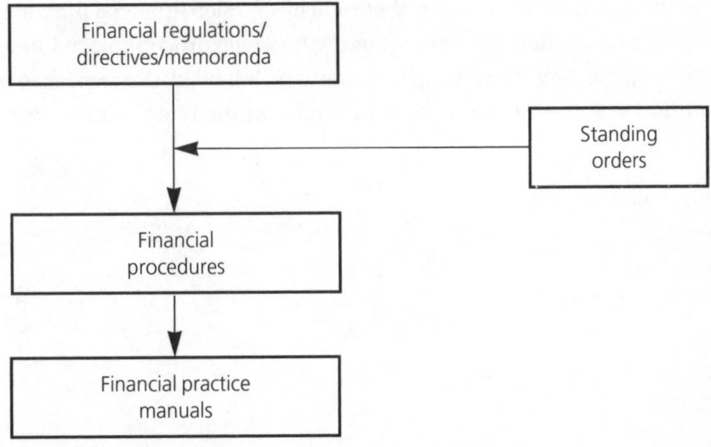

Figure 21 Financial control framework

FINANCIAL REGULATIONS, DIRECTIVES AND MEMORANDA

They provide the minimal statutory requirements for financial control on which the PSO must base its financial procedures. The main issues covered will include:

- the need to approve annual budgets
- the need to monitor financial performance
- the need for safeguards on the organization's resources
- the duty not to overspend its budget
- powers regarding borrowing.

STANDING ORDERS

PSOs require a framework for the overall conduct of business in the organization and this is provided by the standing orders of the organization. Standing orders will cover a wide range of matters including:

- appointment of chairman and vice-chairman
- conduct of board meetings
- arrangements for delegation to officers or other agencies
- tendering and contract arrangements.

FINANCIAL PROCEDURES

PSOs usually have a financial procedures manual which describes, in broad terms, the way in which the organization will control and manage its financial affairs. This manual will cover such matters as:

- roles of directors and managers in financial control
- powers to recruit and appoint staff
- security of the authority's assets
- internal audit arrangements
- delegated spending limits for directors and managers.

FINANCIAL PRACTICE MANUALS

Following on from the financial procedures there will be detailed financial practice manuals which lay down, in considerable detail, how the content of the financial procedures manuals are to be applied. They will indicate the various processes and systems to be followed, the records to be kept and the persons who can authorize various transactions. Examples of the types of procedure notes that will be needed include:

- ordering of goods and services
- payment of creditors
- collection of income
- payment of salaries and wages
- stock control
- fixed assets
- budgetary control.

It is the role of internal audit to evaluate the robustness of systems of financial control in the organization and to monitor compliance. This will be discussed in a later section.

AUDIT ARRANGEMENTS

An issue which sometimes causes confusion among non-financial staff in public sector is audit arrangements. This is because of the wide range and diverse nature of audit activities to which PSOs can be subject. Basically, various PSOs could at various points in time be subject to several different types of audit, as shown below:

- internal audit
  - in-house team
  - contracted service.
- external Audit
  - National Audit Office
  - Audit Commission
  - private audit.
- other audit
  - Funding Council audit (HE and FE sectors)
  - European Court of Auditors.

Each of these types of audit will be discussed in turn.

INTERNAL AUDIT

In this section consideration is given to the role and approach of internal audit in PSOs.

INTERNAL AUDIT: THE ROLES

Reference was made earlier to financial procedures, and one section of those procedures usually requires the Director of Finance to ensure that an adequate internal audit service is in place. In practice, an internal audit service may be provided in two main ways:

- internal audit staff directly employed by the PSO
- by means of a contract with an external organization such as a private firm of accountants or another PSO or a consortium of PSOs.

The scope and objectives of internal audit will vary from organization to organization. However, best professional practice suggests that the role of internal audit can be summarized as being to review, appraise and report to management on:

- the soundness, adequacy and application of financial and other management controls
- the extent of compliance with, relevance and financial effect of established policies, plans and procedures
- the extent to which the organization's assets and interests are accounted for and safeguarded from losses of all kinds arising from:
  - fraud and other offences
  - waste, extravagance, inefficient administration, poor value for money or other cause.
- the suitability and reliability of financial and other management data developed within the organization.

A number of points should be emphasized regarding the above roles including the following:

- Internal audit should not just be concerned with the effectiveness of financial controls in the organization but should also review the effectiveness of non-financial managerial controls.
- As well as being concerned with the effectiveness of systems, internal audit should also review the robustness of the policies and plans of the organization. Thus internal audit should be looking at, for example, the business plan and financial strategy of the organization.
- Internal audit should be concerned with reviewing financial information in the organization but also should look at non-financial information. Thus, it should be reviewing the suitability and reliability of activity, human resource and fixed asset information in the organization.
- Internal audit has a clear role in identifying ways in which the organization can improve its use of resources.

These comments are important because too many internal audit sections still restrict themselves to the audit of financial systems and fail to undertake much broader roles. Failure to do this must raise question marks about the value for money being given by internal audit itself. The recently published Turnbull report emphasizes these points even further.

INTERNAL AUDIT – THE APPROACH

A large component of modern internal audit is undertaken using a systems-based approach. Thus, instead of manually checking large volumes of financial transactions such as payment vouchers to assess their accuracy and correctness, internal auditors concentrate on the underlying systems and procedures in place. A systems-based approach would work as follows:

- The auditor examines the system involved and assesses the strengths and weaknesses making up the system. Such systems could include the payroll system, the income collection system, the ordering system or the manpower recruitment system.
- The auditor test-checks a small number of transactions processed through the system to reveal if they had conformed with the procedures laid down. The number of items checked depends on the evaluation of the strengths and weaknesses of the system.
- Where weaknesses in a system or non-compliance with the requirements of that system are identified, the internal auditor would report to management and recommend a course of action to be undertaken. Traditionally, internal auditors have reported to and been accountable to the Director of Finance of the organization, as part of this role is ensuring effective financial control in the organization. This has changed in that the principles of the Cadbury Report on corporate governance are now applied to PSOs and consequently, internal audit may be seen as part of a wider reporting relationship to board level in the organization via the Audit Committee.
- Some months later the internal auditor will follow-up to see if his recommendations have been implemented.

It is important to emphasize that internal audit cannot look at everything and cannot guarantee finding systems weaknesses or detecting fraud. Internal audit has limited resources and must focus those resources on what are regarded as the areas of greatest risk in the organization. Thus, internal auditors will need to assess the risks associated with different activities and systems in the organization, and focus its efforts on those areas of greatest risk. In assessing risks, internal audit will look at a number of factors including:

- the magnitude of a system or activity in terms of numbers of transactions or expenditure
- the dependency of the organization on particular systems and activities and thus the risks of a breakdown in system control
- the effectiveness of the management of a particular system or activity and the degree of organizational change taking place in that area
- the inherent weaknesses in a system and its controls.

Thus, the modern role and approach of internal audit in evaluating systems is very different from the traditional role and approach.

A growing trend in internal audit which will probably impact on PSOs in years to come is the concept of risk self-assessment. Under this approach it is line managers themselves, rather than internal auditors, who will assess the various risks being faced by the organization and the strengths and weaknesses of the existing control framework. Managers will then propose and implement new controls where these are perceived to be necessary to deal with unacceptable risks. Under a system of risk self-assessment the role of the internal auditor will become one of training line managers in the tasks of risk assessment and control design, and undertaking quality assurance of the work being done by those line managers. Clearly, such an approach has a strong flavour of placing responsibility for managerial control on line managers and empowering them to take appropriate action.

EXTERNAL AUDIT

In this section consideration is given to the role, approach and organization of external audit in the public sector.

EXTERNAL AUDIT: THE ROLE

Whereas internal audit is a tool of management whose reporting relationships are determined by the management itself, external audit is independent of the organization and provides an external view of the organization. In the private sector, external auditors formally report to the shareholders of the company. In the public sector, although external auditors will submit copies of their reports to the organization itself, their primary function involves reporting to the relevant Secretary of State on the financial management and control of the organization.

The main roles of the external auditor can be described under three headings, namely:

- To examine the adequacy of financial control systems and procedures in the organization and the extent of compliance with those procedures. In doing so, the external auditor will wish to rely upon the work of the internal auditor in this area.
- To examine the annual financial accounts and underlying financial records and systems of the organization to establish whether or not those accounts give a fair representation of the financial performance and position of the organization.
- To examine the way in which the organization has used the resources at its disposal, to establish the extent to which value for money has been achieved.

EXTERNAL AUDIT – THE APPROACH

In limited companies the primary role of the external auditor is to comment on the accuracy or otherwise of the company's published accounts. To assure themselves about the accuracy of these accounts the external auditor must 'go behind the books' and examine the systems and records on which the accounts are based. If the external auditor cannot state that the accounts show a true and fair view then the accounts will be suitably qualified. In the public sector the external auditors must issue a number of key documents:

- to the organization itself: a management letter
- to the Director of Finance: a letter setting out any weaknesses revealed in internal audit
- exceptionally, to the Secretary of State: the auditor may also issue a report directly where there are serious matters of concern.

ARRANGEMENTS FOR EXTERNAL AUDIT IN THE PUBLIC SECTOR

Currently, the arrangements for external audit of PSOs show considerable variations in practice. Table 10 on the next page shows the current arrangements for external audit of the main PSOs in England and Wales and indicates whether the individual PSO involved has any discretion over the choice of external auditor. Slightly different arrangements apply in Scotland and Northern Ireland where the Accounts Commission for Scotland and the Northern Ireland Audit Office operate.

NATIONAL AUDIT OFFICE

The head of the NAO is the Comptroller and Auditor General (CAG) who has the statutory role, on

Table 10 Public sector external audit arrangements

Public Sector Organization	*External auditor*	*Discretion*
Central government departments	National Audit Office	None
Executive agencies	National Audit Office	None
QUANGOs	National Audit Office	None
Local authorities	Audit Commission	Limited
Health authorities/NHS Trusts	Audit Commission	Limited
Further education colleges	Private auditor	Yes
Higher education institutions	Private auditor	Yes

behalf of Parliament, of auditing the accounts of all government departments and a wide range of accounts of other publicly-financed bodies. The CAG is an officer of Parliament who reports to the Public Accounts Committee, and is independent of the executive arm of government. Dismissal from post can only be by a resolution of both Houses of Parliament. Not surprisingly, many of the reports of the NAO can be extremely critical of the government of the day.

The NAO is responsible for auditing appropriation accounts within government departments and, ultimately, for certifying the correctness of those accounts when they are laid before Parliament. In discharging the duties, the NAO must be satisfied about the adequacy of systems of financial control operating in the PSO. Aside from being the primary external auditor of government departments, agencies and quangos, the NAO also undertakes various types of review in other parts of the public sector. For example, it undertakes value-for-money audits testing the economy, effectiveness and efficiency of government department activities and also undertakes investigations into matters of public concern on behalf of the Public Accounts Committee.

THE AUDIT COMMISSION

External audit of NHS organizations and local authorities is the responsibility of the Audit Commission which, although being a public sector organization, is largely independent of central government. In practice the Audit Commission discharges its external audit duties in two ways:

- about 70 per cent of audit workload is undertaken through the District Audit Service, the operational arm of the Audit Commission
- the balance is undertaken through firms of private sector auditors who are contracted to the Audit Commission to undertake these external audit duties.

Irrespective of who actually conducts the audit, audit fees are based on a common scale of fees negotiated centrally by the Audit Commission. Both types of auditor are required to work to the Audit Commission's Code of Practice.

PRIVATE AUDIT

Private audit means audit services provided by a firm of accountants and auditors. Private audit of PSOs may take place in two ways:

- As already noted, 30 per cent of the work of the Audit Commission is contracted-out to private firms of auditors. The Audit Commission runs a competitive tendering process in which district audit and private firms compete to win audit contracts. The various local authorities and NHS organizations who are to be audited are involved in the selection process.

- HE and FE institutions are free to choose who should be their external auditor, and usually will choose a private firm. However, in choosing an auditor they must make reference to guidance provided by the various funding councils.

OTHER AUDIT

Finally, there are some additional audit activities which may impinge on PSOs to a lesser or greater extent:

EDUCATION FUNDING COUNCIL AUDIT

The further and higher education funding councils, described in Chapter 2, both have their own audit sections. These audit sections undertake various reviews of further and higher education institutions respectively. These reviews are in addition to the internal and external audit arrangements of the institutions themselves.

EUROPEAN COURT OF AUDITORS

Sometimes PSOs may receive funds from the European Commission to undertake specific projects in specialist fields. They will be required to prepare financial statements and certify that the funds have been spent for the approved purposes. Although it is not a common event, the organization may be visited by an auditor of the European Court of Auditors who will be concerned with verifying the correctness of the financial statements submitted.

PUBLIC AUDIT FORUM

No discussion of public sector external audit could be complete without mention of the work of the Public Audit Forum (PAF). It is undoubtedly the case that the PAF has been created in response to government and public concerns about the effectiveness and consistency of the audit process in the public sector. The PAF was set up by the four national audit agencies, the National Audit Office, the Northern Ireland Audit Office, the Audit Commission for Local Authorities and the National Health Service in England and Wales and the Accounts Commission for Scotland, to provide a focus for developmental thinking in relation to public audit.

Specific elements of the PAF's remit are to:

- Provide a strategic focus on issues cutting across the work of the national audit agencies.
- Build visibly on the existing co-operation between the national audit agencies to enhance the efficiency and effectiveness of public audit whilst, in all matters, respecting the statutory and constitutionally independent status of the agencies in the selection, execution and reporting of their work and in determining how this work should be organized and staffed.
- Establish definitions of what constitutes public audit insofar as this differs from and goes beyond the current interpretation of company audit.
- Advise on the application of standards and the practices of the auditors of bodies delivering public services, including on the quality of service to be provided to such audited bodies, having regard to the statements issued by the Auditing Practices Board.

- Develop standards for use by auditors of bodies delivering public services where none have been issued by the Auditing Practices Board.
- Advise on the resolution of common technical problems and disseminate good and innovative practice in tackling common issues.
- Provide the considered view of the national audit agencies on any developments or proposals which impact on public audit, whilst avoiding comment on the merits of government policy objectives.

As well as the four national audit bodies the PAF also involves various stakeholders in the public audit process, including government departments, local government, the NHS, the audit profession and the Consumer's Association. The main role of the PAF is consultative and advisory. It is not able to direct the national audit agencies and other bodies involved in public audit. However, the PAF will undoubtedly try to influence and improve audit practice in the public sector and either has provided or will provide guidance on the following issues:

- the principles of public sector audit
- the audit of propriety and governance in the public sector
- the service which auditees can expect from public auditors
- the implications for accountability of the Better Government agenda
- the implications for public auditors of the use of data matching techniques
- the implications for public auditors of the trend for greater involvement by the public in the decision-making process of public bodies, and of the freedom of information legislation.

SPECIALIST AUDIT ACTIVITIES

In describing the roles of the different types of auditors, reference was made to a number of general audit activities such as assessing the strengths and weaknesses of financial control systems. In addition, three specialist audit activities are undertaken by either external or internal auditors. These are:

- value-for-money audit
- information systems audit
- capital audit.

VALUE FOR MONEY AUDIT

Auditors have a clear role in evaluating the extent to which PSOs achieve value for money (VFM) in their use of public resources and for identifying ways of improving VFM. The term VFM is shorthand for the three 'E's of economy, effectiveness and efficiency in resource use. There are clear definitions in each case:

- **Economy** – concerns the amount paid by the organization for the acquisition of real resources. It includes the cost of obtaining supplies and employing staff.
- **Effectiveness** – concerns the output of the organization and the extent to which the organization has achieved its predetermined strategic objectives.
- **Efficiency** – concerns the amount of resources used to produce a certain level of service output, or the so-called input–output ratio. Examples could include patient throughput per bed and cost per surgical procedure. Cost-effectiveness is often used to mean efficiency but it should be noted that the term 'cost-efficiency' is meaningless.

It has also been suggested that a fourth 'E' of equity is also important to consider, but auditors have not involved themselves in this matter.

Internal auditors have a key role in VFM audit and they will conduct such audits in two main ways:

- Systems reviews – examine and evaluate certain management systems and make recommendations that will improve VFM. An example might be a review of the estates maintenance system which could produce a recommendation for improving the targeting of resources.
- In-depth reviews – review a specific activity or department, in-depth, and recommend improvements in operational practices.

VFM audit could comprise up to 40 per cent of the external audit effort. The Audit Commission undertakes a series of national VFM studies into particular issues and the external auditors look at the potential to apply the results locally. Such national studies can be concerned with aspects of professional practice such as nurse management, maternity services and school management. In addition, external auditors undertake a series of local VFM studies.

The skills of the VFM auditor are very different to those of the general auditor. Often VFM auditors have a background away from general audit, such as management consultancy, buildings management and IT management.

INFORMATION SYSTEMS AUDIT

In most organizations, the last thirty years or so have seen an increasing use of computers in financial and management systems, to the point where the vast bulk of systems are now computerized. The extensive use of computers in information management creates considerable areas of risk of loss or fraud for the organization. Consequently, auditors, both internal and external, must continually pay attention to a number of different aspects of computerization. Various audit roles can broadly be classified into the following types:

- **System design** – where the organization is planning to design new or amended computerized systems which will contribute to the financial management of the organization, and the auditor will need to be involved at an early stage to ensure that the planned system will incorporate sound financial control principles and enable the auditor to undertake audit checks once it is up and running.
- **System operation** – when computer systems are operational, the auditor will wish to review and be assured that financial control is maintained. This will include the following aspects:
  - Physical security of computers and their environment.
  - Controls on the ability to input data and access to information held on files.
  - Maintenance of 'audit trails'.
  - Reconciliation between the input and output of data. For example, ensuring that the total sum of creditor invoices submitted for payment equates to the total of cheques drawn.
- **VFM of Information Systems** – the computer auditor will wish to be involved in assessing the organization's achievements in value for money from information systems and information technology. This should include a review of the benefits actually achieved compared with planned benefits.

CAPITAL PROJECTS AUDIT

Traditionally, PSOs have spent large sums each year on major capital buildings projects. Clearly, they need to be assured that contracts meet the specifications and tender terms and prices. Internal and external auditors have a strong role here. Some of the matters which they will examine concern the:

- adequacy of the planning procedures leading up to the commissioning of capital schemes, and adherence to those procedures
- appropriateness of and adherence to procedures for letting contracts
- procedures for authorizing variations to contracts
- procedures for approving the final accounts of contractors
- post-project appraisal including value for money.

The nature of much of this work is extremely technical. It is often the case that the internal auditors involved have a background in building or engineering, rather than accountancy.

However, capital project audit in the public sector is of declining importance. The emergence of the Private Finance Initiative (PFI) means that a very large proportion of public sector capital expenditure will be financed and built by the private sector and not by the PSOs themselves. Hence it is for the private company to assure itself that its contracts meet the specifications and tender terms and prices. Public sector auditors will be concerned to ensure that PSOs have correctly followed the established PFI procurement procedures and that the correct accounting treatment has been applied to capital projects financed under the PFI.

INTERNAL AND EXTERNAL AUDIT COMPARED

There is often confusion about the respective roles and reporting relationships of internal and external auditors, and some clarification is needed. Firstly, with regard to role, there are some similarities between the role of the external auditor and that of the internal auditor. Both are concerned with evaluating systems of control in the organization and duplication of effort should be avoided because the external auditor will usually place great reliance on the work done by, and the findings and recommendations made by, the internal auditor. External auditors will thereby contain their effort within the minimum audit fee. However, one major difference concerns the statutory accounts of the organization. The external auditor has a clear role in assessing the veracity of the accounts of the PSO and the underlying financial systems that generate those accounts. The internal auditor has no such role. Also it was suggested that the role of internal audit is wider. External audit concentrates primarily on financial control, whereas internal audit should be less financially-oriented and should be concerned with all aspects of management planning and control, financial and non-financial, in the organization.

Secondly, with regard to reporting relationships, external audit is external to the PSO and usually reports to the relevant Secretary of State on the financial affairs of the organization. However, internal audit is internal to the organization and while internal auditors may be independent of individual senior managers, the function is not independent of the PSO as a whole and internal audit is sometimes referred to as a tool of management.

CORPORATE GOVERNANCE

Corporate governance is an issue which originated in the private sector but soon entered the public sector arena and is now a key feature of public sector management. Corporate governance can be thought of as the means by which the top levels of an organization (the Board) can be confident about its ability to monitor and control what is happening in the organization. Twenty years ago the term 'corporate governance' was virtually unheard of. In the UK, the corporate governance debate came into the spotlight due to several high-profile corporate scandals such as Polly Peck, Maxwell and BCCI. In these cases, directors were not only seen as acting against the shareholders' interests, they were acting in dereliction of their duties to the company. A perceived growing public distrust of the corporate sector meant that action was needed, lest a legislative response was found to counter public disquiet. In the aftermath of these cases, a committee, chaired by Sir Adrian Cadbury, was formed in 1991 to examine the financial aspects of corporate governance in publicly-quoted UK companies. The subsequent Cadbury Report, which was published in 1992, focused the corporate governance debate in four main areas:

- the responsibilities of executive and non-executive directors for reviewing and reporting on performance to shareholders
- the case for establishing audit committees
- the principal responsibilities of auditors
- the links between shareholders, boards of directors and auditors.

Although corporate governance was originally concerned with private companies, the problems of control and governance also existed in the public sector. Hence corporate governance has had significant relevance in PSOs and, as reports of the House of Commons Public Accounts Committee will testify, the public sector has not been immune to scandals, which include:

- large scale overspends on major IT projects
- ineffective and expensive overseas visits by public sector managers at the expense of their employer
- poorly-handled privatisations of in-house activities
- poor financial performance leading to large-scale financial deficits.

These events often represented failures in corporate governance since actions were taken by managers, *without* Board approval or knowledge. Thus, since the advent of the Cadbury Report, PSOs have generally mirrored much of what has happened in the private sector and have dealt with such matters as the clarification of the roles of executive and non-executive directors and the creation of audit and remuneration committees.

There have been a number of corporate governance reports since Cadbury, namely: Ruttemen (Financial Guidelines), Greenbury (Directors' Remuneration), Hempel and Turnbull. The most recent report (the Turnbull Report) is concerned with the organizations' systems of internal control and risk management and it must be strongly emphasized that, whereas the early initiatives on corporate governance were concerned, primarily, with financial controls and risks, the Turnbull Report takes a much broader view and emphasizes the whole gamut of controls and risks (financial and non-financial) in the organization. This point is of great relevance to PSOs where there may be a wide variety of risks including such matters as poor quality services, health and safety, political concerns, and so on.

Although PSOs do not have shareholders they do have boards of directors who owe a duty of accountability to various stakeholders including the general public. Thus the principles of corporate governance which were developed for public companies are as relevant to PSOs. Hence most PSOs (with the exception of central government departments who are seemingly immune from such requirements) generally apply the principles of corporate governance in a number of ways, including:

- **Director responsibilities** – preparation of statements outlining the roles and responsibilities of executive and non-executive directors in the organization.
- **Annual reports** – publication of an annual report that is publicly available, which describes the activities of the organization and its use of resources.
- **Audit committees** – the creation of an audit committee to consider all audit matters, including audit plans and audit findings. Membership of the audit committee is an important matter. Maintaining a high level of independence may preclude executive directors and, generally, audit committees will comprise only non-executive directors of PSOs, although executive directors may be in attendance for some or all issues.
- **Remuneration committees** – to examine and set the remuneration of PSO senior managers.
- **Effectiveness of internal control** – under Turnbull, responsibility for the effectiveness of systems of internal control (both financial and non-financial) is placed firmly at the feet of the Board of the PSO. Turnbull requires that the Board should review the robustness of internal control and risk management by means of ongoing reports and through the conduct of an annual assessment. Internal audit has a key role in assisting the Board to undertake this task.

CHAPTER SIX

Human Resource Management in the Public Sector

This chapter is concerned with human resources in PSOs and the effective management of these resources. As will be discussed below in greater detail, human resources are still, perhaps, the key resource in relation to the delivery of public services (although the IT revolution may change that). The last twenty years have seen enormous changes in the industrial relations climate in the UK, and in the use of human resources both in the private and public sectors. Hence, not surprisingly, there have been radical changes in the scope and function of human resource management (HRM) in the public sector. Indeed, it would not be an exaggeration to suggest that prior to 1979 HRM was virtually a non-existent function in the public sector but has now evolved to a situation where it ranks alongside financial management in terms of its degree of importance.

In the various sections of this chapter three broad issues will be addressed:

- the way in which the use of human resources in the public sector has changed in recent years
- changes in the public sector environment and the way, in broad terms, that these have impacted on HRM
- the process of HRM in the public sector and the way it has evolved in recent years.

THE IMPORTANCE OF HUMAN RESOURCES IN THE PUBLIC SECTOR

Human resources are of great significance in PSOs for two main reasons as described below.

PROPORTION OF NATIONAL WORKFORCE

Public sector employees traditionally and currently constitute a large proportion of the total workforce of the nation. For example, in 1994 public sector employment represented some 21 per cent of the total workforce of the nation. However, in recent years public sector employment, as a proportion of the total workforce, has declined through a combination of an increase in the total size of the nation's workforce and reductions in public sector employment. This latter point is illustrated in the table below.

Table 11 Public sector employment: headcount (000)

Year	*Central government*	*NHS*	*Local government*	*Other public sector*	*Total public sector*
1961	1215	575	1869	2200	5859
1979	1235	1152	2997	2065	7449
1984	1136	1223	2942	1599	6900
1992	1090	1230	2897	565	5782
1994	1010	1171	2642	467	5290

These figures conceal a number of trends which are of great interest and importance:

- **Sectoral trends** – it will be noted that total public sector employment rose to a peak in 1979 and continuously declined from that point in time. However, that overall picture conceals a number of specific trends including the following:
  - the transfer of large numbers of other public sector employees to the private sector following privatization of state utilities
  - growth in the numbers of NHS employees between 1961 and 1979
  - substantial growth in police and social services staff within the local government sector
  - decline in local authority manual staff resulting from the outsourcing of certain functions to the private sector
  - continual decline in the numbers of armed forces personnel
  - reduction in numbers of civil servants and transfer of many civil service posts from government departments to executive agencies.
- **Employment trends** – modern employment trends worldwide have created a shift from a situation where organizations employed virtually all their staff on a permanent and full-time basis to one where organizations have three kinds of staff:
  - a proportion of core staff employed as full-time permanent employees of the organization
  - a range of specialist services provided, on contract to the organization, by employees of a different organization
  - a flexible army of casual, part-time workers whose numbers increase and decrease according to need.

  There are a number of reasons why this trend has taken place, including the need for a flexible workforce and as a means of avoiding the potential costs of employee protection associated with large numbers of permanent employees.

  To a large extent, PSOs have reflected this trend. Many PSOs, either voluntarily or by compulsion, now outsource a considerable range of activities on contract to private sector organizations. Some examples of this would include internal audit, IT management, training and development and specialized maintenance. Furthermore, there has been substantial growth in part-time employees in a number of areas including part-time teachers, part-time nurses and part-time clerical posts.
- **Workforce trends** – there have also been trends in the overall composition of the public sector workforce. The main aspect of this is an increasing proportion of female workers in the public sector workforce. However, two points concerning this trend should be noted:
  - The male:female ratio varies greatly according to the type of employment involved. Thus, female workers are usually more highly represented among part-time staff than are male workers. For example, in 1994 whereas 36 per cent of total NHS employees were part-time female workers, only 4 per cent were part-time male workers.
  - The percentage of female employees in the workforce varies substantially between different sectors and different types of post. For example, in 1994, in the police force some 83 per cent of full-time posts were occupied by men while in education and social services the relevant percentage of male workers was 21 per cent and 14 per cent respectively.

  Nevertheless, in spite of these comments the overall increase in the proportion of female workers in the public sector has implications for employment and working practices in PSOs. This covers such matters as flexible working hours and provision of childcare facilities.

COSTS OF EMPLOYMENT

Traditionally the delivery of public services has been, and continues to be, a strongly labour-intensive activity. Some obvious examples of this labour-intensive activity include classroom teachers, nurses and social workers. Consequently, employment costs constitute a very large proportion of GDP and hence total public expenditure in all developed countries, as illustrated in Table 12.

Table 12 Public sector employment costs as a % of GDP

	UK	*USA*	*Germany*	*France*
1970	11.6	11.4	8.8	10.8
1980	13.5	10.6	11.0	13.8
1990	12.0	10.5	9.7	13.2
1997	7.9	9.6	10.0	14.4

As will be seen, in some countries, most notably the UK, there have been substantial reductions in PSO manpower and associated costs of employment. To a large extent this has been due to the programme of privatization and the consequent transfer of many employees into private sector employment. However, there have also been reductions in manpower due to basic improvements in productivity, organizational simplification and so on. Various attempts have been made to substitute technology for labour in the delivery of public services. Some examples of where this is the case include the following:

- the use of computer-aided learning and video packages in place of formal lecturing
- the use by managers of personal computers and word processors in place of secretarial services
- the use of electronic networks for transferring documents and information in place of physical transfer by porters or administrators
- the use of automated testing equipment in laboratories
- the use of optical character recognition technology in place of manual data input
- the use of automated telephone advice lines for consumers.

However, in spite of these various advances in automation and productivity, human resources are likely to comprise a substantial proportion of public expenditure well into the foreseeable future.

FACTORS IMPACTING ON THE USE OF HUMAN RESOURCES IN THE PUBLIC SECTOR

Clearly, there have been substantial changes in the use of human resources in the public sector, particularly since 1979. There are, probably, four key factors which have influenced this level of change and these are summarized below.

EMPLOYEE RELATIONS CLIMATE

The 1980s and 1990s saw significant change in the employee relations climate in both public and private sector organizations with the strong reassertion of 'the right of managers to manage'. This coincided with the decline in the organized power of employees and the lessening influence of trade unions. This is a controversial area of discussion but it is probably true to say that there were several main reasons for this change in climate:

- **Employment legislation** – following its election in 1979 the government of the day embarked on a wide range of legislative and policy changes relating to employment and industrial relations. It is beyond the scope of this book to discuss these matters in any detail, but it will suffice to say that these legislative changes reduced the employment safeguards available to individual employees and reduced the powers of trade unions representing those employees. In recent years there has, however, been something of a reversal of these trends.

- **Managerial revolution** – the 1980s and 1990s saw something of a revolution in managerial practices with the public sector adopting many of the managerial practices of the private sector. There are many reasons for this including:

  - the involvement of private sector managers on the boards of PSOs such as colleges and NHS Trusts.
  - the increased emphasis placed on management development in PSOs
  - the recruitment of private sector managers into PSO managerial posts
  - the increased involvement of management consultants in the work of PSOs.

- **The 1983–84 miners' strike** – the national miners' strike of 1983–84 represented a massive blow to the power of organized labour in this country. The main striking force of the trade union movement had gone down to ignominious defeat and was forced into a humiliating return to work. The implications of this defeat were substantial enough for the coal industry itself, with its size being cut to a fraction of that in 1983 and its subsequent privatization. However, the implications of this defeat were much more widespread, and it could be argued that it destroyed much of the myth of trade union power and encouraged managers, in both private and public sectors, to be more assertive about their right to manage. This matter of managerial authority should not be underestimated, and it can be argued that this assertion of the right to manage was a key factor in enabling the government to force through its agenda of change on the public sector. Consideration of many of the controversial changes in the public sector (for example privatization, local government competition and NHS reforms) shows that these took place some years after the passing of new employment legislation and the defeat of the miners' strike.
- **Changes in pay bargaining arrangements** – this will be discussed in a further section but for the moment it will suffice to say that the employee relations climate in the public sector was substantially affected by changes in pay bargaining arrangements. Predominant in this change was the breakdown in national collective bargaining arrangements and moves towards, on the one hand, the use of pay review bodies, and on the other hand, the decentralization of collective bargaining to the local level.

TECHNOLOGY AND AUTOMATION

The IT and technological revolution has had substantial impacts on the operational activities of PSOs, their human resources and their contacts with their client base. As noted above, this may be undertaken with the aim of improving efficiency and/or to improve the quality and effectiveness of service provision. Take, for example, the introduction of computerized X-ray equipment in hospitals. Such equipment involves the patient getting a lower dose of X-rays, with obvious benefits, but also enables the X-ray image to be stored in digital format with lower storage and retrieval costs. However, technological developments such as these have two main impacts on the human resources of the organization:

- They result in a substitution of technology for labour, meaning that the same amount of work can be undertaken with less staff. Thus the organization is faced with the task of shedding staff.
- The need to interface with the technology means that the remaining staff need to learn and adopt new working practices. Thus there is a substantial change management agenda relating to the introduction of technology.

ORGANIZATIONAL CHANGE

It was noted in Chapter 3 that over the last twenty years the public sector has gone through a large number of organizational changes in terms of:

- configuration
- internal organization and culture
- expenditure and financing methods.

Clearly, these changes have had a substantial impact, in many ways, on human resources in the PSOs.

CONTINUOUS PERFORMANCE IMPROVEMENT

It was also noted, in Chapter 3, that the last twenty years have seen a requirement for PSOs to demonstrate continuous performance improvement in terms of economy, effectiveness and efficiency. As discussed above, a large element of this performance improvement has come about through the introduction of new technology, but there have also been other changes as well. Reductions in overall staffing levels have meant that many staff in PSOs have had to accept more flexible working methods involving multi-skilling and the elimination of restrictive practices in terms of the range of duties undertaken and the timing of their work. To achieve this flexibility of working it has also been necessary for PSOs to invest heavily in training and development. If anything, the remaining restrictive practices in PSOs now reside in the domain of professional staff such as doctors, teachers and police officers, and it will be interesting to see if any government will try to eliminate these constraints on performance improvement.

THE CHANGING PRACTICE OF HUMAN RESOURCE MANAGEMENT

The practice of HRM in the public sector has radically altered over the last two decades. This is for a number of reasons, including public policy trends as described in Chapter 3, changes in domestic employment legislation, changes in EU employment legislation and a changed industrial relations climate.

There are two aspects to this change:

- the expansion in the scope of HRM practice
- the expansion in the degree of involvement in HRM practice.

SCOPE OF HRM PRACTICE

The traditional practice of HRM in the public sector was often termed 'personnel administration', and involved little more than the administrative procedures of processing staff joiners and leavers. In recent years HRM practice in PSOs has changed substantially for the reasons mentioned above, and this has led to an expansion in the size and status of the HRM function in PSOs. Although HRM still involves the traditional and important administrative functions relating to joiners and leavers, its role has expanded to incorporate a number of other specific aspects including:

- legal and procedural advice regarding employee relations matters such as disciplinary matters, redundancy and dismissal
- improved procedures for staff recruitment
- local pay negotiation machinery in the light of devolved pay negotiations
- systems of employee appraisal

- improved systems of training and development
- various aspects of organizational development and change management.

EXTENDED ORGANIZATIONAL INVOLVEMENT IN HRM PRACTICE

As with financial management it must again be emphasized that the HRM involvement is no longer the province of the HR professional. There has been a substantial and increasing involvement of general managers and service professionals in various aspects of HRM, necessitating them having some knowledge of various aspects of HRM. This was not always the case. Twenty years ago such managers had little involvement in HRM, as illustrated by the following points:

- employee appraisal was virtually non-existent
- remuneration and conditions of service were usually nationally determined
- industrial and employee relations including disciplinary matters were managed centrally
- training and development was limited in scope
- in some PSOs, such as the civil service departments, line managers had no involvement in the recruitment of staff in their own departments since recruitment was undertaken centrally for the organization as a whole.

Today, line managers in PSOs are usually involved, to some degree, with virtually all aspects of HRM. Hence they need a minimum knowledge of employment legislation and various aspects of HRM. However, they can never hope to obtain the depth of knowledge and experience of the HRM professional, and so the organization must ensure that sufficient professional HR support is available.

KEY ASPECTS OF HUMAN RESOURCE MANAGEMENT

Modern HRM is concerned with a diverse range of different activities concerning human resources in the organization. Within the public sector, the practice of these various activities has been substantially affected by the various factors described above and the public policy changes outlined in Chapter 3. The HRM activities covered in this chapter are as follows:

- strategic human resources planning
- recruitment of employees
- retention of employees
- appraising employee performance
- employee remuneration arrangements
- training and development
- organizational development
- change management.

STRATEGIC HUMAN RESOURCE PLANNING

As already noted, the provision of public services is a strongly labour-intensive activity. Hence it is essential for the public sector and individual PSOs to think many years ahead about the numbers and types of manpower it will need and where such manpower will come from. Thus, the process of strategic human resources planning is a vital management task, and is discussed below. The basic process of strategic HR planning is summarized in Figure 22.

What this figure shows is that the strategic HR plan must be underpinned and influenced by the overall mission and strategy of the PSO or the sector concerned. The overall strategy could be

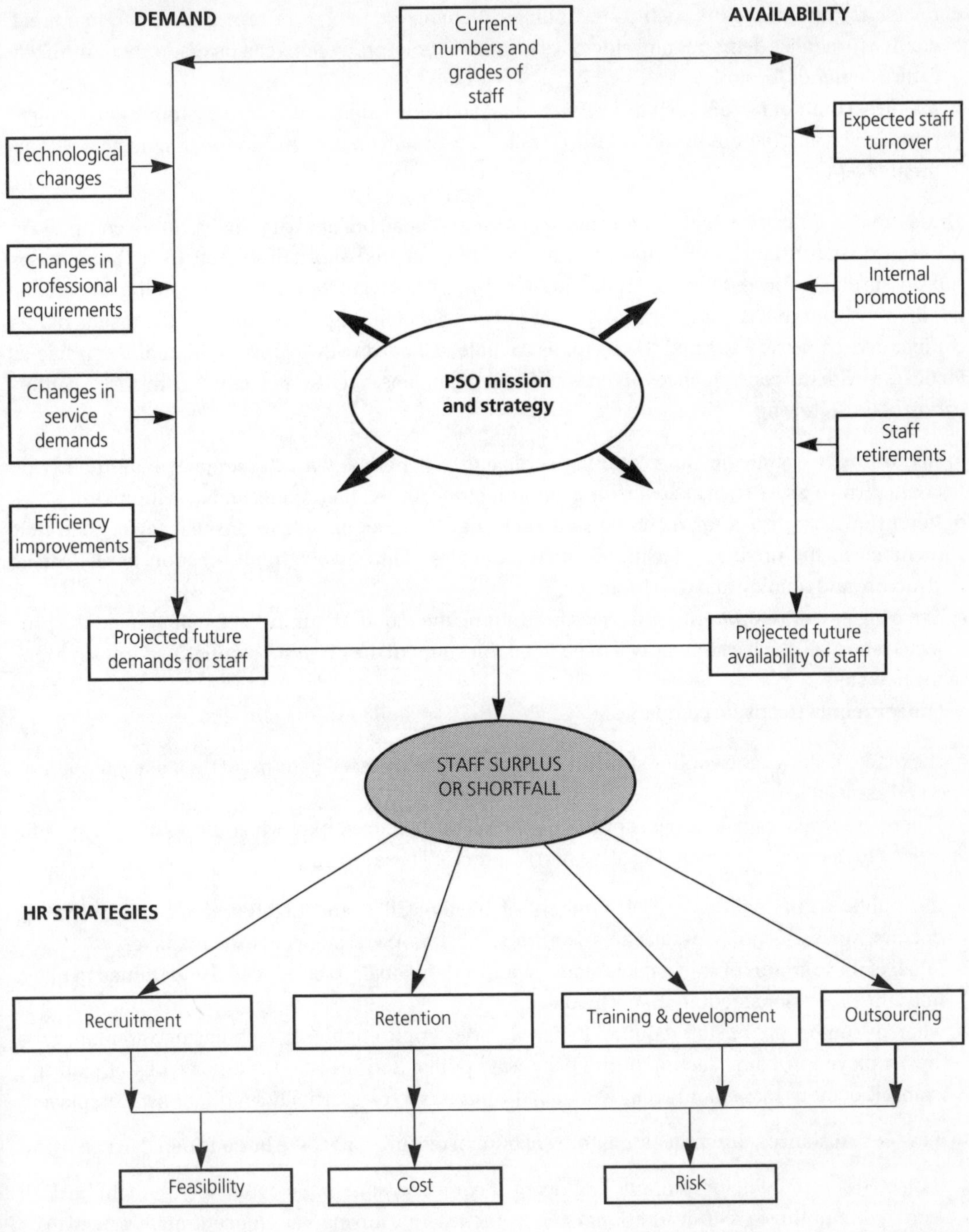

Figure 22 Strategic human resource planning

concerned with improved service effectiveness, improved consumer satisfaction or improved efficiency, and these factors must be taken account of in the strategic HR plan. Then, starting from the existing position of numbers and grades of staff, two types of projection can be made for several years ahead:

- taking account of factors such as technological changes, changes in professional requirements, changes in service demands and efficiency improvements, projections can be made about the likely future demands for staff
- taking account of factors such as staff turnover, staff retirement and internal promotions. projections can be made about the likely future availability of staff on the assumption that no new recruitment takes place.

These projections can be made for any number of years ahead but at each point in time a comparison between demands and availability will indicate the estimated shortfall in staff (or in some cases staffing surplus) expected to occur at that point in time. Clearly, there will be considerable uncertainties involved, but that is inherent in any form of strategic planning. Depending on the results of this comparative exercise, PSOs and the sector as a whole will need to develop and implement strategies for dealing with the consequences of these staffing projections. Such strategies will comprise a combination of the following:

- **Recruitment** – strategies for recruiting sufficient staff to deal with the projected shortfall. This could involve issues such as advertising, remuneration levels and training and development.
- **Retention** – strategies for retaining staff such that the level of staff turnover is lower than that included in the original projections. Such strategies could involve remuneration levels, career structure and training and development.
- **Training and development** – strategies for training the required numbers of staff to meet the projected shortfall. Such a strategy will need to take account of the often substantial lead time in training new staff.
- **Outsourcing** – to private companies.

As the diagram shows, the various strategies will need to be assessed in terms of their likely feasibility, cost and associated risk.

There are three specific aspects of the public sector labour market which necessitate a specific approach to the long-term planning of human resources. These are that:

- the public sector employs large numbers of highly-skilled and highly-trained staff including doctors, nurses, technicians, teachers, lecturers, social workers, engineers and managers
- for all of these groups of staff it takes many years for individuals to be educated and trained to meet, fully, the professional requirements involved
- whereas some types of staff required by PSOs (for example engineers, technicians and managers) are employed in many sectors of the economy, public and private, for other types of staff (for example doctors, nurses and social workers) the public sector is virtually a monopolistic employer.

In these circumstances, the strategic planning of human resources needs to be considered in two parts:

- Projected shortfalls of, for example, engineers or computer staff in the public sector might be dealt with by attempting to recruit additional staff from the larger job market. Hence strategies need to be developed, for individual PSOs and sectors, to enable such staff to be recruited. This might not be easy and might require a consideration of factors such as remuneration structures, training and development, career structures and working environment .
- Projected shortfalls of, for example, doctors, nurses and teachers, cannot or perhaps should not be addressed in the same way since no alternative sources of supply are available. Individual PSOs might attempt to 'steal' staff from other PSOs by offering better pay and so on, but such approaches

are often inflationary and offer little benefit to the public sector as a whole. Instead, the sector might develop and implement strategies to try and ensure that there are sufficient staff available to meet projected future demand. This could involve a combination of the following approaches:

- **education and training** – manipulating the numbers entering the education and training process for the various professions, early enough for trained staff to come on-stream at the right time
- **overseas recruitment** – attempting to recruit suitable staff from overseas
- **recovery** – attempting to recover staff who for various reasons had left the profession concerned.

With all of the above classes of employee there is both a national and local dimension to the development and implementation of such strategies:

- **National** – for certain groups of staff (for example doctors and teachers) certain approaches are probably most effectively applied at the national level. Thus, for example, the numbers of students to be recruited for medical or teacher training must be addressed at the national level.
- **Local** – for other groups of staff, although it may be appropriate to apply such approaches at the national level, locally-based approaches may also be applied. Thus, for example, national advertising campaigns designed to attract retired nurses back into the profession can be supplemented by campaigns undertaken at the local level by individual or groups of NHS Trusts.

EMPLOYEE RECRUITMENT

PSOs need to employ large numbers of staff of different types and levels of skills in order to undertake their activities and serve the public. This means they must recruit suitable numbers of staff and retain those staff in employment. There was a time when some PSOs, somewhat arrogantly, assumed that there were virtually limitless numbers of potential employees in the market-place, and that very little care was needed to select employees since most of the applicants would be capable of doing the job to the required standard. Hence the recruitment processes employed were often simplistic and ineffective. At worst, in some local authorities, this might have involved an advertisement in the local newspaper followed by a selection process where applicants had a five-minute interview by a committee of councillors, and were asked to answer 2–3 pre-set questions, supported by written references which were often of dubious value. At best, they might have involved national advertisements followed by a longer interview.

In general, PSOs did not, historically, pay too much attention to matters such as performance, efficiency and strategic objectives and hence did not have to pay too much attention to the recruitment of high-quality staff. However, times change. It has already been noted that, over the last twenty years, the pressures on PSOs to perform and achieve ever more challenging objectives means that they must be more diligent in recruiting appropriate high-quality staff. Furthermore, the recruitment of staff can be an expensive business, with costs incurred on advertising, selection, induction and so on. Hence, to minimize these costs it is important for PSOs to appoint the right staff for the job, thus avoiding potential high turnover of staff. Thus, recruitment approaches in PSOs have become much more sophisticated and professional and in many cases are the equal of best practice in the private sector.

Many vacant posts in PSOs will be filled by internal promotion. In the private sector, best practice will involve the use of sophisticated succession planning arrangements, whereby current members of staff are developed and groomed for promotion to more senior posts several years in advance of the post becoming vacant. In this way, the risk associated with recruiting an unknown employee from another organization on the basis of a limited selection process are dramatically reduced. By and large, this approach is not applied in PSOs, since it is felt to be unacceptable for an internal candidate to just be appointed to a post without any sort of competitive selection process. Thus, at the very least, vacant posts will be advertised internally and internal applicants may apply. However, most middle and senior graded posts in PSOs will be open to external competitive recruitment. Figure 23 summarizes what is involved in recruitment.

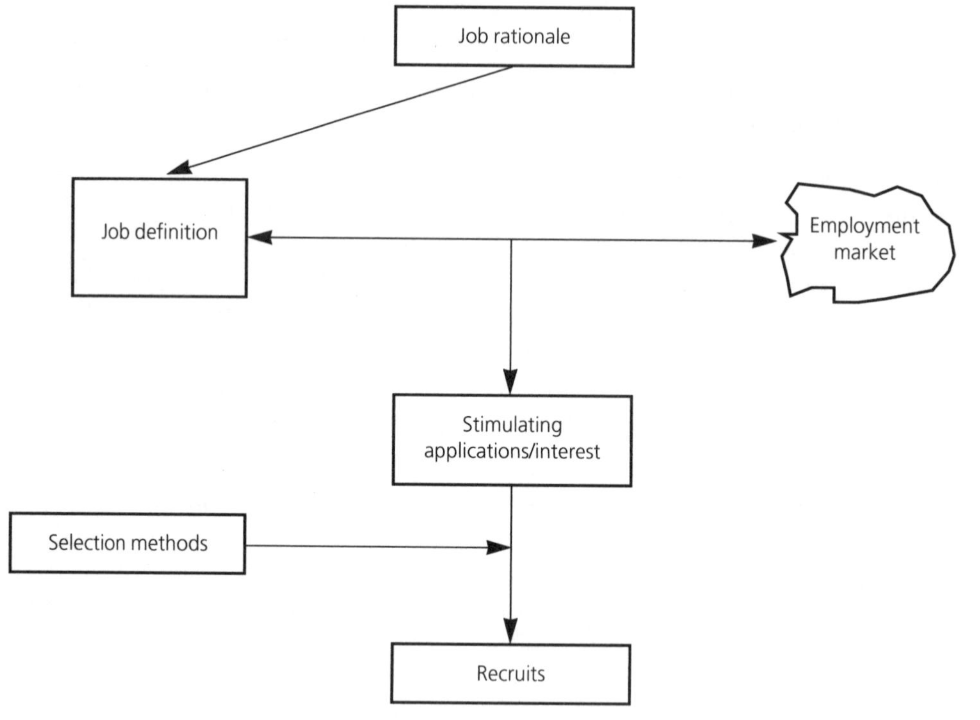

Figure 23 Employee recruitment process

There are four issues to be addressed here, as discussed below.

JOB RATIONALE

Many years ago the relatively stable organizational arrangements that existed in PSOs meant that when a post became vacant it was usually quite appropriate to proceed to fill the vacancy without any further consideration. Hence the main rationale for recruitment was a vacant post. Today, the pressures on PSOs mean that no vacant post should automatically be filled and consideration should always be given to the various prior options that may be available. These might include any or all of the following:

- merging the responsibilities of one post with another post
- sharing the responsibilities of the post among other postholders
- eliminating or reducing the functions undertaken by the postholder
- contracting-out the functions of the post
- recruitment of a new person to the vacant post.

These various options need to be evaluated, and a rationale for the preferred approach developed.

DEFINING THE JOB

Prior to advertising, a job needs to be properly defined. There are two main aspects to this:

- **Job description** – when a job is vacant it may be filled without any changes to the existing job description. However, these days, the pace of organizational change is such that few job descriptions will remain unchanged. Minor changes may be needed and where major changes are contemplated it may be necessary to undertake a job analysis exercise.
- **Job terms** – a number of issues need to be addressed here including the remuneration package, applicability of PRP, fringe benefits and so on. Although the post may have previously been subject to a job evaluation exercise, this may need to be reconsidered in the light of organizational developments and changes in the job market.

STIMULATING APPLICATIONS AND INTEREST

Where an organization has identified a potential need to recruit staff, and has defined the job, it must then interface with the job market to stimulate interest in the post and to identify sufficient numbers of people with an interest in the post. The more effective this process the greater the pool of candidates the PSO will be able to choose from. Traditionally, this has involved media advertising, but when placing an advertisement in the media considerable care needs to be taken and the following points should be borne in mind:

- **Choice of media** – careful consideration needs to be given to where the post should be advertised and this, in turn, will be influenced by the kind of applicants being sought. Use of local newspapers is relatively cheap but obviously has limitations in terms of readership. National newspapers are very expensive but clearly will have a wide readership, although the type of readership will vary from paper to paper. Professional journals will attract applicants from within an existing profession but not applicants from outside that profession.
- **Style of advert** – some public sector employers are sometimes too arrogant and assume candidates will flock to join their organization. In actual fact, the advertisement must be a selling process and must contain information which will be attractive to candidates. Thus, the post should be given an attractive title (titles are more important to the individual than to the organization) and care should be taken to spell out all of the advantages and benefits of the post. Interested parties should be invited to request an information pack.
- **Contact point** – it is very desirable to give the name of someone in the PSO (for example the current post-holder) who can be contacted to discuss details of the post.
- **Response time** – employers sometimes give very short response times, often in the summer period when people are on holidays. They are then surprised if they get a limited number of applications. Advertisements should give potential applicants sufficient time to consider the post, undertake some preliminary investigations and submit an application.
- **Selection date** – it is advisable to indicate at an early stage the date when the selection process will take place, since this enables candidates to plan accordingly. This is particularly the case when a PSO is attempting to attract candidates from the private sector, since many private sector employees will not be sympathetic to their employees having interviews for a new job and may not be co-operative.
- **Application form or CV** – generic application forms are often unsuitable for senior and middle-ranking posts. Thus, if such a form is to be used, applicants should be given the opportunity of submitting a supplementary career resumé.

As an alternative to advertising, some PSOs have made use of recruitment agencies. The agency will be responsible for finding suitable applicants for the post and may do this by a number of means including advertising, direct approaches (headhunting) or through identifying suitable candidates from those already on its books. The agency may also produce a shortlist of potential candidates for the employer by interviewing applicants itself. Using this approach the PSO has effectively contracted-out one part of the recruitment process and thus saved itself a considerable amount of work. However, there are a number of potential drawbacks in using agencies:

- the process may be expensive, since the agency needs to be paid commission which is usually a certain percentage of the salary of the post
- it is possible that the agency will not have a full understanding of the requirements of the post
- the employer never gets a real feel for the nature of the employment market involved
- many applicants may be deterred from applying to an agency, particularly if the prospective employer is anonymous or they are unable to speak to anyone in the organization about the nature of the post on offer.

Given these disadvantages, employers need to be very cautious about the use of agencies but in certain circumstances such as where the employer lacks time and/or skills they may be appropriate.

SELECTION

From the range of applicants available, the organization needs to select the most suitable person for the job and this requires an appropriate selection mechanism. The traditional approach in PSOs was, initially, for a shortlist for applicants to be drawn up. References (especially from their current employer) would be obtained for shortlisted applicants and they would be subject to an interview by a panel. As already noted, sometimes little interview preparation was undertaken, the interview was poorly structured and too much emphasis was placed on the employer's reference.

In recent years substantial improvements in selection have been made by many PSOs and these include the following:

- **Interview improvements** – the use of a more rigorous interview process. This could involve training for prospective interviewers in the use of interview techniques, and a greater commitment of time in the planning and rehearsing of interviews.
- **Interview supplements** – the use of various techniques to supplement and complement the basic interview process. This could involve any or all of the following:
  - The use of psychometric tests. One group of tests might measure candidates' basic numeric, verbal or reasoning proficiency and thus aim to assess their basic skills in relation to the job. Other tests would attempt to establish the personality profile of the candidate and would assist in assessing their likely 'fit' to the team or organization.
  - The use of assessment centres. This could involve candidates being asked to undertake a range of assessable activities including in-tray exercises, simulation exercises or case studies.
  - Prospective candidates might be required to prepare and deliver a verbal presentation to the interview panel, on a relevant topic, and respond to questions on their presentation.
- **References** – less reliance being placed on pre-interview employer references which are often suspect and which can deter applicants from the private sector. It is becoming more commonplace for PSOs to follow the private sector practice of asking for references only after the position has been offered to an individual subject to the receipt of satisfactory references.

- **Evaluation** – the use of a structured framework for evaluating each of the interviewees. This framework would set down the various criteria being assessed during the selection process and the weighting to be given to each criterion. Possible criteria might include:
  - physical appearance
  - qualifications
  - experience
  - skills and attributes
  - achievements
  - personal characteristics.

Each member of the interview panel would be required to complete a form which scores each candidate against each criterion. The total scores for each candidate would then inform the panel discussion on the candidates, rather than be used solely as the decision-making method.

EMPLOYEE RETENTION

It is probably true to say that no organization would wish to see a zero turnover of its employees. In any organization, new employees are essential to introduce new blood, new ideas and enthusiasm in the workplace. Furthermore, staff vacancies often give the opportunity for specific units to reorganize themselves relatively painlessly without the need for redundancy. However, it is equally true to say that no organization should wish to see labour turnover rates which are excessively high, since such high turnover has a number of negative implications including:

- loss of organizational memory (that is, background on the activities of the organization)
- high cost involved in recruiting replacement staff
- high cost of inducting and training new staff
- loss of continuity in, for example, client relations
- general organizational disruption.

Hence, all PSOs need to ensure that they have effective policies in place to retain staff and ensure that labour turnover does not become excessive. There are a number of matters that can be addressed to contain labour turnover within tolerable limits and many PSOs will have introduced some or all of these:

- **Exit interviews** – the conduct of exit interviews with all departing employees to establish the reasons for their leaving. By this means trends can be monitored and specific recurring problems identified.
- **Appraisal** – the establishment of a well-structured and maintained employee appraisal system. If conducted properly, this will give the employee a feeling of being valued and will encourage them to stay, but if conducted badly it will have the opposite effect.
- **T&D** – adequately resourced and planned training and development programmes. Employees see T&D as a necessary part of career progression and in its absence may look at other jobs as a means of obtaining such T&D.
- **Career development** – the establishment of proper career development arrangements within the organization so that employees are aware that they will have real opportunities for progression within the organization, as an alternative to gaining promotion by going elsewhere. Some PSOs, somewhat strangely, take the opposite view and make it clear to employees that they will only progress by moving elsewhere.

- **Change management** – one of the main reasons for employee turnover is organizational change. Hence, good and effective change management arrangements can contribute to reducing turnover of staff.
- **Remuneration** – the reality is that many employees will leave for better remuneration and the nature of public sector pay arrangements means that it is often difficult for PSOs to do much about this, since most pay is still determined nationally. Although there is little that can be done in the case of the individual employee leaving for more money, where this becomes a trend in specific parts of the organization then consideration could be given to undertaking a reorganization and regrading exercise and/or the introduction of a system of performance related pay.

APPRAISING EMPLOYEE PERFORMANCE

Although employee performance has, in many ways, always been appraised informally, until twenty years ago the formal appraisal of employee performance in the public sector was virtually non-existent. Today, formal employee performance appraisal is widespread throughout PSOs and is an important issue in HRM.

WHY APPRAISE PERFORMANCE

Performance appraisal usually concerns staff and managerial performance and is undertaken for three main reasons:

- **Promote improved performance** – the appraisal process is a mechanism for establishing existing employee performance, any shortfalls in performance and the reasons thereof. It should then form the basis for identifying an individual's training and development needs for the year ahead, and for motivating individuals and giving them a sense of being valued by the organization.
- **Career development** – the appraisal is the mechanism by means of which an individual employee's future role and career development in the organization can be mapped out. It can also form the basis for succession planning within the organization as a whole. In some cases an employee's future career development might best be undertaken elsewhere and this is a matter also to be considered during the appraisal process.
- **Remuneration** – where a PSO operates some form of performance related pay or merit pay then there needs to be some systematic basis for establishing the size of the pay award. The appraisal process can form the basis for establishing the performance of an individual employee, to which remuneration will be related.

STRUCTURE OF THE APPRAISAL PROCESS

The appraisal process can be summarized as laid out in Figure 24:

- **Appraisal objectives** – The starting point of the appraisal process will be the objectives which will have been set for the employee at the previous appraisal interview. Appraisal objectives should be limited in number (perhaps six as a maximum) and, as far as possible, should be capable of quantification and measurement with the aim of reducing the subjective element of the appraisal process. There is often resistance from public sector employees, particularly service professionals, to the setting of individual objectives. Some will claim that the nature of their work makes it impossible to quantify and measure their performance, but this is a difficult argument to sustain since any of the following may be quantified and measured:

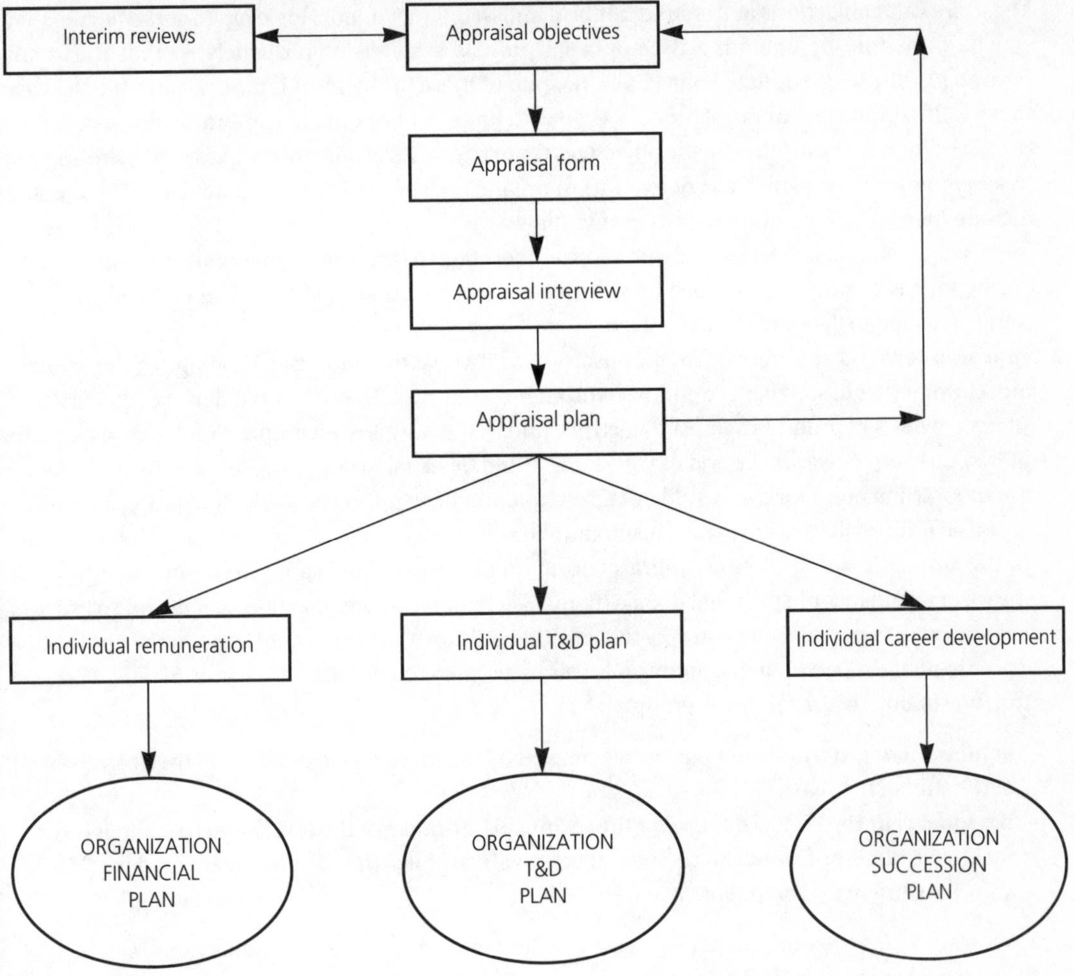

Figure 24 Employee appraisal process

- mortality rates of individual surgeons
- examination success rates of individual teachers and lecturers
- arrest rates of police officers, and so on.

A much stronger argument against the setting of such objectives is that the setting of quantified objectives in certain areas may result in other areas of activity being excluded from the appraisal process. In turn, this might affect the behaviour of the appraisee in a negative manner. This would be particularly the case where the appraisal process was being used to determine the performance related element of an employee's pay. Some examples might illustrate this objection:

- setting examination success rates for teachers might lead them to ignore other educational objectives such as understanding, creativity or citizenship
- setting mortality rate objectives for surgeons might lead them to avoid complex procedures and risky patients.

These are valid objections and should not be dismissed out of hand. However, to some degree they can be overcome by operating the appraisal process sensitively and widely so that it extends beyond just those quantifiable objectives. In spite of these problems it is almost certainly the case that a well-conducted appraisal process, even with flaws, is better than no appraisal process.

In addition to these job-specific objectives there may also be other objectives which are applied to all employees and which are derived from organization-wide core competencies. These could include such factors as courtesy and confidentiality.

Finally, it should be recognized that some amendment to these objectives may have taken place during the year and if this has been done those amendments should have been agreed with and communicated to the individual involved.

- **Appraisal form** – best practice in appraisal would involve the appraiser keeping regular contact with the member of staff being appraised throughout the year. They would undertake informal and interim reviews of progress against objectives, and in this way any major problems would be highlighted early on. Towards the end of the year it would be usual for a full appraisal to be undertaken and the starting point for this would be the completion of an appraisal form. The design and use of appraisal forms will vary greatly from situation to situation. However, a typical approach would be for the appraiser to complete an appraisal form on the person being appraised prior to interview. The form would include personal details (name, age, time with organization, salary and so on) and details of activities undertaken during the year. In addition, the form would contain the appraiser's assessment of the person being appraised. This assessment could include a combination of criteria from one or both of the following groups:

  - **achievement criteria** – what has been achieved by the individual compared to the objectives set at the start of the year
  - **personal criteria** – this would cover the technical attributes of the individual (knowledge, technical skill, quality of work and so on) and personal attributes (for example team working, leadership, judgement or discretion).

  There are various ways in which these assessments could be recorded, including rating scales, multiple choice boxes or just free-form text.

  The appraisal form would also include space for the person being appraised to make their comments on the appraisal and to record the outcomes of the appraisal process.

- **Appraisal interview** – the appraisal process involves a face-to-face meeting and discussion between the appraiser and the appraisee. The issue critical to the success or failure of the appraisal process is the style adopted by the appraiser. Conducting an appraisal interview is a difficult task and there are many bad habits to avoid including the following:

  - **Over-critical** – the appraiser adopts a negative approach and focuses unduly on the failures and problems of the appraisee and not on achievements.
  - **Halo effect** – the appraiser judges the appraisee positively on one particular criterion but this positive halo spills over into other areas. Thus appraisees are also judged positively in areas where they are actually weak. The reverse effect termed the 'horns effect' is also possible.
  - **Aggression** – the appraiser is over-aggressive and threatening. This is unlikely to result is a positive appraisal interview.
  - **Failure to listen** – the appraiser does most of the talking and tries to persuade the appraisee of the correctness of his assessment and proposed future plans. It is important that the appraisee is encouraged to talk about his achievements, any problems encountered and any concerns.

- **Lack of seriousness** – the appraiser gives a clear impression that he does not take the appraisal process seriously. Common signs of this are not allowing sufficient time (at least one hour) for the appraisal and allowing interruptions during the appraisal interview.

Even the most perfectly-structured appraisal process will fail if the appraiser operates an inappropriate style involving any or all of the above bad habits.

- **Appraisal plan** – there will be four main outcomes of the appraisal process. Firstly, there will be the agreed performance basis on which the employee's future remuneration can be established. Secondly, there will be an agreed training and development plan for the individual employee and thirdly, the employee should have a clear idea of career development opportunities within the organization. It should be noted that these three outcomes from individual appraisal interviews can be aggregated to provide input into the financial, T&D and succession plans of the organization as a whole. Lastly, the appraisal process will generate a set of employee objectives for the year ahead and these will form the basis for the next appraisal process.

KEY APPRAISAL ISSUES

There are three issues to mention which will assist with the success of the appraisal process:

- **Bias and safeguards** – with any employee appraisal process there are always concerns about managerial bias creeping into the process. While this concern can never be completely resolved, it is wise to have some safeguards on the appraisal process itself. One aspect of this is the parent and grandparent approach whereby all the appraisals conducted by individual managers (the parent) are reviewed by their immediate superior (the grandparent) with a view, among other things, to identifying bias. Another approach is the '360 degree' appraisal whereby employees are appraised by other staff above, below and to the side of them, and possibly also by consumers and other external parties. Finally, it is common for the personnel department to also review appraisal documents as a means of quality-assuring the appraisal work being done.
- **Training** – available evidence suggests that many PSO managers do not like undertaking appraisals, particularly the face-to-face interview. Furthermore, many managers conduct the appraisal process very badly and thus the process can be counter-productive. Thus, appropriate training is a necessity.
- **Monitoring** – regular monitoring and review of performance is undertaken and objectives are modified as required to meet the changing needs of the organization.

TRAINING AND DEVELOPMENT

The training and development of employees is now recognized as one of the key aspects of HRM in both private and public sector organizations. This was not always the case, and until relatively recently much of training and development in some PSOs was often limited to asking employees what courses they might like to attend in the current year. Even now, where T&D approaches in PSOs have become more sophisticated, there are still examples of substantial and unfocused training activity. However, by and large, the public sector revolution of the last twenty years has radically changed the approach to training and development in PSOs. The pressures of competition, performance improvement and the need to achieve strategic objectives have meant that PSOs now have to ensure that their employees have the skills needed to undertake their jobs both now and in the future. Furthermore, because of the existence of flatter organizational structures it is frequently the case that employees have to do several jobs and so have to be multi-skilled. Also, as already noted, PSOs have had to face an environment of continual organizational change which contrasted with the period of relative stability prior to 1979. This degree of change has posed severe challenges for employees and hence, training and development has also had to address issues of change management which were not relevant in previous eras.

WHAT IS TRAINING AND DEVELOPMENT?

There is often considerable confusion about the use of the terms 'education', 'training' and 'development' and different persons will use the terms in different ways. For the purposes of this chapter the following interpretations will be applied:

- **Education** – this is broadly concerned with meeting the basic needs of a person to fulfil their role in society as an individual, an employee, a family member or as a member of a community. Examples might be the provision of basic literacy and numeracy skills, the basic requirements for entering an occupational role or the development of a particular talent such as music or art. In general, educational activity is the province of schools, colleges and universities and thus falls outside the scope of this chapter.
- **Training** – this is any learning activity which is primarily concerned with the acquisition of skills required to undertake an occupational task. Hence, the focus of training is the job or task. Examples of training might include safe operation of equipment, effective conduct of a surgical operation or competent use of a budgetary control system.
- **Development** – the focus here is the future, and a development activity is any learning activity concerned with meeting the future manpower needs of the organization and the career growth needs of the individual. Examples of development activity might be the development of middle managers to fill senior management positions or the preparation of employees to meet the challenge of future organizational change.

WHY TRAINING AND DEVELOPMENT?

Training and development is an expensive activity and can amount to a substantial oncost on the employment costs of an individual. Thus PSOs need to be clear about why they are making such a large-scale investment and to be assured that their T&D activity is suitably focused and effective. There are three key reasons for making this investment:

- **Achievement of strategic objectives** – as has already been seen, PSOs today are faced with a number of pressures including competition, the need to maintain client satisfaction and the need for continual performance improvement. The reality is that much of the activity of PSOs is people-based and thus requires the employees of the organization to be suitably skilled and competent. This applies not just in the professional field such as doctors, nurses and teachers but also in relation to skilled manual employees (for example electricians and technicians) and semi-skilled employees (refuse collection workers, cleaners, telephonists and so on). A failure by any of these classes of employee to work to adequate standards will inhibit the extent to which the organization can achieve its strategic objectives. Broadly speaking, training and development can be needed for four main reasons:
  - to meet the needs of new employees to the organization to ensure they are adequately skilled and competent
  - to deal with any shortfall in performance by existing employees

- to promote improved performance among employees and to contribute towards employee development
- to deal with the implications of organizational change.

- **Employee recruitment** – the availability of high-quality training and development is often a substantial incentive to prospective employees of the organization, and is thus a potentially important factor in recruiting high-quality staff. This is particularly so in relation to professional occupations. In today's world no employer can guarantee employment for life, but what they can promise is that they will maintain an individual's employability through the provision of T&D designed to maintain their level of competence and marketability in the employment market.
- **Employee retention** – the arguments here are similar to employee recruitment, and the availability of high-quality training and development is often a means of retaining high-quality staff in the organization. This is often a more important factor than remuneration.

Thus it is vital that the PSO invests adequate resources in the training and development of its employees and uses those resources appropriately.

STRATEGIC ASPECTS OF TRAINING AND DEVELOPMENT

Leaving aside the detailed aspects of T&D, there are a number of broad issues which need to be considered at a strategic level and which underpin the detailed aspects of T&D. These are:

- **Individual-oriented versus corporate-oriented** – some modern learning theory advocates approaches to T&D which have the following characteristics:

  - they should be employee-centred and not organization-centred
  - they should be highly participative in practice
  - they should be flexible in approach
  - they should emphasize learning by experience (that is, experiential learning).

  Not surprisingly, much of T&D practice in most organizations, public and private sector, does not match up to these criteria since it tends to be focused on the needs of the organization and is fairly structured in nature. Hence the development and implementation of T&D strategies will need to recognize and reflect this conflict between the individual and the organization.
- **Professional versus managerial** – as has been noted many times, PSOs employ large numbers of highly-trained and highly-skilled professionals. Consequently, these professionals often have substantial T&D requirements in order to maintain levels of professional competence. At the same time, the increasing involvement of service professionals in the management of PSOs implies a substantial need to develop and maintain managerial skills. This often results in a conflict of both time and resources to be devoted to professional and managerial issues, and the development and implementation of T&D strategies will need to recognize and reflect this conflict.
- **Skill-specific versus cultural change** – T&D activities may be directed towards specific areas where there are perceived to be weaknesses which need to be eradicated. Such weaknesses could be in a variety of fields including professional, technical or administrative. On the other hand, T&D activities could be directed towards the achievement and consolidation of cultural change in the organization and could be concerned with matters such as innovation, learning organizations or entrepreneurialism.

THE TRAINING CYCLE

The process of delivering T&D in any organization can be thought of as a cyclical process something like that illustrated in Figure 25.

Each of these aspects of the training cycle will be discussed below.

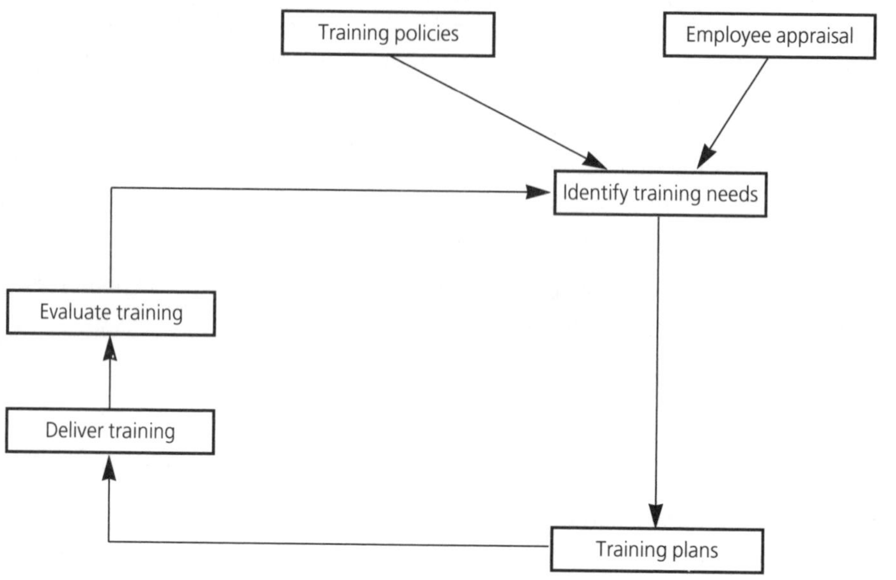

Figure 25 Training cycle

TRAINING POLICY

Most PSOs will have a T&D policy as part of their wider HR policies, and this T&D policy will set out what the organization is prepared to do to develop its employees. As with mission statements, discussed in Chapter 4, a training policy may be a short succinct statement or a much longer description of policy. However, the wording of the policy statement will indicate how far the organization is prepared to go to develop its people. Consider the following two examples:

- **Organization A** – the organization will ensure that every employee is adequately trained in the basic tasks of their employment
- **Organization B** – the organization believes it is in its own and its employees interests that full support for training and development be given, and pursuance of T&D activities will be regarded as a key part of an employee's role.

Clearly, the training policy of organization B is far less restrictive and more forward-looking than that of organization A. Also, one might expect organization B to be devoting more resources to T&D than organization A. This is not to imply that the T&D policy of organization A is wrong. If they operate in a relatively stable and unchanging environment then their more restrictive T&D policy might suffice. A less stable and more dynamic environment such as the direct services organization of a local authority might require a more proactive T&D policy, since it has to operate in a dynamic and constantly changing environment.

The organization may also have policies regarding the delivery of training. Some organizations may decide to contract-out most of the T&D activity while others will have a substantial internal training function.

IDENTIFYING TRAINING NEEDS

The training cycle (Figure 25) begins and ends with training needs. The assessment of training needs is, therefore, a key component of training and the route towards effective use of training resources. However, in many PSOs it is often not done at all, or is done badly. Training needs can often be thought of as being a combination of the needs of:

- the corporate organization
- the individual department
- the job, profession or occupational group
- the individual employee.

However, although all of the above needs may be taken into account, the reality is that the training needs of the organization will take precedence over the needs of the individual, and this is reflected in the requirements of the Investors in People Standard which is discussed below.

Training needs can be summarized as shown in Figure 26.

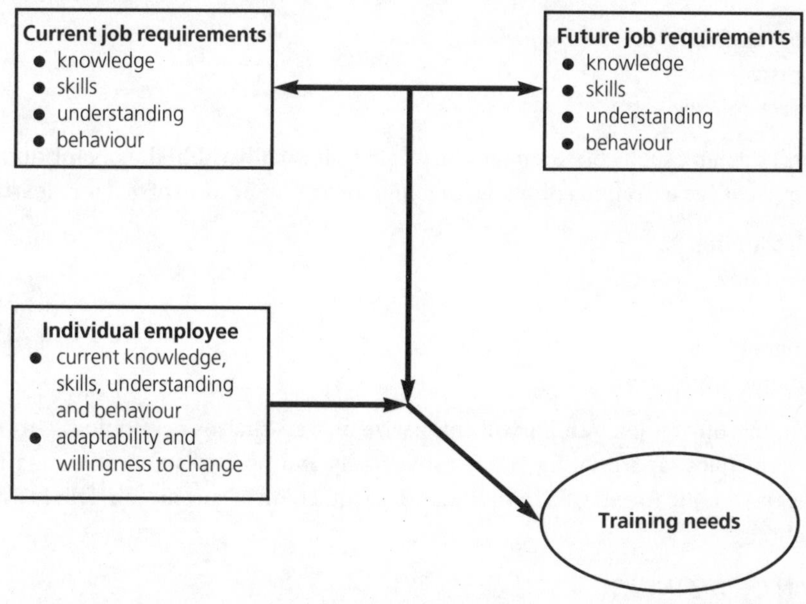

Figure 26 Training needs

Basically, this diagram shows that the training needs of the individual are (1) the sum of requirements of the job both now and in the future less (2) the sum of the individual's current skills and adaptability and willingness to change. A mismatch between (1) and (2) implies a training need.

The training needs of the organization as a whole will basically be the summary of individual training needs. These individual training needs can be identified in a number of ways including:

- as an output to employee performance appraisal (see above)
- specific surveys of training needs

- review of data on performance of activities or quality of outputs
- employee questionnaires and interviews
- client feedback.

The results of a training needs analysis (TNA) then feed through into the training plan for the organization.

PREPARE TRAINING PLANS

As with most things in life, the resources that can be devoted to training and development are limited. There are the costs of purchasing training provision and the costs in terms of lost productive time by those being trained, and these must be carefully planned and controlled. A training plan is a systematic statement of training intentions and the means by which they are to be delivered. Hence the training plan will need to cover, for each training programme, the points shown in Table 13 using the example of a training plan for business planning in a local authority.

Within PSOs, training and development was often traditionally seen as attendance at external courses, often with the aim of acquiring additional qualifications. However, there are many approaches to T&D and effective training can be delivered in a number of ways. These different approaches can be classified in terms of being 'on the job' or 'off the job' as shown below:

- **Off-the-job training**
  - short courses
  - longer-term courses.

  Although 'off the job', such courses might be located internally within the organization, provided externally by a college or training provider, or might involve some form of distance learning.

- **On-the-job training**
  - job instruction
  - coaching
  - secondments
  - special projects, and so on.

  In general terms, off-the-job training will emphasize matters such as developing an understanding of general principles, appreciating comparative ideas and practices and obtaining background knowledge. On-the-job training will emphasise the acquisition of specific job skills in a real working environment.

EVALUATION OF TRAINING

As has been repeatedly stated, T&D is an expensive investment for any organization and some attempt must be made to evaluate what has been achieved for the cost incurred. The evaluation process needs to cover the training programme as a whole and the individual courses or elements within the programme.

Although the evaluation of T&D is a complex and difficult task, whatever the difficulties it must be emphasized that some evaluation is better than no evaluation. Basically, an evaluation of T&D can focus on two distinct but related matters:

- **Initial response** – this concerns the initial response of those being trained to the training event itself. In most PSOs this form of evaluation would be undertaken, and would comprise an

Table 13 Training plan

Topic	*Description*	*Example*
Aims	The training aims for each programme	To gain an understanding of the purpose of business planning To understand the relevance of business planning in local government To develop skills at preparing business plans
Target	The target groups of employees to be trained	All senior officers in all departments (50 people)
Content	The content of each training programme covering: • curriculum content • learning methods employed	Content • why business plans • content of business plans • information requirements • difficulties of preparation Methods • lectures • exercises • case studies
Approach	The training approach to be applied such as internal training, external courses, secondments etc.	Use of external trainers experienced in business planning in local government
Evaluation	The evaluation approach to be adopted for each programme	Post-course questionnaire Follow-up interviews, three months later, with selected course participants
Costs	The costs associated with each programme: • direct • indirect	Direct costs • five courses at a cost of £1000 per course = £5000 Indirect costs • 50 days at a daily rate of £200 per day = £10 000
Administration	Administrative arrangements for each programme (e.g., location, timing)	Board room Each Monday in April (9–5)

evaluation of such matters as the structure of the training event, the issues covered, the methods of presentation, the quality of course materials, the approach of the tutors and the quality of the training accommodation. This would usually be done by getting each person at the event to fill in a questionnaire giving their reactions to the event and its relevance to them. However, more sophisticated approaches can be applied including:

- face-to-face interviews with attendees
- direct observation of the training event by an assessor
- controlled tests of what individuals have absorbed through the training.

- **Longer-term impact** – this form of evaluation involves an assessment of the longer-term impact of the training event and the benefits it has produced in terms of productivity, efficiency, quality, consumer satisfaction and so on. This is a notoriously difficult task since it is always difficult to separate out the impacts of the training activity from other factors impacting on the organization. However, whatever the difficulties, the principle should always be that some evaluation is better than no evaluation. A number of possible approaches could be employed including:

- **Comparative studies** – comparisons might be made of improvements in productivity, quality and so on in those departments or teams which had received training compared with those which had not.
- **Behavioural change** – the longer-term impact of training might be assessed by reference to the behavioural changes which have taken place among those employees who have received training. Thus, simple questionnaires might be developed and managers asked to assess the impact of training on changes in employee behaviour. The results of all the questionnaires could be analysed and an overall picture gained of the impact of T&D activity.

INVESTORS IN PEOPLE (IIP) STANDARD

No discussion of T&D would be complete without consideration of the IIP standard since many PSOs have devoted considerable time and effort towards gaining the standard. IIP is a national quality standard developed in 1990 with the aim of encouraging employers to invest in T&D. The standard provides a benchmark against which an organization can compare its T&D policies and practice in relation to T&D. The standard has four key principles which are:

- **Commitment** – the organization must be able to demonstrate a commitment to the development of all of its employees. This commitment is usually demonstrated by means of some form of policy statement or press release, but the views and attitudes of senior managers in the organization will also be taken into account.
- **Planning** – the organization needs to show that it has a system in place which identifies the training and development needs of *all* of its employees, and plans to meet those needs. These T&D needs should be identified primarily in the context of the strategic objectives of the organization and not the wishes of the individuals concerned. The emphasis on *all* of its employees must be noted. This means that in PSOs it is not sufficient to identify the T&D needs of professionals and managers but one must also look at the T&D needs of support staff and manual workers.
- **Action** – the organization needs to be able to demonstrate that it is taking action to meet the identified T&D needs of *all* of its employees throughout their period of employment. Part of this will involve demonstrating the degree of investment in T&D activity.
- **Evaluation** – the organization needs to show that it has systems and procedures in place to evaluate its investment in T&D both in terms of individuals and the organization as a whole.

IIP can be awarded to a whole organization or a department within that organization. Thus using a university as an example, IIP may be awarded to the university or one or more of its departments. The IIP standard will be awarded by the local Training and Enterprise Council (TEC) following the recommendation of a recognition panel of senior business people. The decision will be based on the findings of an independent licensed assessor who will have visited the organization, will have reviewed and assessed the T&D policies and practices of the organization, and will have sought evidence that the above key principles are being applied. Evidence will be required to show how the organization is performing against twenty-four indicators of effective practice. Prior to this assessment, quite often an organization will have commissioned its own review by an independent and specialist consultant to assess the shortfalls between what it currently does and what is required to achieve IIP. Remedial action can then be taken prior to the visit of the official assessor.

The practical benefits of working towards and achieving the IIP standard are claimed to be many including the following:

- improved productivity, since skilled and motivated people work harder and better
- reduced costs and wastage, since skilled and motivated people constantly examine their work to contribute to reducing costs and wastage
- enhanced quality, since investing in people significantly improves the results of quality programmes: Investors in People adds considerable value to BS 5750, ISO 9000 and other total-quality initiatives
- improved motivation through greater involvement, personal development and recognition of achievement, motivation is improved
- improved consumer satisfaction, since Investor in People is central to helping employees become customer-focused
- public recognition, since Investor in People status brings public recognition for real achievements measured against a rigorous national standard
- staff recruitment, since being an Investor in People helps to attract the best-quality job applicants
- competitive advantage, since through improved performance, Investor in People organizations develop a competitive edge.

Given these potential benefits it should be no surprise that many hundreds of PSOs including schools, colleges, NHS Trusts and public agencies have attained IIP status and yet more have indicated a commitment towards its achievement. However, the IIP standard is not without its critics and the following points have been made:

- **Standards** – concerns are sometimes expressed that the standards of assessment being applied when awarding IIP status are not seen as high enough to gain universal recognition of excellence, or that there seem to be inconsistencies in the application of standards in different parts of the country.
- **Continuity** – once an IIP award has been made there is no robust process for checking if the organization is maintaining the standards required.
- **Form over substance** – there is a feeling that some organizations are more concerned with the status which achievement of the standard brings (the flag, the certificate and so on) rather than the actual substance of training and development in the organization.

Thus, although IIP has certain advantages in terms of a benchmark against which existing policies and practices can be compared, it does have limitations. It is predominantly a process-driven comparison which requires evidence that systems and procedures are in place regarding planning, action and evaluation of T&D. What it does not do, however, is assess whether the organization has a real T&D culture where T&D activity is seen as vitally important and valued accordingly.

EMPLOYEE REMUNERATION ARRANGEMENTS

Until twenty years ago the vast majority of remuneration arrangements within PSOs could be described as being as follows:

- National pay scales existed for each pay grade for each type of job. Thus, the pay for a particular grade would be the same everywhere in the country, except in London where the London weighting also applied. The rates of pay for the many different types of job in the public sector were negotiated nationally by a series of joint councils (or Whitley Councils) which involved employer and trade union representation. Thus, there would be Whitley Councils for nursing staff, teaching staff, police officers, administrative and clerical staff and so on. In these circumstances the degree of discretion that an individual PSO had over its pay costs was extremely limited and consisted, perhaps, of some flexibility in the precise grade to be assigned to a particular job.
- The grade assigned to a particular post involved an incremental scale. Each year, the employee holding the post, automatically received an annual increment on the anniversary of their appointment, until they reached the top of the scale. This increment was given without any reference to the performance of the individual employee during the year, or their disciplinary record. It was usual, although not universal, for new employees to be appointed to the bottom increment of the scale, whatever their previous experience.

It would be wrong to over-emphasize the degree of change which has taken place in the public sector since 1979 since national pay negotiation and national pay grades are still very much the norm. However, there are three specific developments which have taken place and these are:

- the introduction of systems of performance related pay (PRP)
- the development of local pay bargaining
- the use of pay review bodies.

PERFORMANCE RELATED PAY

Systems of PRP have been introduced into some parts of the public sector, most notably the NHS and some parts of the Civil Service. PRP has also been proposed for other parts of the public sector such as for the teaching profession. In other cases PRP has been proposed but has been rejected. For example, the Sheehy Report on police service management recommended the implementation of PRP in certain parts of the service, but in the face of fierce resistance from the service itself the government of the day backed down on this issue.

Usually the implementation of PRP has not been applied throughout an organization, but has generally been found among senior and, perhaps, middle management. Thus it is a different concept from that of bonus schemes which have been operated with manual employees for many years. There are two main arguments for PRP:

- when filling vacant posts the existence of PRP will attract a greater number of high-quality applicants
- the use of PRP will actually motivate employees to achieve greater performance than they otherwise might have achieved in its absence.

However, there are a number of severe difficulties which can be associated with PRP:

- It is likely to be inflationary and will result in a higher wage bill overall.
- Although there is some evidence within the private sector that PRP can lead to higher performance and hence profitability, in the public sector there is no clear evidence that PRP generates employee performance over and above that which might have been achieved in its absence.
- It is administratively complex to operate.

- It may lead to undesirable behaviour on the part of the public sector employee. An example often quoted was that of police officers increasing their total numbers of arrests, in order to get their pay increased, while paying less attention to serious crime. Similar arguments can be created for teachers, doctors, nurses and so on.
- It can be very divisive in an organization, particularly where the process for setting PRP is not robust or transparent.

These are substantial disadvantages and one might seriously question why PRP was introduced into the public sector. Nevertheless, in spite of these difficulties, PSOs often do not have any choice about implementing a PRP scheme since it forms part of government policy. Hence the emphasis must be on designing and implementing a PRP scheme which minimizes these difficulties. The following features need to be considered:

- **Scheme design** – a PRP scheme needs to be properly designed. Particular attention needs to be given to the following issues:
  - **Basis of payment** – usually the payment of PRP will be linked to the employee appraisal process and PRP will be triggered by individuals' achievement of the objectives set for them as part of the appraisal.
  - **Annual payment or consolidation** – the issue here is whether the performance related element of pay should be a once-off annual bonus payment or should be an increase consolidated into the employee's basic pay. Arguably, the bonus system is a more effective catalyst for continued high performance, but the consolidation approach is more prevalent in the public sector.
  - **Maximum payment** – clearly, in the public sector, the performance related element of pay cannot be open-ended and there must be some limits on the amount to be paid. An annual payment PRP scheme needs to have some maximum payment, while a consolidated PRP scheme needs to have an annual maximum payment and a time limit for the award of PRP. Thus, a typical consolidated PRP scheme might involve employees achieving up to a maximum payment of 5 per cent of their basic wage each year for a four-year period. At the end of the four-year period their pay would then be fixed apart from inflationary increases. Clearly, the PRP element should replace the annual increment in traditional public sector pay schemes.
  - **Partial payment** – clearly, if employees achieve all of the objectives set for them then they will be entitled to their total performance related pay. However, the issue here is what should be the arrangement if employees only partially achieve their objectives. Under one scheme it could be that they will receive no PRP since they did not achieve their objectives, while under another scheme they will receive partial PRP in line with their achievements. If the latter, then there need to be some clear rules about what level of PRP will be payable for what level of achievement.

- **Robust appraisal process** – a PRP scheme must be underpinned by a robust, transparent and properly managed employee appraisal process in which employees have confidence. This should go a long way towards reducing the divisiveness of a PRP scheme.
- **Financial appraisal** – it has been noted already that PRP schemes tend to be inflationary. To some extent this is inevitable since it is clearly important for a PRP scheme to be equitable and to be seen to be equitable by employees. This means there is likely to be a cost implication. This is a particular concern in the public sector where PRP increases cannot usually be offset by increased sales or higher prices, since most PSOs operate within a cash-limited environment. Hence, every new PRP

scheme needs to be financially appraised to establish the financial impact of its implementation. This may seem obvious but is not always done.

LOCAL PAY BARGAINING

As noted above, the traditional approach with regard to public sector pay was for there to be negotiations at national level between employer and employee representatives. Thus, the individual PSO had little influence on pay negotiations for their employees. In recent years these arrangements have somewhat broken down and there has been a move towards a certain amount of pay negotiations at a local level. In the NHS, for example, it is now usual practice for NHS Trusts to undertake pay negotiations at a local level for certain classes of employee. However, it is still the case that other groups of employees in the Trusts (for example doctors) do not form part of these local pay negotiations but have their pay determined at national level.

As with PRP there are advantages and disadvantages to local pay bargaining, the main ones being:

- It gives the employer flexibility to vary pay rates to meet local employment market conditions.
- It can be time-consuming to operate.
- Many personnel officers in the public sector are inexperienced in the conduct of local pay bargaining. Thus, they may negotiate poorly with trade union officials backed by national negotiation resources.
- It can result in instability in a situation where staff move from one organization to another because of higher pay rates being offered.
- It can be inflationary if there is not collaboration between neighbouring organizations to avoid competing for a fixed pool of employees by offering higher rates of pay.
- It can be inflationary if there is not a proper financial appraisal of the pay arrangements.

As with PRP, some PSOs often do not have any choice about implementing local pay bargaining since it forms part of government policy. Hence the emphasis must be on designing and implementing an arrangement which minimizes these difficulties.

PAY REVIEW BODIES

It was noted earlier that the Whitley Council pay machinery involved negotiation at national level by employer and employee representatives. Thus the government was not a direct party to these negotiations although, since the government set the size of the annual cash limit inflation addition for PSOs, it was bound to have some influence on the size of the final settlement. However, within the public sector there are some groups of employees whose pay is strongly influenced (as opposed to being directly determined) by the work of a series of pay review bodies (PRBs). These PRBs came into creation for various reasons. In some cases it was as a result of great public concern about actual industrial action or threats of industrial action by groups of essential workers such as nurses, while in other cases (for example teachers) it was as a result of government frustration with the slowness of the existing Whitley system. The PRBs are supposed to provide an independent perspective on the pay of the particular group of employees under review and make recommendations accordingly. However, the recommendations of a PRB are not binding on the government and there have been examples of where the government has not fully accepted the recommendations of a PRB. Aside from the examples mentioned above, PRBs exist for doctors and dentists, MPs, top people (for example judges, generals and senior civil servants) and police. Whether the PRB approach is extended to other groups of public sector workers remains to be seen.

ORGANIZATIONAL DEVELOPMENT

As already discussed, PSOs have had to undergo major changes over the last twenty years and will continue to face change for the foreseeable future. Consequently, there have been (and will continue to be) significant changes in the way they are organized and in their use of human resources. In this section consideration is given to some aspects of organizational development which have taken place in the public sector, and to what should be the correct approach to organizational design and development.

ASPECTS OF ORGANIZATIONAL DEVELOPMENT IN PSOs

Although much of the organizational change which has taken place is organization-specific there are some generic themes which can be identified. Some examples of these generic changes which have been applied in many PSOs are as follows:

- **Restructuring of central functions** – the process of delegated decision making, referred to in Chapter 3, has implications for internal organizational structure. As decision making power is delegated downwards, many centralized functions start to lose some of the rationale for their continued existence in a centralized form. Take, for example, the finance and personnel departments in a PSO. As middle- and lower-level managers in the organization start to exercise decision-making power they need their own source of advice and information on finance and human resources respectively. This need often results, over a period of time, in some finance and personnel staff being relocated away from the central finance or personnel departments and located in proximity to the managers who they advise. This means that the centralized functions are often reduced in size and concentrate on those activities best undertaken on a centralized basis.
- **De-layering** – in common with many private sector organizations throughout the world, PSOs have also undertaken substantial amounts of organizational de-layering. By this is meant the complete removal of a tier of management, with a corresponding enlargement in the span of control of certain managers. A good example of this concerns the senior management structure of local authority departments and this is illustrated below using the education department as a model:

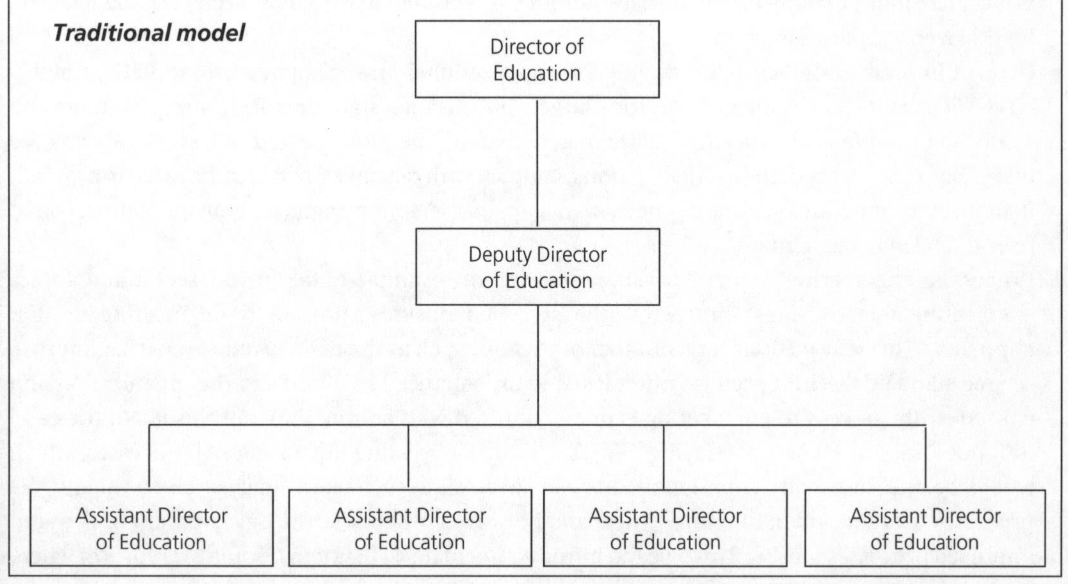

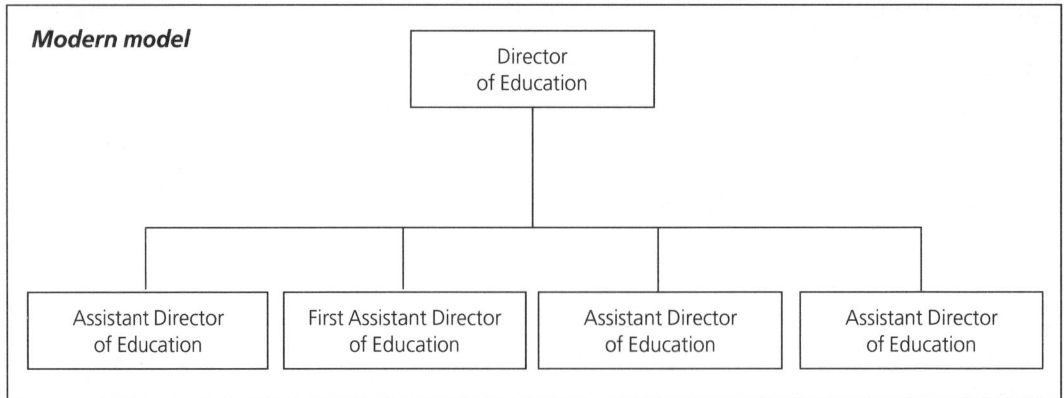

It can be seen that whereas the traditional model had a deputy tier, this tier has been eliminated in the revised model and all four assistant directors report directly to the Director. In the absence of the director one of the assistant directors will be nominated to act in the role of director for the duration of absence. This may be done in rotation, or one of the assistant directors might be regarded as *primus inter pares*.

The above example is based on the senior management structure of a department but similar de-layering could be taking place at lower levels in the department and in other departments. The theoretical arguments for de-layering are that:

- with modern information systems senior managers can directly access information and no longer need tiers of management to collect, analyse and present information to them
- de-layering reduces bureaucracy, increases flexibility, and thus permits a faster response to change.

While there may be some truth in this, the author suspects that in the public sector the main reason for de-layering is cost saving.

- **Growth in managerialism** – the traditional organizational arrangement in some PSOs, notably NHS Trusts and HE/FE colleges, was for a largely professional staff (doctors, nurses, lecturers and so on) to be supported by a small cadre of general administrators. Over the last 10–15 years the increasing complexity of these organizations, coupled with resource pressures, have led to a growth in managerial functions such as financial management, personnel management, marketing, IT and operational management.
- **Process re-engineering** – many PSOs are following the example of the private sector and are re-engineering their business processes (the so-called business process re-engineering or BPR approach). This may be done for a number of reasons, such as the need to reduce costs or improve service standards. A BPR exercise often leads to an enhanced role for IT in the organization and consequently process re-engineering is often confused with automation, but this is not the case. BPR does not just involve overlaying new IT systems on existing organizational processes, which would be the case with automation. Instead, BPR aims to review, analyse and evaluate the processes with the aim of developing new and improved processes. The development of new and improved processes may well involve the introduction of new IT systems. Some examples of where BPR has been applied in the public sector include:

- The re-engineering of the provision of services to women in an NHS hospital. The aim was to provide a more integrated and user-friendly range of services to women.
- The re-engineering of student administrative services in a university. The aim would be to provide a faster and more accurate service to students on all administrative matters such as registration, examination, fees and grants, accommodation and welfare. The streamlining of such administrative services is seen as something which would attract students in the competitive HE environment.
- The re-engineering of the process concerned with the billing and collection of local authority council tax. This could provide a more responsive, accurate and efficient service to taxpayers.

Process re-engineering has significant implications for the human resources of the organization, particularly where the re-engineering involves the increased use of sophisticated IT systems. Not surprisingly, surveys of the application of BPR in the private sector have suggested that its achievements have been limited due to the problems of organizational resistance. Such problems may be even more acute in the public sector. Nevertheless, the ongoing pace of technological advancement coupled with the need for performance improvement must mean that process re-engineering will continue to be of great relevance to PSO.

- **Changes in staffing mix** – it was noted at the beginning of the chapter that there has been a shift in PSOs away from a homogeneous staffing establishment comprised of largely full-time permanent employees, towards one which has a mixture of full-time, part-time, temporary and permanent staff. Such changes can often have profound organizational implications. Take, for example, FE colleges which have shifted strongly from a situation of employing largely full-time lecturers to a situation where there are a large number of part-time staff paid on a sessional basis. Such part-time staff are often contracted to do little more than prepare, deliver and assess in relation to the course curriculum. Thus, the burden of other functions such as marketing, administration and student welfare tend to fall on a smaller number of core staff. If this trend is substantial enough it may require some reorganization of duties within the college.

APPROACH TO ORGANIZATION DESIGN AND DEVELOPMENT

All of these situations described above (and others) demand and will continue to demand an understanding of the key features of organizational development in both specialist personnel managers, line managers and service professionals. Figure 27 shows the key features to be addressed in considering the design and development of an organization (or part of the organization).

- **Strategic objectives** – the achievement of strategic objectives should be the starting point of organizational development. Strategic objectives may involve such matters as improved quality, lower costs or improved customer satisfaction. The nature of these objectives should underpin the decisions made about organizational development.
- **Organizational processes** – it is process which defines an organization, not its structure. For example, it is possible to have two organizations with the same structure but which are very different in nature because of the processes employed within them. Thus, a golden rule of organizational development should be that process precedes structure. By this it is meant that before issues of organizational structure, numbers of posts, gradings and so on are addressed, there must be consideration of the organizational processes employed to achieve strategic objectives. Issues of process are vital whether one is considering the provision of education, the conduct of policing, the provision of medical services or the issue of social security benefit, and often substantial

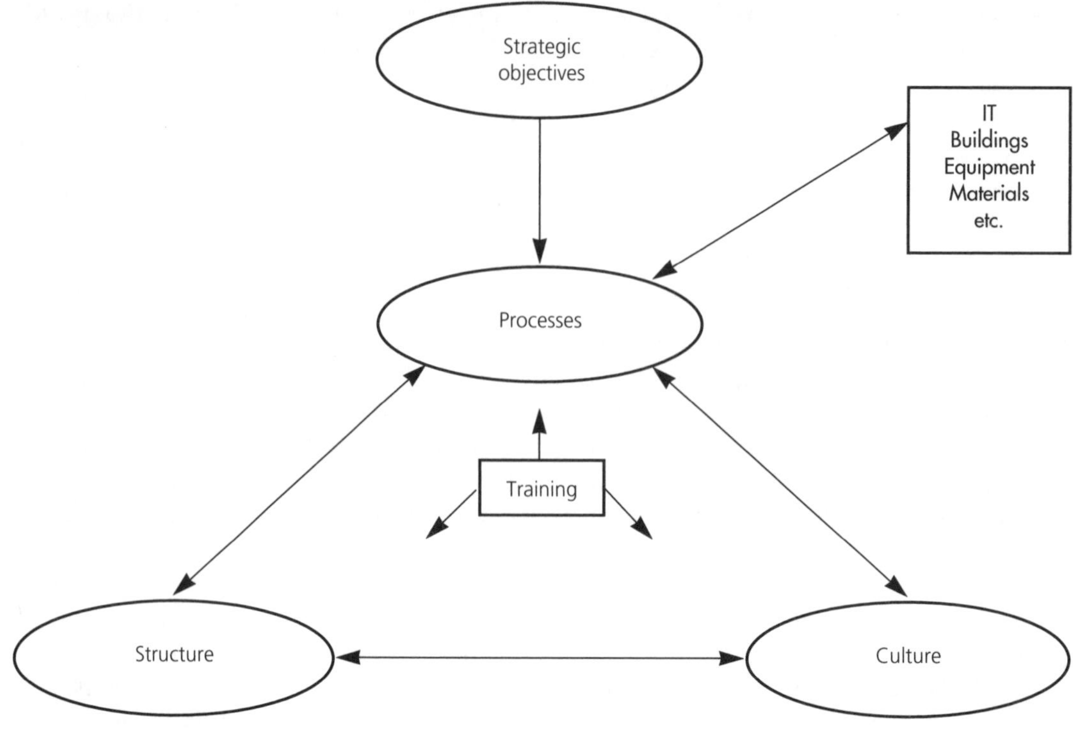

Figure 27 Key features of organizational design and development

improvements in performance can be achieved by making changes to the processes being employed. Too often, organizational development in PSOs has involved organizational restructuring with little or no consideration being given to the processes employed. As the diagram also shows, consideration of process also involves looking at other related matters such as the use of IT, and the suitability of buildings and equipment.

- **Organizational structure** – organizational structure should be built around the revised processes to be employed and their use of IT, equipment, consumables and so on. Once a new structure has been established then individuals can be allotted to new posts in the revised structure in a variety of ways. Thus, people should be fitted to posts and not posts built around the available people. In practice, however, political pressures often mean that this approach cannot fully be applied and the organizational structure will be, at least, partly built around the people currently employed within the organization. However, in designing the structure the following need to be addressed:

  - specific tasks to be undertaken by individual post-holders
  - expected task performance required from post-holders
  - skills and competencies required by post-holders
  - numbers, gradings and remuneration of posts
  - accountabilities, hierarchies and reporting arrangements.

  In addressing these matters suitable use should be made of techniques such as job design and job evaluation.

- **Organizational culture** – for a new process and structure to work effectively it will also be necessary to address issues of organizational culture and attitude. In the public sector some of the cultural changes that have taken place in recent years include:

  – greater flexibility of working
  – greater responsiveness to client needs
  – greater use of individual discretion
  – increased emphasis on team working
  – greater cost-consciousness.

  The achievement of these cultural changes requires an emphasis on the management of change and this is discussed further below.

- **Training** – there will be very few types of organizational development which do not require a substantial investment in training. This could involve training in new practices, training in the use of IT, change management and so on. However, this has not always been done. Take, for example, the policy of transfer of mentally-ill patients from long-stay institutions into smaller community-based units. This development required considerable process, structural and cultural change to the provision of mental illness services. Particularly important was the issue of change management since many staff (and patients) had been in an institutional environment for upwards of twenty years. However, in some cases the investment in staff training was minimal.

CHANGE MANAGEMENT

One of the major themes of this book has been the degree of organizational and cultural change that has taken place in the public sector over the last twenty years. Such change has been wide-ranging as the following examples illustrate:

- The requirement for many local authority direct service departments, such as highways maintenance, to operate in an openly competitive market.
- The requirement for executive agencies such as the Passport Agency and the Benefits Agency to operate in a more customer-friendly manner and to be responsive to customer needs.
- The implementation of a delegated system of management such as that of a clinical directorate arrangement in an NHS Trust or LMS in a school.
- The merger of two or more PSOs such as NHS Trusts or FE colleges.
- The implementation of a strategic plan requiring substantial changes in the organization arrangements and operational practices within the PSO.
- The introduction of modern IT as a means of delivering public sector services in a more effective and efficient manner.

Organizational changes such as the above can have substantial implications for staff in a number of different ways including:

- relocation of their place of work
- redefinition of their job
- changes in working hours
- loss of their job
- the requirement to work with new equipment such as IT
- the need for a change of attitude in dealing with customers or clients.

Not surprisingly, changes such as this are often so radical that they may generate fierce opposition and resistance to change from many parts of the organization. Furthermore, it is important to dispel the myth that change can be enforced by dictat. Resistance to change rarely comes about by direct obstruction but rather by more insidious methods such as delay, loss of morale and performance and so on. Hence, managers in PSOs charged with implementing change must have an awareness of the various issues involved and must develop the skills of managing the change process.

Thus, a key aspect of HRM is change management and it is important to understand that organizational change does not happen of its own accord but has to be managed. In this section the following matters are discussed:

- the nature and causes of change
- planning the change
- implementing the change
- consolidating the change.

THE NATURE AND CAUSES OF CHANGE

Emphasis has already been given to the extent of organization change that has taken place in the public sector in recent years. The world is dynamic and it is clear that such change will continue to take place in the future as a result of a number of pressures including:

- technological developments implemented in PSOs
- socio-economic changes in the client base being served by the PSO
- changes in the professional practices of service professionals employed in PSOs
- changes in the national and local economy which will impact on PSOs (for example private sector competitors to public service providers)
- political and policy changes of the government of the day and changes in government.

There is, however, no standard pattern of change and the precise nature of change required will never be the same in any two organizations or any two periods of time. However, in very simple terms, the type of change can be thought of as being one or other of the following types:

- **Evolutionary or gradual change** – this type of change takes place gradually over a period of months or even years.
- **Radical change** – this implies a sharp degree of change in a short period of time such as that involving an organizational merger. The radical nature of the change may come about as the result of some crisis situation or may be thought to be more likely to be effective than a gradual process of change.

The principles of change management are the same in both cases although the detailed aspects and emphasis of the approach will clearly differ. Change management comprises three stages of planning, implementation and consolidation and these are the subject of the next three sections.

PLANNING THE CHANGE

It is probably self-evident that a successful change process requires adequate planning. Even the most dedicated and skilled implementation team will struggle if the plans on which the change process are based are in some way flawed or inadequate. Planning an effective change management process requires managers to focus on the following issues:

- **Clear objectives** – the change process requires that clear and unambiguous objectives for the change process are identified, agreed and ultimately communicated to all those involved. In some cases, such as an office reorganization, these objectives might be fairly clear-cut but in other cases, such as the introduction of improved methods of handling queries from the general public, the objectives might be more complex and lack clarity. A lack of clarity can easily lead to the change process failing to achieve what it was intended to achieve and this can, in turn, be counter-productive since many staff might see that all the hard work and discomfort associated with change has been for nothing. In the author's experience there is often a tendency, in the public sector, to obfuscate the objectives of the proposed changes as a means of avoiding difficult decisions which, in turn, limits the effectiveness of the proposed changes.
- **Resources for change** – to be effective, a change process needs to be adequately resourced and there must be a project manager and a number of change agents who are able to devote sufficient time to managing the change process. In addition, in some circumstances it may be necessary to buy in additional external support for specialist areas such as training, and budgets for this need to be made available. Too often in PSOs, change management is undertaken on a shoestring, with those involved being unable to devote sufficient time to the change process and training needs being underestimated. Not surprisingly, in such circumstances the change process often fails to deliver the planned changes.
- **Identify key aspects of change** – applying the Pareto principles to change management suggests that about 20 per cent of the tasks in a change management process will generate about 80 per cent of the problems. In any change process there will be a large number of tasks to address, but it is important early on in the planning of change to identify the key tasks likely to cause problems and to focus effort on them.
- **Identify main pressures for and against the change** – in any organization there will be those staff who are enthusiastic about the changes proposed, and who will support it, and those who will be hostile to the change and will resist it. Hence, as part of the planning of change it is important to try and identify, early on, where these pressures will come from and what may be done about them. Often organizations might employ a number of techniques such as the use of questionnaires, telephone surveys or focus groups to try and gauge employee attitudes towards change and to get a picture of the pressures for and against the changes proposed.
- **Identify training needs** – in the author's experience, the training needs of change management programmes in PSOs are often underestimated. Take, for example, the transfer of mental illness patients from an institutional care setting to a community care setting. This was a major change in the organization and culture of such care delivery which had major implications for care staff who had been working in an institutional setting for many years. However, frequently much of the planning emphasis concerned physical buildings and numbers of staff, with minimal attention being paid to the cultural changes involved and the training needs of care staff. In these circumstances, perhaps it is not surprising there have been many problems associated with such changes.
- **Develop a robust written plan** – a robust and written plan needs to be developed which will encompass a number of things including:

  - the nature of the change and its objectives
  - the key aspects of the change
  - the activities to be undertaken and the individual's responsibilities
  - the timescales for the change process

 - means of assessing progress
 - contingency plans.

IMPLEMENTING THE CHANGE

Once the planning is complete the required changes must be implemented. The following issues should be addressed as part of this process:

- **Leadership** – for the change process to be successful there needs to be effective leadership at all levels. There will be a need for overall leadership provided by a nominated project manager who is enthusiastic about the proposed changes and can communicate a vision of the changes throughout the organization. Clearly it is important that the project manager has good communication and organizational skills. Also there will need to be a series of change agents. These change agents will be nominated members of staff, who are enthusiastic about the proposed changes and who can adopt a number of roles including:
  - the generation of ideas
  - participation in project planning and monitoring
  - communication of information to staff in the organization
  - communication of staff concerns to the project manager
  - the conduct of specific tasks relating to the changes.
- **Communication** – this is perhaps the most important aspect of the change management process and effective communication is needed about the objectives of the change and the conduct of the change process. In the absence of effective communication, rumour is almost certain to be fostered and widespread resistance generated. Managers involved in the change process must not underestimate the burden of communicating to staff, and frequently the burden on those managers involved in a major change management process is so great that it results in periods of ill-health. Communication can be achieved in a number of ways and all should be considered:
  - in-house newsletters
  - verbal presentations
  - electronic mail
  - training sessions
  - via change agents, and so on.
- **Employee involvement** – wherever possible staff should be actively involved in the change process and should see change as something they are undertaking rather than something which is being done to them. This will require staff to be enabled to undertake specific tasks in relation to the change process. There are clearly risks in doing this since staff have the ability to inhibit change as well as promoting change but it is probably a risk worth taking.
- **Limiting resistance** – resistance to change may come about actively in terms of direct obstruction or passively in terms of non co-operation or lack of enthusiasm. In either case the success of the change process depends on overcoming such resistance. It is important to try and limit the degree of resistance to the change process and a number of approaches can be employed:
  - good communication as described above
  - employee involvement as discussed above
  - making limited amendments to the proposed changes to assuage serious resistance
  - one-to one-discussions with known 'rebels' to persuade them to accept the changes.

- **Changing culture** – where the degree of organizational change is substantial, this often implies the need for a substantial change in organizational culture. Take, for example, the following:
  - the need to introduce a commercial and entrepreneurial culture into a local authority direct services organization
  - the need to introduce a less defensive culture into executive agencies needing to improve customer relationships
  - the introduction of modern IT as a means of delivering services.

  In these circumstances a number of specific actions can be undertaken to reinforce the need for cultural change in the organization, including:

  - physical changes such as the reconfiguration of the buildings layout or changes to staff uniforms
  - the introduction of employee appraisal with clear objectives
  - the introduction of performance related pay
  - substantially changed managerial attitudes such as the encouragement of success rather than criticizing failure
  - the delivery of training programmes.
- **Monitoring progress** – to ensure a successful implementation it is important that progress against plan is monitored throughout the implementation, and that remedial action is taken where necessary.

CONSOLIDATING THE CHANGE

With any change process there is always a possibility that the organization will lapse back into its traditional pre-change mode of operation unless care is taken. Hence a number of actions need to be taken to consolidate the changes made, and these include:

- **Measure success and publicize impact** – it is important to measure the success of the change process, be that in terms of additional income generated, improvements in customer satisfaction or reductions in time taken to undertake tasks. These improvements should be publicized throughout the organization. If no such improvements can be identified then one must question either the rationale for the change process and/or the implementation approach adopted.
- **Provide ongoing training** – it is more than likely that the training provided during the implementation period will be insufficient and ongoing training will be needed to consolidate the changes effected.
- **Recruitment profiles** – when recruiting new staff it is important that the PSO recruits staff who will help consolidate the change process rather than inhibit it. This may require amendments to the job specification of particular jobs in the organization.
- **Maintain momentum** – these days change tends to be an ongoing process. Thus it would be a mistake for staff to think that once the main implementation period has ended they can now expect a long period of stability. In most organizations today, both public and private, the need for continuous improvement in performance means that change is an ongoing process and the momentum for change needs to be maintained since it will, in turn, facilitate the next series of changes required to be implemented.

CHAPTER SEVEN

Marketing and Public Relations in the Public Sector

If this book had been written twenty years ago then it is very unlikely that there would have been any mention of marketing, let alone a chapter devoted to the subject. Equally, the organizational culture of the times would probably have meant that although PSOs were interested and involved in some aspects of public relations, it is likely that it would have not been regarded as that important a subject. The changes that have taken place over the last twenty years have substantially altered this situation and marketing has become an increasingly important activity. This is illustrated by the fact that a report of the Association of Market Survey Organizations showed that market research expenditure by public bodies amounted to £17.2 million in 1993 which was an increase of 29 per cent over the previous year. The following policy changes which took place over this period have contributed to the growth in interest and activity in marketing and PR in PSOs:

- the introduction of market testing and competition
- pressure for PSOs to generate additional income streams
- the need for PSOs to be able to demonstrate improved performance
- the need for PSOs to improve the degree of consumer satisfaction with their services.

If anything, it could be argued that the tools of marketing and market research will become of increasing importance to the public sector in the future. There will be increasing pressure on PSOs to identify the needs and wishes of their consumers and to meet those needs and wishes. Indeed, the Best Value initiative in local government places strong emphasis on assessing and meeting the needs for services of consumers. Hence, the marketing function in PSOs is likely to grow in importance.

This chapter aims to consider some specific aspects of marketing and their actual or potential applicability in the public sector. The aspects of marketing that are discussed are:

- the scope of marketing and PR in the public sector
- market research
- market segmentation
- marketing strategy
- public relations
- evaluation of marketing.

However, before considering these specific matters, consideration is first given to the ways in which marketing and PR techniques have been or could be applied within the public sector.

THE SCOPE OF MARKETING AND PR IN THE PUBLIC SECTOR

Like most management activities marketing is, in essence, a simple activity which aims to address three key questions:

- In what business areas, both current and prospective, do we wish to be involved in future ?
- Within the chosen business areas, who are the customers and what are their needs and wishes?

- Taking account of customer needs and competitor strengths, how are we to compete and be successful?

For obvious reasons these three questions sometimes need to be amended for public sector activities. For example, some public services are provided free of charge to customers and other public services are provided by a PSO in the absence of competition. However, the change factors listed above have meant that marketing and PR are now seen as key management activities in many if not most PSOs and it is appropriate for all public sector managers to have some knowledge of the tasks involved. The examples shown in Table 14 illustrate the scope for marketing and PR in the public sector. They also illustrate that marketing and PR techniques can be used for two main purposes:

- As a means of sustaining or increasing the level of 'business' activity in the PSO and as a means of generating additional sums of money for the PSO itself.
- As a means of promoting the activities of the PSO and assisting it in achieving its strategic

Table 14 Public sector marketing and PR activity

Organization	*Marketing activities*	*Purpose*
Local authority direct services organization	Market research and marketing of services within the parent local authority and to other external clients	Cash generating
FE college/sixth-form college	Market research and marketing of the college in order to attract sufficient students	Cash generating
University	Market research and marketing to attract students and to develop research and consultancy activity	Cash generating
Local education authority advisory unit	Market research and marketing of education advisory services to other LEAs and schools	Cash generating
Benefits Agency	Market research and marketing of the availability of benefits in order to ensure adequate uptake	Non-cash generating
GSO	Market research and marketing of the sales of official publications for income generation purposes	Cash generating
Regional economic development agencies	Market research and marketing of the potential of region to potential inward investors	Non-cash generating
NHS Trusts	Market research and marketing of health care services to general practitioners and primary care groups	Cash generating
	Market research and marketing of private patient facilities	Cash generating
Health promotion agency	Research into and promotion of healthy lifestyles such as no smoking, diet, exercise	Non-cash generating
Local authority leisure services department	Market research and marketing of leisure services as a means of generating additional leisure activity among the population	Cash generating/non-cash generating
Local authority	Market research about consumer attitudes towards service provision as part of a best value exercise	Non-cash generating
Most PSOs	General public relations activity to encourage the general public to view the PSO positively	Non-cash generating

objectives. These purposes do not necessarily involve the need to generate additional sums of money for the PSO itself. This is sometimes referred to as social marketing.

In some cases the marketing activity might be undertaken for both purposes. For example, the local authority leisure centre may wish to market its services as a means of generating cash and of stimulating its catchment population to undertake more exercise.

The above list is not exhaustive, but does give a good indication of the widespread applicability of marketing in the public sector and the need for PSO managers to have some knowledge of marketing and PR techniques.

KEY ASPECTS OF MARKETING

The issues discussed above show that marketing is a key aspect of management for the public sector. Moreover, the development of policies such as Best Value in local government mean that PSOs will have to pay even more attention in the future to the assessment of consumer needs and so on, which are at the core of marketing management. Hence, PSO managers will need to develop an understanding of marketing in the same way as they have had to develop an understanding of strategy, finance and HR. The key aspects of this, which are discussed below, are:

- market research
- market segmentation
- marketing strategy
- public relations
- evaluating marketing activity.

MARKET RESEARCH

The marketing of goods and services is an activity which generally operates in a competitive environment. Clearly, in a commercial setting in both public and private sectors, this is the case where an organization is trying to persuade customers to purchase their goods and services in preference to those of competing organizations. However, it also applies in less commercial situations. Consider the example of health promotion referred to above. Health promotion agencies are concerned with 'selling' their particular message, such as non-smoking, in preference to other competing messages from tobacco companies about the benefits of smoking. Similarly, the Benefits Agency would be trying to sell the idea that people should claim the benefits to which they are entitled by law even if the time and effort associated with making such claims means that they have to forgo other activities. Hence marketing is essentially concerned with:

- identifying the needs and wants of potential consumers
- satisfying those wants more effectively and efficiently than the competition.

To achieve these aims it is necessary to understand the minds of those in the target markets – their attitudes and value systems – and this is, essentially, the province of market research. Market research is concerned with collecting, analysing and interpreting information to establish what people want and why they want it.

TYPES OF MARKET RESEARCH

There are different types of market research activity and it is important to be clear about the distinction between them. These approaches can be classified by the main purpose or objective of the particular research activity, and the four main classifications are as follows:

- **Exploratory** – where a PSO is undertaking market research for the first time or where a particular market researcher is undertaking work in an unfamiliar sector, it will be necessary to undertake some basic exploratory research. This involves some preliminary analysis of the markets in which the organization is operating and lays the foundation for future and more detailed research activity. Thus, for example, an executive agency which sold government publications (such as GSO or ONS) and which might be conducting market research for the first time, would need to obtain some basic information about the nature of its existing market and potential competing products.
- **Descriptive** – this type of research is intended to provide descriptive and fairly detailed information about factors such as market conditions, consumer opinions and attitudes, purchasing behaviour and competing products. Thus, a local authority leisure centre may obtain detailed information on:

  - the use of leisure services by different sectors of the community
  - their reasons for using those facilities
  - potential alternative leisure activities which they had considered, and so on.

  Such information is only intended to provide a detailed picture of the current situation but may lead on to predictive and conclusive research as described below.
- **Predictive** – this is clearly concerned with predicting the future. Thus, the research would be concerned with predicting future trends, such as changes in the size and composition of the market, changes in customer tastes and changes in price levels. For example, in the public sector, universities which offer a range of different degree courses might be interested in predicting changes in attitudes and demands of future generations of students as to the curriculum content of courses and the methods of teaching and learning. Various techniques can be used to obtain base data such as interviews, questionnaires and group discussions, and this data can be input into formal forecasting models which would provide an analysis of likely outcomes and confidence levels.
- **Conclusive** – this type of market research is concerned with trying to establish a formal causal link between the sales and consumption of a product and key marketing variables such as price, packaging or advertising. The way in which this research would be carried out would be by means of an experiment. Consider the example of the Benefits Agency referred to above. The agency may wish to identify if there was any causal link between uptake of benefit and factors such as advertising or the handling of client queries. Thus, an experiment may be conducted whereby in certain offices a different approach to advertising or client handling might be employed, and the impact on the take-up of benefit measured. To obtain meaningful results it would be necessary to undertake the experiment in a sufficiently large number of offices to ensure there were statistically reliable results.

MAIN RESEARCH AREAS

Market research activity can be conducted in a number of specific areas which reflect the components of marketing strategy. These areas of research are summarized below and the example is used of a local authority leisure services department to illustrate the distinction between them.

- **Product research** – this concerns research about the nature of the actual product itself, any proposed changes to its make-up and the likely response of consumers to the product. Thus, for example, the local authority leisure services department might be thinking of amending its approach to and timing of the provision of cultural events, and might wish to assess likely attitude and reactions of consumers to this change. This would require research to be undertaken specifically on this issue.

- **Pricing research** – this concerns research into the attitude and reaction of consumers to changes to the pricing structure of an organization's product range. Using a local authority leisure centre as an example, this could cover a number of matters such as the impact on consumer behaviour of basic price increases, the introduction of different prices for different times in the day, or prices based on a membership scheme coupled with lower basic prices.
- **Distribution research** – this concerns the way in which goods and services are made available to consumers and the impact on consumer behaviour of changes in the distribution network. In the commercial field this could cover, for example, a shift from selling and distribution via high street shops to mail order. In the local authority leisure field this could involve the impact on consumer demand for evening classes of shifting the provision of courses from a large number of disparate centres in individual schools in the area to a smaller number of centres focused on the local FE college. Intuitively, one might expect a reduction in demand, but market research could throw light on the scale of the reduction and whether it would be significant.
- **Promotion research** – this area of research is concerned with evaluation of the methods of promoting the organization's products, and the impact of changes in promotion practice. Thus, the local authority leisure services department may wish to assess the effectiveness of its current approach to promoting its local theatres and the impact of possible changes in the methods employed. This could cover activities such as mass-media advertising, sponsorship, mail-shots, telephone marketing, Internet web-sites or membership arrangements.

In practice, the organization involved may wish to consider changes in several of the above areas of marketing, but it is important that market research is undertaken which tries to identify, separately, the impact of each element of the marketing strategy.

STAGES IN MARKET RESEARCH ACTIVITY

Any market research exercise should comprise five main stages although, clearly, the detailed aspects of the approach will vary from case to case. The five stages are as follows:

- **Stage 1: Define objectives and scope** – there needs to be a definition of the objectives of the research, whether it is descriptive or predictive, and the particular issues that need to be addressed, such as consumer attitudes, product knowledge or aspirations. Also some broad definition of the scope of the project needs to be defined, particularly in terms of the collection and use of primary and secondary data.
- **Stage 2: Obtain and review secondary data** – whatever type of market research is being considered it is quite possible that some relevant work has already been undertaken and published. Thus, for example, a study may already have been conducted about what factors influence general practitioners in deciding where to refer patients for private health care. Hence, before undertaking any detailed work it is important to obtain and review the information already available. Such information may come from a number of sources such as government publications, professional bodies, trade associations, academic journals or the Internet.
- **Stage 3: Design primary data collection approach** – this stage is concerned with obtaining new information about the nature of the relevant market or markets. Possible approaches are discussed in more detail in the next section but basically these include interviews, questionnaires,

observations and experimentation. In this stage it is also necessary to establish the parameters of the exercise such as sample size and sample methods.

- **Stage 4: Conduct data collection exercise** – the actual data collection needs to be carried out. This may be undertaken in a number of ways:
  - data collection exercise managed and undertaken by staff of the organization
  - data collection exercise managed by staff of the organization but actual data collection undertaken by contracted staff
  - data collection exercise contracted out entirely to a specialist market research organization.
- **Stage 5: Analyse and interpret results** – once results of both the primary and secondary data collection exercises have been obtained it is necessary to analyse the results and draw inferences accordingly. Various statistical techniques can be used to do this and some of these are outlined in a later section. However, it is also important that the results are reviewed to see if they provide a commonsense picture.

MARKET RESEARCH TOOLS

Within market research there are a number of specific tools which can be used according to the approach described in the previous section. These tools can be classified as being data collection tools or analytical tools as shown in Table 15.

Table 15 Market research tools

Data collection tools	*Analytical tools*
Questionnaires	Forecasting
Interviews	Optimization
Observation	
Experimentation	

Each of these techniques is summarized below.

Data Collection Tools

- **Questionnaires** – many people are used to the face-to-face market research questionnaire whereby the interviewer goes through a pre-set list of questions with the interviewee. However, such questionnaires can also be used by mail or over the telephone. There are both advantages and disadvantages to this approach to gathering information, as described below:
  - large numbers of such questionnaires can be administered in a short time
  - the interviewer does not need to be highly skilled
  - while the interviewer records responses they are unlikely to get 'under the skin' of the issues being discussed.

Such approaches can be used in PSOs but it is important to distinguish between their use for quality assurance purposes and for marketing purposes. The former approach, which is quite common in the public sector, usually involves asking questions about the degree of satisfaction with the service that has already been received. This could involve, for example, asking questions of leisure centre customers as they leave the leisure centre or telephoning patients after they have left hospital. Market research is much wider and involves getting information from customers, former customers and prospective customers about the goods and services the organization currently offers and might offer in the future. Thus, in using questionnaires for market research it is important to ensure that the sample used will be representative of the market in which the organization is likely to operate and will therefore contain no substantial bias.

If a PSO is planning to use questionnaires to obtain market research information it must recognize that questionnaire design is a complex task, and considerable thought needs to be given to the issues involved. The following points should be borne in mind:

- obtain a balance of open-ended and closed questions
- use clear, simple and unemotive language
- do not use questions which rely on the interviewee's memory to answer
- questions must not be too complex
- don't ask loaded questions – be neutral
- limit the questionnaire size to essentials
- ***always*** pilot the questionnaire with a small sample before undertaking the full study
- ensure the interviewers are properly trained to ensure consistency
- ensure the interviewers have a clear and practical means of recording responses (for example ticks in a box).

- **Interviews** – this approach involves the conduct of an in-depth interview either face to face or via a telephone. Such an approach does not involve the use of a questionnaire and an unskilled interviewer but requires a skilled interviewer who understands the issues being discussed, can 'get under the skin' of the issues and relate to the interviewee. The results of the interview will be more qualitative information about beliefs, values and so on, rather than quantified information. Given the need to prepare and undertake the interview, only a fairly small number of such interviews can be undertaken and thus the data obtained will be limited. A variation on this theme involves the use of the focus group where the interviewer facilitates and encourages discussion within a group format. Again, the group will need to comprise people who represent the target market in which the organization is interested.
- **Observation** – this involves the direct observation and recording of actual consumer practices. This can be done by human observation or indirect recording of actual events, possibly using some form of technology such as close-circuit TV, tape recorder or some other recording device such as a bar code reader. For example, in the retail field, electronic point of sale (EPOS) devices record actual transactions and can produce an analysis of sales patterns. In smaller organizations it may be necessary to obtain such information by direct observation of purchases. In the public sector, similar techniques can be used to capture information in the following areas:

  - take up of promotional literature in conferences (for example regional development conferences)
  - sales of publications in GSO
  - applications for prospectuses in FE colleges.

- **Experimentation** – this has already been described as a means of undertaking conclusive research. Changes to key marketing variables are made and the impact on sales or consumption of the various goods and services are measured.

Analytical Tools

It is beyond the scope of this book to outline these in any depth, since they require a certain level of mathematical and statistical knowledge. However, the sections below give a brief outline of the nature of each approach and the way in which it can be used. The interested reader is referred to more technical books on the topic.

- **Forecasting** – forecasting the future with absolute precision is obviously impossible. However, some attempt to forecast, for example, future market size, consumer demand and sales is important in marketing and should be attempted. Forecasting techniques are varied but can be classified as using:

  - subjective methods
  - objective methods
  - a combination of subjective and objective.

  Subjective techniques are qualitative in nature and rely on human judgements rather than quantitative analysis. An example of this is the use of consumer juries where groups of consumers, in an interactive group, review different forecasts and give their opinion on which is the most realistic. Alternatively, consumer views could be elucidated by some form of questionnaire.

  Objective techniques involve the use of statistical or mathematical methods and fall into two main types: time series models and causal models. Time series models are most useful for short-term forecasting (6–12 months) and involve identifying patterns which occur over a period of time. Thus, for example, a time series analysis could identify the pattern of demand for buildings repairs for each month or quarter over an annual period. On the other hand, causal models try to establish relationships between sales and other independent variables such as price and advertising. The purpose of the model would be to forecast the impact on sales of changes in price, advertising and so on.
- **Optimization** – this requires the use of a technique termed 'linear programming'. It is a technique often used in relation to production decisions where a firm which manufactures several products (with differing financial returns) has to assess the optimal production level in a context of limited amounts of raw materials and labour. This is illustrated in Figure 28.

  Such an approach may also be used in relation to marketing decisions where different products, which produce differing financial returns, also require different amounts of scarce marketing resource to generate that return. Thus the organization needs to decide how best to use its limited marketing resources to optimize the overall financial return.

MARKET SEGMENTATION

One of the key concepts in marketing is that of market segmentation. Rather than consider a market as a homogeneous whole, market segmentation involves breaking down the total market for a particular range of goods and services into several segments where each segment represents a separate market which requires a distinctive approach to marketing. Thus, for example, whereas the marketing of a service in one market segment might be addressed through mass media advertising, in another market segment the same service might be best marketed through telephone selling.

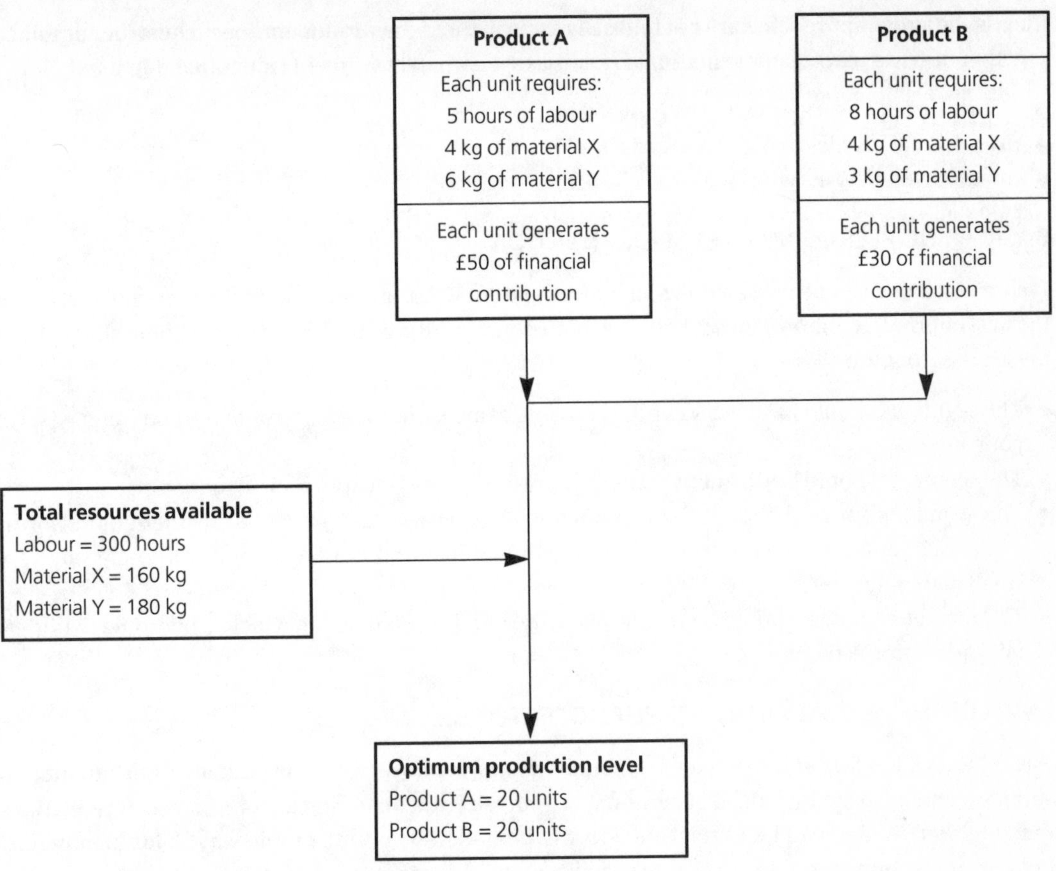

Figure 28 Approach to linear programming

APPROACHES TO MARKET SEGMENTATION

There are a number of different ways in which a market can be segmented and these are:

- **Consumer type** – at its simplest a market could be segmented between individuals as consumers and organizations as consumers. In saying this, it is recognized that organizations themselves comprise individuals who will be responsible for purchasing decisions.
- **Geographic** – the total market could be broken down into a number of geographic areas such as different parts of the country or different areas within a particular city or town.
- **Demographic** – the market could be broken down in terms of males and females and/or in terms of different age groups in the population.
- **Social class** – there are a variety of ways in which the market population could be segmented into different social classes including employment category, income band or educational attainment.
- **Lifestyle** – the market population could be segmented according to different types of lifestyle led. Some aspects of this could include those who:
  - are physically active
  - enjoy artistic pursuits
  - travel extensively overseas.

Clearly the above approaches are not mutually exclusive and the various approaches can be combined together to give a market segmentation. Thus, particular market segments identified might be:

- elderly males who travel extensively overseas
- professional females living in particularly affluent wards in a city
- unemployed persons who are physically active.

BASIC PRINCIPLES OF MARKET SEGMENTATION

Clearly, a market can be broken down in many different ways, and some guidelines are needed about the best approach to be employed. In doing this a number of basic principles need to be employed and these are as follows:

- The segments should be identifiable and capable of measurement in terms of numbers and types of consumers.
- The segments should be distinctive enough to justify a different approach to marketing.
- The segments should be substantial enough in size to make the process of segmentation worthwhile. Marketing can be an expensive function and it would not be economical to identify very small market segments.
- The market segments should be readily accessible to the organization which is planning to undertake marketing activity.

MARKET SEGMENTATION IN THE PUBLIC SECTOR

The relevance to PSOs of the market segmentation approach will vary substantially from situation to situation and needs to be judged accordingly. For those PSOs operating in commercial-type markets market segmentation will be as relevant and will be undertaken in the same way as for commercial organizations. However, there are some specific aspects of market segmentation which are of specific relevance to the public sector and these include:

- **Health promotion agencies** – the agency will be concerned to project messages (for example no smoking, anti-drugs, or healthy eating) to the community at large. In doing this it will recognize that different approaches to marketing will be needed for different market segments. Thus, for example, messages might be projected to young people via the medium of posters, leaflets or videos in schools and youth clubs. On the other hand similar messages might best be projected to elderly people via mass media advertising on television and radio. For the unemployed, the best approach to marketing the health promotion messages is through some form of community development organization.
- **Benefits agency** – to promote the uptake of benefit it is necessary to communicate to potential recipients the availability of such benefits and the procedures to be followed. However, the agency assesses claims and makes benefit payments to many different groups of people in society such as the elderly, single parents and the disabled, and a standardized marketing approach is unlikely to be successful. Instead, it is necessary to segment the benefits market into a series of groups and develop a marketing strategy for each discrete group.

MARKETING STRATEGY

Having developed strategic objectives as part of its strategic planning process, undertaken market research and segmented its market where appropriate, the PSO now needs to prepare a marketing strategy which will both complement and supplement the other aspects of its strategy. In simple terms marketing strategy can be thought of as the application of the '4Ps', namely:

- product
- price
- place (distribution)
- promotion.

The combination of these four factors is often referred to as the 'marketing mix', and this mix will vary between the type of goods or service and the market segment being addressed. Each of these aspects of the marketing mix will be considered in turn.

PRODUCT

This is perhaps the most important aspect of the marketing mix since without goods and services as products the other aspects of marketing become redundant. In both the private and public sectors, the organization needs to give considerable thought to its product range and the relationship with its markets. In any organization there will be a combination of existing products which will have been around for some time and products which are newly developed. Similarly, there will be a combination of existing markets in which the organization is involved and new markets which it wishes to penetrate. This is illustrated in Figure 29.

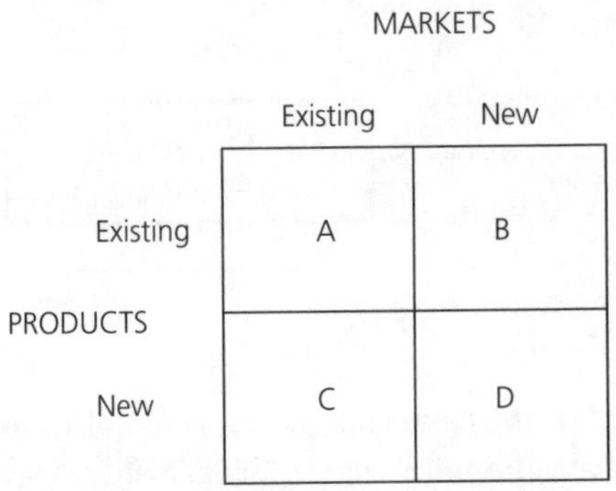

PRODUCTS \ MARKETS	Existing	New
Existing	A	B
New	C	D

Figure 29 Products and markets

Thus, in terms of marketing the organization can be faced with four possible options and these are discussed below using a university department as a public sector example.

- **A: Marketing existing products in existing markets** – this involves either continuing to market products to the existing customer base or to new customers within the same market segment. Thus it is a strategy of market maintenance or market penetration. In the case of a university department this implies the ongoing marketing task undertaken, each year, of marketing the existing range of courses to the main market which is the A-level school-leaver.
- **B: Marketing existing products in new markets** – this is often referred to as a strategy of market development. A university department might decide to market its existing range of educational activities in another country or to a new client base such as the unemployed.
- **C: Marketing new products in existing markets** – this is a strategy of product development and involves 'selling-on' to existing customers. Thus a university department which already provides a wide range of training courses to local employers might try to diversify and offer market research and consultancy activities to those same range of employers.
- **D: Marketing new products in new markets** – this is the most risky and probably most time-consuming approach but also the one most likely to give the greatest return. Thus, a university department which traditionally has focused its activities around full-time degree courses might decide to try and market short training courses to local employers. This approach implies both a new product and a new market.

The above options are not mutually exclusive and organizations might pursue several approaches simultaneously. However, it must be recognized that each option will require a differing degree of commitment to new product development and a differing approach to the other elements of the marketing mix (pricing, distribution and promotion).

There is no single correct approach here and in developing a marketing strategy PSOs must assess the following matters:

- **Product development** – the time and resources likely to be available for new product development. If a product cannot be developed properly then it should not be developed at all.
- **Marketing resources** – the time and resources available for marketing will be finite. A balance will therefore need to be struck between the competing demands for marketing resources of each of the above options. Again, for example, if there are insufficient resources to market a new product adequately in a new market, then it should not be attempted.
- **Market conditions** – consideration needs to be given to market conditions, particularly when considering new products and new markets. Thus, for example, delaying the launch of a new product might mean 'missing the boat' since competitors will enter the market.

PRICE

The price charged for a product will be a key element in marketing that product. Given that goods and services are sold in some form of market (for example perfect competition or monopoly), in setting a price two factors must be taken into account, as shown in Figure 30.

Figure 30 Pricing considerations

The financial return from a product will be heavily influenced by the price charged, and basically the higher the price the higher the return and vice versa. However, the price charged will also have an impact on certain strategic marketing objectives such as market share and rate of sales growth. Again, in simple terms, the lower the price the higher the rate of sales growth or market share and vice versa. Thus, the price charged will reflect the balance between these two competing factors and in some cases the achievement of the marketing objectives might be so paramount as to justify a negative financial return (that is, a loss leader).

Furthermore, the price to be charged will depend on where the product is in the product life cycle. At the time of product launch the need for sales growth might be so important as to justify a low or even negative financial return resulting from a low sales price. As the project matures, sales growth might be seen as less important and so the price charged will be such as to produce high financial returns.

Thus, overall, organizations need to address the questions shown in Figure 31 in relation to each product. This iterative process needs to be followed until a suitable balance between financial return and marketing objectives is achieved.

This approach is applicable in the public sector, except in those circumstances where price is not a relevant issue.

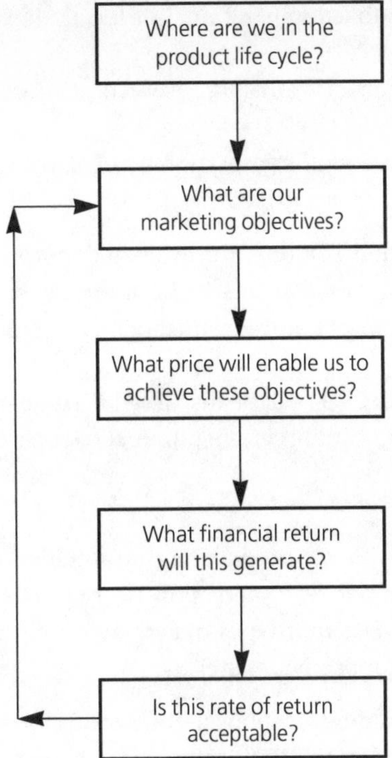

Figure 31 Pricing policy

PLACE (DISTRIBUTION)

Marketing has sometimes been defined as the process of getting the right goods and services to the right place at the right time. This raises the key issues of:

- where goods and services should be made available to the consumer (for example retail outlets, wholesale outlets or mail order)
- the logistical process of distributing the goods and services to the place where they can be acquired by the consumer.

Consider, for example, the marketing of personal computers. These may be marketed (and purchased) through specialist computer stores, large chain retail outlets or by mail order direct from the manufacturer. From the point of view of the manufacturer each of these distribution options will have implications for sales volumes and revenues, and costs and distribution processes. Hence an evaluation of these factors is required before any decision is made.

These distribution considerations are also very relevant to PSOs, as the following examples will illustrate:

- **universities** – educational courses delivered via distance learning courses or via traditional attendance-based courses
- **local authorities** – adult education delivered at a wide range of centres (for example schools and village halls) or limited to a few locations

- **GSO** – marketing and selling of publications by mail order, by Internet, through GSO shops or through general bookshops
- **regional economic development corporations** – provision of services to potential inward investors from local offices, from overseas offices or via the Internet
- **health promotion agencies** – provision of information by mail, by means of public exhibitions or by visits to organizations such as schools and factories.

In PSOs, sometimes these distribution options are evaluated purely on the basis of cost. This is a mistake and a full financial evaluation needs to be undertaken taking account of both the likely outcomes (for example sales volumes and revenues) deriving from each option as well as the costs.

In Chapter 9 the future role of IT in PSOs will be discussed at some length. It is important to note the potential role of the Internet in distributing certain public services in the future.

PROMOTION

Promotion is effectively concerned with communicating information about the organization and its products and activities to its potential customers. For this reason it is sometimes referred to as marketing communications. It comprises four types of activity which will have different degrees of applicability to different PSOs. These four activities are:

- **Advertising** – some form of mass communications in the various forms of media (newspapers, TV, radio and so on) which is paid for by the PSO undertaking the advertising. The advertising can concern the PSO itself or focus on specific products or activities. Again, the potential future role of the Internet in marketing public sector services should be borne in mind at this point. This is discussed further in Chapter 9.
- **Personal selling** – the use of one-to-one selling by a salesperson to a potential range of customers.
- **Sales promotion** – this can comprise a number of disparate activities concerned with promoting the PSO as a whole and/or its products and activities. Some examples might include exhibitions, sponsorship, product demonstrations, display materials, competitions and mail shots.
- **Publicity** – this is some form of mass media communication which has not been paid for by the PSO undertaking the marketing activity. Thus, it can involve editorial comments, new stories, letters and so on. The fact that it is not paid for means that the timing and content is not under the complete control of the PSO, which can cause problems. However, one of the main purposes of public relations activity is to try and ensure that such news is presented in the most positive manner. This is discussed further in the section on public relations.

It is important to emphasize that there is no single correct model for the marketing mix. Each of the above approaches will differ in a number of ways including:

- cost
- short-term impact
- long-term impact.

Hence, any PSOs contemplating a marketing strategy will have to assess the best marketing mix for their particular circumstances. To do this they could undertake the following:

- commission a specialist marketing consultancy exercise as to the best marketing communications mix

- review the marketing communications mix arrangements of other similar organizations which have been successful
- undertake pilot studies of different promotional approaches and assess the results prior to undertaking a full implementation
- consult relevant professional or trade associations for guidance.

PUBLIC RELATIONS

Public relations (PR) is basically concerned with the strategic management of information in such a way that desired publicity objectives are achieved. It is an extremely important activity for private sector organizations but especially so for the public sector. The process of PR is illustrated in Figure 32.

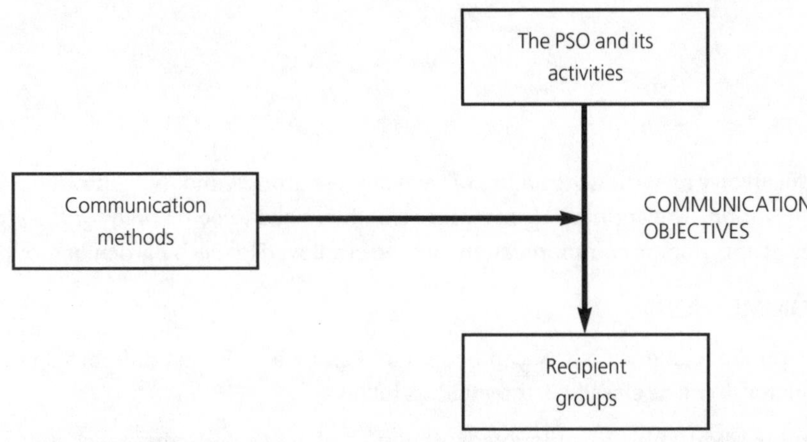

Figure 32 The public relations process

The various aspects of this are discussed below.

THE PSO AND ITS ACTIVITIES

PR can be considered as being of relevance to PSOs in two main ways:

- **Product marketing** – as a component part of the marketing strategy for products and activities provided by a PSO. Thus the aim of PR will be to communicate positive messages about the specific products and activities. In this case products could mean:
  - courses run by FE colleges
  - clinical services provided by NHS Trusts
  - local authority advisory services.
- **General** – PSOs operate in a very political environment, sometimes involving elected representatives and sometimes not. Thus it is always desirable to present the PSO itself in the most positive light, in the light of circumstances which may be sometimes positive and sometimes not. PR is a key activity in this area.

RECIPIENT GROUPS

PR involves communication between the organization and the various recipient groups or publics with which it is involved. Each of these groups will have a different knowledge of and perspective on the organization in question and so communication messages will need to be adjusted accordingly. As with marketing, this implies segmenting the public into a series of groups or publics to which specific communication objectives are addressed in a particular way. There are several ways in which this segmentation can be undertaken but one with specific application to PSOs is as follows:

- employees
- the electorate
- government
- the business community
- suppliers
- consumers
- the media
- opinion leaders.

Thus, PR activity will involve analysing the nature of each of these groups, and their knowledge of and interest in the organization. The appropriate messages will then need to be tailored for the group in question and the most appropriate communication method employed for each particular group.

COMMUNICATION METHODS

As with marketing, public relations activity can be undertaken by a variety of different methods of communication, but these can be classified, threefold, as follows:

- **Personal communication** – this is undoubtedly the most effective and persuasive approach to public relations, provided it is done well. A polished presentation coupled with a confident response to questions will do much to communicate the desired messages of the organization. Equally, it is perhaps the most risky approach if things are not well planned and prepared.
- **Printed communication** – this involves any form of printed document which communicates the organization's desired messages. It could involve:
  - direct mail
  - literature
  - press releases.
- **Visual communication** – this can involve any form of visual image designed to communicate the desired message. It could involve:
  - photographs
  - films
  - television
  - Internet web-sites
  - exhibitions.

EVALUATING MARKETING ACTIVITY

Although it is accepted that marketing is an essential managerial activity, in most organizations – in both private and public sectors – there are usually a number of concerns, including:

- the organization of marketing activity and whether it should be centralized or decentralized
- the effectiveness of marketing activity and the mix of marketing activities undertaken
- whether the correct amount of resource (too much or too little) is being devoted to marketing.

The evaluation of the effectiveness of marketing activity is notoriously difficult to assess. The apocryphal story is often told of the business tycoon who stated that half of his marketing budget was being wasted but he didn't know which half it was. However, in spite of these difficulties it is imperative that some form of evaluation of marketing activity is undertaken. This is especially true in PSOs, where it is often the case that marketing activity does not generate any additional income streams to cover the cost of marketing but absorbs scarce resources which might otherwise have been used for direct service delivery.

Some possible approaches to evaluating marketing activity which might be considered are given below.

BENCHMARKING

The PSO could benchmark its marketing activity against those of comparable organizations. This is likely to mean comparable organizations within the same service sector (for example health or education). The benchmarking exercise could cover such matters as resources devoted to marketing, numbers of marketing staff and organization of marketing activity. Where a PSO showed considerable divergence from the sector norm then it should look closely for reasons and benefits or costs associated with this difference.

CONSUMER ASSESSMENT

A survey of actual consumers could be undertaken to establish their views on the marketing approaches of the organization. In particular, this survey could identify whether consumers had been aware of the promotional activity of the organization and whether it had had any influence upon them.

BEHAVIOURAL ASSESSMENT

More formal and scientifically-based studies could be undertaken of the extent to which marketing effort has actually influenced consumer behaviour. For example, in the health promotion field, studies have been undertaken to evaluate whether particular advertising campaigns on alcohol consumption or smoking have actually changed the short-term and longer-term behaviour of those who observed these campaigns.

CHAPTER EIGHT

Managing Quality and Consumer Satisfaction in the Public Sector

Traditionally, the public sector had an image of being inflexible, unresponsive and having little concern with the people they were serving and their degree of satisfaction with the services provided to them. Whether this view was justified in all cases is a debatable point but, historically, there can be no doubt that public sector management systems were traditionally based on a bureaucratic model which emphasized conformity and uniformity of approach. At the same time, the public sector organizations were largely monopolistic providers and thus consumers of services had limited or no alternatives. In recent years, fuelled by initiatives such as the Citizen's Charter, a significant change among PSOs has been the emphasis they now place on consumerism and keeping consumers satisfied.

At around the same time that issues of consumerism came to the fore, concerns were also being expressed about the absolute and comparative quality standards being achieved in certain public services (such as literacy in schools) and the variations in quality standards of other services across different parts of the country (for example cancer treatment outcomes). Thus, in recent years there has been a significant drive in many PSOs to improve the quality of the services they provide.

In view of the above, it is hardly surprising that the issues of consumerism and quality have become inextricably linked (and sometimes confused) in the minds of service users and service providers. Hence this chapter aims to look at both the management of consumer satisfaction and of quality of service outcomes.

QUALITY AND CONSUMER SATISFACTION: THE DISTINCTION

The above comment immediately begs the question as to what is meant by service quality and consumer satisfaction, whether there is a distinction between the two concepts and, if so, what the difference is. In broad terms the distinction shown in Figure 33 can be drawn:

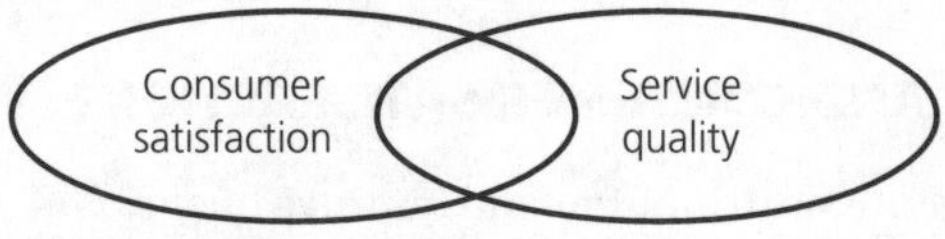

Figure 33 Consumer satisfaction and service quality

These two concepts are described below:

- **Consumer satisfaction** – this is a simple concept to describe even if it is sometimes difficult to assess. Very simply, it is the degree of satisfaction which consumers of services have for the service they have received from the PSO. The degree of consumer satisfaction can be influenced by a number of different factors such as:
  - the attitudes (good or bad) of staff providing the services
  - the pleasantness of the physical environment in which the services are provided

- the actual outcome of receiving the service (for example outcome of surgical operation)
- the waiting time for service
- the response time to queries
- the response time of the telephone switchboard.

In some cases, such as street cleaning or postal services, consumer satisfaction may legitimately incorporate a direct assessment by consumers of the quality of service provided in terms of litter-free streets or prompt and accurate postal deliveries. This is illustrated by the overlap of the two ellipses in the above diagram. However, in other cases, for example medical care and education, consumers are not always able to assess the quality of service received because such an assessment requires a degree of technical expertise they do not possess.

- **Quality** – this is more to do with the inherent quality of service being provided by the PSO. It can be thought of as an objective professional assessment of the standards of service being provided by the PSO. The quality of service should be capable of being measured or assessed in some way such as, for example:

  - comparison with service quality in other similar PSOs
  - comparisons of service quality over time
  - comparisons of actual service quality with some predetermined standard.

  As already mentioned, in some cases, the degree of consumer satisfaction may indicate something about service quality but, in other cases, it may say very little about actual service quality. Although, for example, most consumers can give a reasonably clear view on the quality of a street cleaning service as evidenced by the amount of litter remaining on the streets, with some public services this is not always easy to do. Examples can easily be quoted, particularly in the medical field, of consumers being totally satisfied with the service they had received even though the actual quality of the medical care provided was demonstrably poor in professional terms. Clearly, the converse can also be true. Furthermore, for example in the police service, public satisfaction with policing seems to be influenced more by the visibility of the 'bobby on the beat' than measures of the effectiveness of policing in terms of crime prevention and crime resolution. Hence the measurement and promotion of quality requires different approaches to that of measuring and promoting consumer satisfaction.

WHY PURSUE QUALITY AND CONSUMER SATISFACTION?

Setting up and maintaining systems to monitor and improve quality and consumer satisfaction can be expensive, and the question must be asked as to why PSOs should undertake this investment which, after all, is diverting scarce resources from direct service provision. Outlined below are some of the main reasons:

- **Market pressures** – as has already been noted earlier in this book, in many areas of activity PSOs are monopolistic providers. Thus, if one is not satisfied with the quality of service from your local Benefits Agency office or your local authority consumer protection department one does not have the option of taking one's business elsewhere. However, this argument should not be overstated and, as was discussed in Chapter 3, there are many areas of PSO activity where market situations have been introduced and where competition does apply. Some of these examples are as follows:

  - **Trading services** – many PSOs operate in normal commercial markets and supply goods and services to consumers at a price. In these circumstances the PSO will need to pay attention to the quality of its product if it is not to lose competitive position and hence income.

- **Consumer choices** – even where there is not a true market in terms of the consumer paying for public services, there are situations in the public sector where consumer choices can affect the income streams of the PSO. A good example of this is a university, whose income stream is strongly affected by the numbers of students who choose to go to that university. Hence, universities are concerned about their teaching standards as viewed by current and past students and the results of teaching quality assessments undertaken by QAA.
- **Purchaser–provider situations** – in those areas of service provision where there is a true purchaser–provider split, the purchaser organization (rather than the service consumer) has the option of taking business elsewhere, albeit in a limited manner. Thus the health authority (or PCG) which is dissatisfied with the quality of a particular service being provided by one of its NHS Trusts may have the option to transfer its contract to another Trust.

- **Electoral pressures** – in those PSOs where there is an electoral process, then issues of service quality may influence the electoral outcome. Although it may be naïve to think that general elections might be won or lost on issues of public service quality, it is conceivable that this may happen at the local level. The author is aware of several situations where the ruling party in a local authority is believed to have lost power because of grave concerns among the electorate about the quality of service provision. Clearly, it would have been better for the ruling party if they had addressed issues of quality and satisfaction prior to the election.
- **Professional pressures** – there are often pressures from within various professions represented in the public sector for PSOs to improve quality standards. An example would be the inspections of hospitals by the various Royal Colleges. Caution is needed, however, in distinguishing pressure for improvements in service quality as opposed to professional self-aggrandisement of the worst kind.
- **Central government pressures** – this is perhaps the most important and influential factor. Developments such as the Citizen's Charter, Patient's Charter and Best Value mean that PSOs are being exhorted or forced to make progress against centrally-defined quality targets in a wide range of areas, and to publish their performance against those targets. Whatever the merits or demerits of this approach, it seems inevitable that central government pressures to meet quality targets will only continue to increase.

MANAGING CONSUMER SATISFACTION

PSOs have undertaken a variety of approaches to assessing the degree of consumer satisfaction with the services they provide. These include:

RECORD OF COMPLAINTS

In many types of PSOs there is a formal system, often required by law, for the receipt and processing of complaints about the organization itself or about individual members of staff. Aside from the process of dealing with the individual complaint it is usual for the total number of complaints to be categorized and analysed, and compared over time or compared against the level of complaints in other comparable organizations. Such an analysis can provide useful information on which management can take action, particularly if there is a trend in the total number of complaints over time or compared to other organizations. The nature of the complaints might be capable of being attributed to a specific activity, department or individual and appropriate remedial action taken. However, a moment's reflection will show that although useful, the level of complaints has severe limitations as a measure of overall consumer satisfaction. There is an inherent implication that those who do not complain are satisfied with the service, which may not be the case. Furthermore, an increase in complaints may be due to changes in societal attitudes or local demographic changes and may indicate nothing about the overall consumer satisfaction levels. Hence, other approaches to measuring consumer satisfaction must be examined.

CONSUMER QUESTIONNAIRES

A more comprehensive approach to measuring consumer satisfaction is for each and every consumer to be invited to fill in a questionnaire about their degree of satisfaction with the services provided at the end of their receipt of service. The results of this exercise may be used to follow up individual concerns and may be analysed to provide an overall picture of consumer satisfaction.

CONSUMER SURVEYS

PSOs may undertake sample surveys among their consumers, as to the quality of services they provide. Such surveys may be undertaken by in-house staff or some external organization, such as MORI, may be commissioned to do the survey.

FOCUS GROUPS OR PANELS

PSOs may set up and maintain focus groups or panels to monitor and give an opinion on the services being provided. Indeed, the government has done exactly this on a national basis with a large panel of 5000 people being used to obtain satisfaction ratings on public services.

Clearly, the prime requisite for promoting consumer satisfaction is that the results of the above methods are acted upon and not ignored.

MANAGING SERVICE QUALITY

The management of quality can be a difficult task in most PSOs and a number of complex issues need to be addressed. The main features of a quality management process are shown in Figure 34.

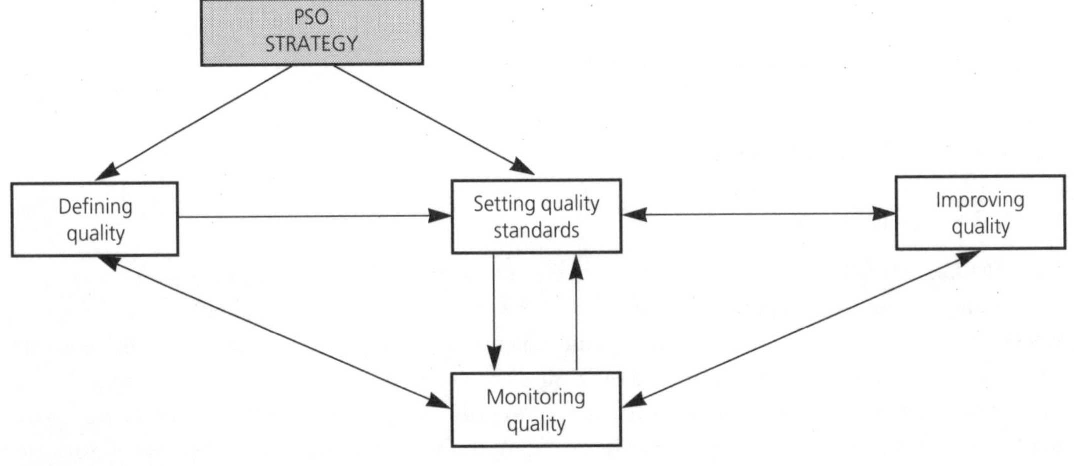

Figure 34 Managing service quality

DEFINING QUALITY

Before considering the measurement of quality it is necessary to be clear about what is meant by the use of the term 'quality' within the PSO. Thus, in considering different approaches to the management of quality one must be clear about what one is trying to achieve. As Figure 33 shows, one of the factors which will affect our definition of quality will be the overall strategy of the organization and the objectives it is trying to achieve. However, it is important not to overcomplicate this issue. The dictionary defines 'quality' of a commodity as being 'the essential attributes' of that commodity. Hence, in measuring quality it is important to concentrate on those essential attributes. Public services are often delivered in a political context and it is often tempting to try and overcomplicate the quality management process through politicization. Thus, factors such as equity and equality, although important issues, are not really quality attributes and should not be treated as such.

There are three main dimensions to the meaning of quality in relation to the delivery of public services. These concern:

- **Technical quality** – the technical quality of the service actually delivered. Some examples of this might include the technical quality of medical and nursing care, of teaching or of buildings maintenance delivered to the consumer. Clearly, to a large extent, as has already been noted, the consumer is unable to assess this dimension of quality unaided.
- **Interpersonal quality** – this aspect of quality includes a wide range of interpersonal factors between the service provider and the consumer. Thus, it would include such matters as courtesy, friendliness and provision of information. Clearly, in this area the degree of consumer satisfaction will give a very strong indication of the quality of service being provided.
- **Environmental quality** – this aspect of quality concerns the physical environment in which the service is delivered. It would include factors such as the condition of buildings, waiting facilities, catering facilities, signposting and ease of access. Clearly, it is possible for a first-class technical service to be delivered in poor physical surroundings and vice versa.

All three of these dimensions of quality are important and need to be incorporated into the quality management process.

In addition to this threefold analysis of quality there are some other distinctions which need to be considered and agreed upon. These are as follows:

- **Effectiveness versus performance** – the basic distinction here is between doing the right things and doing things right, as described below:
  - **effectiveness** – this is concerned with undertaking the most effective activity designed to meet a service need (doing the right things)
  - **performance** – this is concerned with how well the chosen activities are undertaken (doing things right).

  For example, in the medical field the most proven effective therapy for a clinical condition might be surgery but the operation might be performed badly, thus impacting on the quality of clinical outcome. On the other hand, a less effective therapy (for example physiotherapy) might be performed well but again would not give the best possible quality of clinical outcome. Thus, in considering issues of quality and quality improvement one needs to be clear about whether existing shortfalls in quality are the result of ineffective approaches or poorly-performed activities. Once this is done, suitable strategies for improving quality, such as improved performance or implementation of more effective approaches, can be pursued.

- **Absolute outcomes versus value-added outcomes** – absolute outcomes are only concerned with the absolute quality of the final outcome irrespective of the starting point of service delivery. Value-added is concerned with relating the quality of the final outcome to the inputs into the service delivery process. Two examples of this are as follows:
  - **Schools** – the quality of education in a school could be measured in terms of absolute outcomes by looking at the examination success rates of different schools. On the other hand, the quality of education in terms of value-added would require one to compare these examination results against the socio-economic characteristics of pupils entering the school. The argument here is that schools in a deprived area are never going to achieve the same absolute examination results as schools in a rich area, but they may be achieving greater value-added.
  - **Surgical services** – the quality of surgical services could be measured in terms of absolute outcomes by looking at the survival rates for particular operations for different hospitals or different surgeons. On the other hand, the quality of surgical services in terms of value-added would require one to compare the survival rates of individual hospitals or surgeons with the initial health status of those patients receiving the surgical intervention.

SETTING QUALITY STANDARDS

It can be argued that the quality standards are the heart of quality management. Without quality standards there is nothing against which to compare actual quality and no basis for quality improvement. The setting of quality standards in PSOs can be a difficult task for, as has already been seen, there are several dimensions to quality and differing groups will have differing views about what should constitute quality improvement. Hence, the process of setting quality standards is bound to be a process of negotiation which takes account of a wide range of factors. The main factors are shown in Figure 35.

These factors are discussed below:

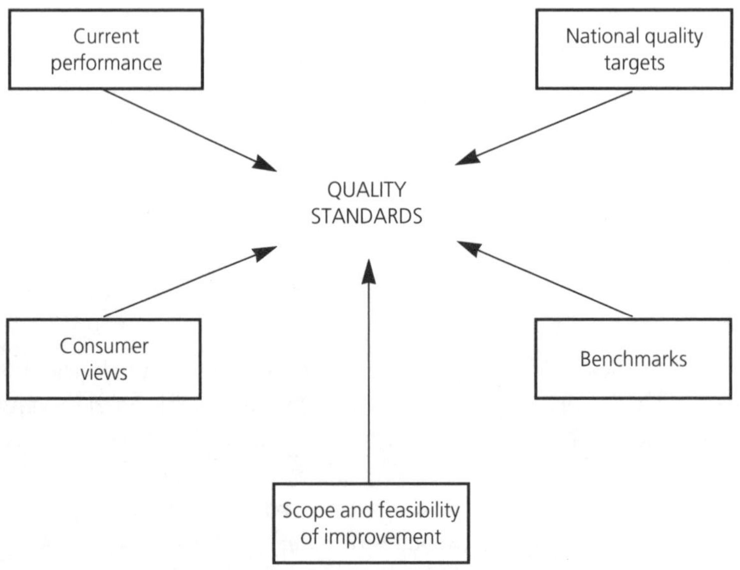

Figure 35 Setting quality standards

- **Current performance** – clearly, in setting quality standards it is desirable for cognizance to be taken of current performance in relation to quality. Thus, it will be necessary to have some information available about current quality performance. This may mean that the quality monitoring systems have to be operated some time in advance of the quality setting process in order that some data on current quality can be made available. If this is not possible then quality standards could be imputed by reference to what is being achieved by other comparable organizations, but this does, of course, run the risk of setting unrealistic and (in the short term) unrealizable standards.
- **National quality targets** – as a result of initiatives such as the Citizen's Charter and offspring such as the Patient's charter there are a considerable number of nationally derived quality targets in various parts of the public sector.
- **Consumer opinions** – local consumers of services and the general public at large will have views on the quality of services that should be delivered, and these views need to be accessed as part of the process of setting quality standards. Clearly, there are potential conflicts that may arise including, for example:

  - Conflicts between national quality targets and local quality aspirations.
  - Conflicts between different interest groups. For example, schoolchildren may have different views about quality of schooling than their parents; prisoners may have different views about quality of prison services compared to the general public.

  This only reinforces the point that the process of setting quality standards is a process of negotiation with several competing pressures. The views of consumers about quality can be elucidated by the methods discussed earlier in this chapter.
- **Benchmarks** – as part of the process of setting their own quality standards, PSOs often try to benchmark their performance against that of other organizations. With service provision activities they will usually try to compare themselves against other organizations in the same sector. Thus, for example, an acute hospital might try to benchmark its service performance against that of other acute hospitals, while an FE college might try to benchmark against other colleges. However, there are other activities which are generic to all organizations and PSOs might benchmark their performance against other PSOs in different sectors or, indeed, private sector organizations. Some examples of such generic activities might include public relations, IT and financial services activities.

  Although such benchmarking is a worthwhile task, some care is needed in the following areas:

  - **Comparability** – although, for example, there are hundreds of acute hospitals in the country they do vary considerably in size, location and so on. Thus, in undertaking a benchmarking exercise one needs to ensure that comparable organizations are being used in the sample.
  - **Sophistication** – benchmarking should not just be a simple but crude comparison of quality performance against others, but should also delve down to consider other factors such as the service delivery methods being used in each comparator organization.

- **Scope and feasibility of improvement** – quality standards are set to facilitate the PSO in maintaining or, most probably, improving the quality of service delivered, however quality has been defined. Thus, in setting quality standards it is necessary to consider the scope and feasibility for improving service quality. There is no point in setting quality standards in the organization in a vacuum, isolated from operational reality and the potential for improving quality. This would most probably result in a complete failure to achieve overambitious standards. There may be many reasons why there are limits on the levels of improvement in quality, some of which may be justifiable and some not so justifiable. These may include matters such as:

- lack of staff time
- inadequate staff skills
- inadequate or inappropriate equipment
- lack of information
- cultural and professional resistance.

Thus, a key aspect of setting quality standards is to identify the feasibility and scope for improvement and to build feasible improvements into the standards.

IMPROVING QUALITY

One (perhaps the main) reason for setting quality standards and monitoring quality is to improve the quality of services being delivered. Hence any quality management process must also incorporate the means for improving quality. There are a variety of possible approaches which can be applied and these are summarized below:

- **Quality control systems** – this is perhaps the most well-known approach to quality improvement. It involves examining the quality of the product ***after*** it has been produced through some form of ex-post inspection procedure which compares the actual product quality with the detailed specification. Measurement of the extent of adherence to the product specification can be made through direct observation, testing or consumer surveys and an assessment of the statistical significance of any deviation from the specification can be tested by the use of statistical sampling.

  Clearly one might question how such an 'after the event' quality control regime can be thought of as a method of improving quality, and there are two responses to this:

  - the actual existence of a quality control regime may put pressure on staff to deliver good product quality in the knowledge that any failures may be picked up
  - in some circumstances it may be possible to 'rework' the unsatisfactory product to a satisfactory standard.

  The problem with quality control in the public sector is that for many of the services to which it might be applied it is either not possible or not desirable to re-work the product, and so quality control is of limited use. Take, for example, the unsatisfactory surgical operation or the badly-taught college course. Although compensation may be offered or there may be the offer to undertake some form of remedial action, this cannot really remedy the effects on the individuals involved of receiving a poor-quality service. However, it is also the case that for many of the less personal services delivered by PSOs (for example local authority housing repairs) quality control systems can be a useful method of improving quality.

  In recent years a number of specific developments have taken place in the public sector which may be regarded as developments in quality control:

  - **Peer review** – in some parts of the public sector some form of peer review is undertaken as a means of identifying poor performance and promoting higher quality of service. An example of this would be the process of clinical audit which is undertaken in all NHS Trusts.
  - **Inspection** – in recent years many PSOs have become subject to an external scrutiny by an independent team of experts. This scrutiny would incorporate an assessment of the service

quality being provided with recommendations for improvement. Examples of this are the OFSTED inspection of schools and the Health Advisory Service (HAS) assessment of mental illness services. With the development of the Best Value initiative in local government the inspection approach will be enhanced substantially, and will be applied to many other types of service. The Audit Commission will have a key role in promoting the development of this service inspection approach.

- **Quality assurance systems** – rather than measuring deviations from quality after the event and taking remedial action where possible and appropriate, an alternative approach is to put in place procedures which minimize the chances of any shortfalls in quality in the first place. This is referred to as quality assurance. Thus, a quality assurance system defines and documents a series of procedures and actions which must be undertaken at each of the various stages in the production process. The underlying assumption is that provided all of these procedures and actions are undertaken then the quality of a product will be assured.

Although an organization may design and implement its own quality assurance process most organizations adopt an established system, most usually British Standard (BS) 5750 which is known internationally as the ISO9000 standard. The BS5750 standard comprises several parts, with differing degrees of relevance to various PSOs. Although many of the parts of BS5750 are more relevant to manufacturing industry in that they deal with matters such as design, production, installation and servicing they do have applicability to the activities of some PSO services such as building design, housing maintenance or street cleaning. However, part 8 of BS5750 is specifically concerned with quality assurance for service delivery and covers matters such as service design and delivery, consumer feedback, marketing and corrective action.

These quality assurance systems lay down the various steps and procedures that are to be followed within the organization for each step in the process of product or service delivery. They will describe in considerable detail the steps to be undertaken, the authorizations required and the documentation to be kept for all stages including:

- design of the product or service
- planning approaches relating to product or service delivery
- marketing methods
- production or delivery methods
- quality control procedures
- testing procedures .

A key element in all of this will be documentation, and every step in the process will have to be documented and recorded. This will enable an audit to be made of the degree of compliance with the quality assurance process.

Many PSOs in various sectors have adopted the BS5750 standard to show their commitment to quality and as a means of generating quality improvements. However, a number of points can be made about these quality assurance processes in general and the BS5750 approach in particular:

- Quality assurance emphasizes systems and procedures rather than outcomes. Examples can be quoted of organizations which had zero non-compliance in terms of their quality assurance system, but quality control indicated that a large proportion of their product needed re-working.
- Quality assurance systems are often imposed top-down in an organization. Thus, employees do not always have wholehearted commitment to the system and often pay lip-service to the

requirements of the system. Clearly, for quality assurance to be most effective its development needs to involve widespread participation by staff.
- Quality assurance systems are expensive to develop and operate, especially in terms of the staff time that needs to be committed to the system and the incremental costs of operating the system. Hence, before going down this road PSOs need to think carefully and rigorously about the benefits that are likely to accrue, the costs involved and alternative approaches to quality improvement that are available. Too often in PSOs one sees BS5750 certification being pursued merely as a badge to be worn by the organization.
- Quality assurance systems are often very bureaucratic and paper-oriented. If one is not careful, the operation of the system can relegate the actual delivery of a quality product or service to a position below compliance with the written procedures.

- **Total quality management** – TQM is a difficult concept to describe since it is as much a philosophy as a management technique. As its name suggests, it is concerned with a comprehensive approach to maintaining and improving quality in an organization. As such, there is no blueprint for TQM and the structure and approach to TQM will vary from organization to organization. Instead, TQM can be thought of as a series of aspects which come together to deliver a TQM approach. These various aspects include:
  - **Organizational culture** – the culture in the organization must be one that is totally committed to the delivery of a high-quality product or service that meets the needs of the consumer. This may be difficult to achieve since other cultural values such as increasing profit (private sector) or maintenance of professional vested interests (public sector) may be more dominant in the organization.
  - **Employee skills** – a TQM approach requires that the skills and competencies of the staff of the organization are maintained and developed as required. This requires a commitment to the development of human resources, possibly along the lines of IIP described in Chapter 6, and sufficient investment in development.
  - **Continuous improvement** – TQM implies a commitment to innovation and continuous improvement within the organization. This may require the creation of specific but informal organizational structures and arrangements to foster continuous development. One example of this would be the formation of quality circles which involve staff in the organization identifying, analysing and recommending changes in operational activities designed to improve quality. In an even more delegated organization, the staff involved would identify, analyse and implement changes without the need for higher managerial authority.
  - **Systems** – the organization needs to have appropriate processes and systems and the associated quality audits in place to set quality standards and monitor quality and consumer satisfaction.

Unfortunately, TQM is often little more than a buzzword and to some extent the term TQM has fallen into disrepute. Many examples can be quoted, in the public and private sectors, of organizations who have declared that they have adopted a TQM approach but in reality have implemented very little of the requirements of an effective TQM approach described above.

In the public sector, perhaps the most difficult barrier to implementing a true TQM approach is that of culture. Some PSOs such as, for example, NHS Trusts employ large numbers of staff who belong to a wide variety of different professions (for example doctors, nurses and physiotherapists). As such, these professionals often have their own professional approaches and their own professional perspectives on what constitutes quality improvement. Hence, it is often an extraordinarily difficult task to persuade them to put aside these professional perspectives and concentrate on a broader and more comprehensive attitude towards quality improvement.

MONITORING QUALITY

The monitoring of quality is really the beginning and the end of the quality management process. On the one hand, it is the end of the process since it shows the organization how successful it has been in improving quality and meeting quality standards. On the other hand, it is the beginning of the process since it informs the development of quality standards in future years.

There are a variety of approaches to monitoring quality in organizations. Some of these are hard quantitative approaches while others are softer qualitative processes. The main approaches are summarized below:

- **Management information systems** – management information systems will capture data about the activities of an organization, analyse that data and present it in a meaningful form. Thus the MIS of an organization may be set up in such a way that it captures information about the quality of the service being delivered. Some examples of this, derived from the public sector, are:

  - **FE college destinations** – arguably one measure of the relevance and quality of FE college course provision is the destination of students who complete courses: how many get jobs, how many go on to higher education, how many become unemployed. Provided suitable data collection facilities and MIS are established then a college can see the pattern of student destinations for each programme and each course, and compare that with information from other colleges and previous years.
  - **Hospital readmission rates** – Hospitals for the mentally ill might capture data on the re-admission rates for patients who had received treatment. Comparisons of these readmission rates with other similar hospitals and/or previous periods may indicate something about the quality of treatment.

- **Sample surveys** – as an alternative to capturing full data via MIS, PSOs may capture similar data on a sample basis. This would require a specific exercise to be planned and undertaken and the results analysed. Such sampling approaches may be undertaken in two ways:

  - ongoing sample
  - retrospective sample.

  Thus using the example of student destination data referred to above, an ongoing sample would involve collecting data from each class as it ended whereas a retrospective sample would be undertaken after the end of a year. Clearly, there are advantages and disadvantages to both approaches. An ongoing sample would involve a captive audience, whereas a retrospective sample would require one to locate students many months after they had left the college. On the other hand, a retrospective sample would allow student destinations to become more clear with the passage of time.
- **Consumer surveys** – earlier in this chapter reference was made to the use of various techniques to monitor the degree of consumer satisfaction with services. Where consumer satisfaction can be regarded as a good proxy for service quality, then clearly these approaches have relevance to the measurement and management of quality. Where they do not provide a good proxy for service quality then clearly caution has to be exercised.
- **Inspection regimes** – inspection of the quality of service output is a key approach to quality

monitoring. The inspection may be undertaken by persons from within or without the organization delivering the service, but clearly it is important that the inspectors have no direct involvement in the actual delivery of the service. Inspection has been used in many types of public service provision for many years. Take, for example, local authority direct service organizations. Under the contractual arrangements that local authorities have with their own DSO there would be provision for there to be an independent inspection of, for example, the quality of street cleaning, buildings repairs or building cleaning. However, within the public sector the inspection approach has also been extended into other more professional areas including:

- the OFSTED inspection of schools
- teaching quality assessments undertaken in universities by the Quality Assurance Agency (QAA)
- inspections by the social services inspectorate of local authority social services.

Clearly, there has been nothing in the past to stop PSOs commissioning independent inspections of the quality of their service provision, but the extent to which this has been done voluntarily has probably been very limited and the examples of inspection quoted above have been compulsorily forced on the PSOs involved. However, the earlier comments about the increasing emphasis on inspection as part of the Best Value regime shows that the level of inspection as part of quality monitoring is set to increase substantially.

- **System compliance audits** – in discussing quality assurance and BS5750 it was noted that audits of the degree of compliance with the quality procedures are an intrinsic part of the quality assurance process. Such audits may be undertaken by internal staff of the organization or by inspectors from BSI. Cases of non-compliance will be reported and corrective action taken. The ultimate sanction for continuous non-compliance would be withdrawal of the BS5750 certification.

CHAPTER NINE

Management of Information Technology in the Public Sector

It needs no emphasis here that the information technology (IT) revolution has impacted on all areas of society, and the public sector is no exception to this. It has been estimated, recently, that the public sector as a whole spends around £2 billion a year on IT, and this is likely to increase substantially each year in real terms. This chapter aims to look at the tasks associated with the management of IT resources. As well as considering issues such as the reasons why PSOs have traditionally invested in IT, the chapter will look ahead to the pivotal role IT will have in PSOs in years to come. This role will involve a substantial change away from the traditional support role to a role where IT is one of the key means of actual service delivery in the public sector. Hence, IT is likely to radically transform the organization, working methods and means of service delivery in PSOs .

In this chapter, the term 'IT' is used to cover a wide range of applications including:

- personal and mainframe computing
- networking
- telecommunications
- workplace automation (for example robotics)
- digital technology
- data and knowledge warehouses, etc.

IT can no longer be regarded as just a technical add-on to the organization. As has already been mentioned, IT is having and will continue to have enormous implications for PSOs in terms of its impact on many aspects of service delivery and on considerations of the organizational culture of individual PSOs. IT is, therefore, set to transform the public sector as it is now known, and it should be no surprise that the development of IT is one of the key themes of the government White Paper entitled 'Modernizing Government' which is discussed in Chapter 10.

This chapter is concerned with the management of IT resources in PSOs, and a number of key questions are addressed:

- what have been the main trends in IT development in the public sector?
- what are the main reasons why organizations invest in IT?
- what have been the main policy drivers behind the development of IT in the public sector?
- what have been the main problems of public sector IT development?
- what will be the future role of IT in PSOs?
- what will be the future impact of IT on PSOs?
- what are the main aspects of IT management in PSOs in the future?
- what factors make for an effective IT function?

The last two items, in particular, are critical parts of this chapter. All too often, IT management in PSOs has been regarded as a purely technical matter which is beyond the understanding of other non-technical managers and thus IT management is often left to technical specialists. This is an issue of real concern since not only is IT a vital resource in PSOs but, as has already been mentioned, IT will be of increasing importance and complexity in the future. Thus it is imperative that all managers and service professionals have some knowledge of the basic principles of IT and are actively involved in its management and development.

TRENDS IN IT DEVELOPMENT IN THE PUBLIC SECTOR

In this section, brief consideration is given to the historic trends in the role of IT in PSOs and these are illustrated in Figure 36.

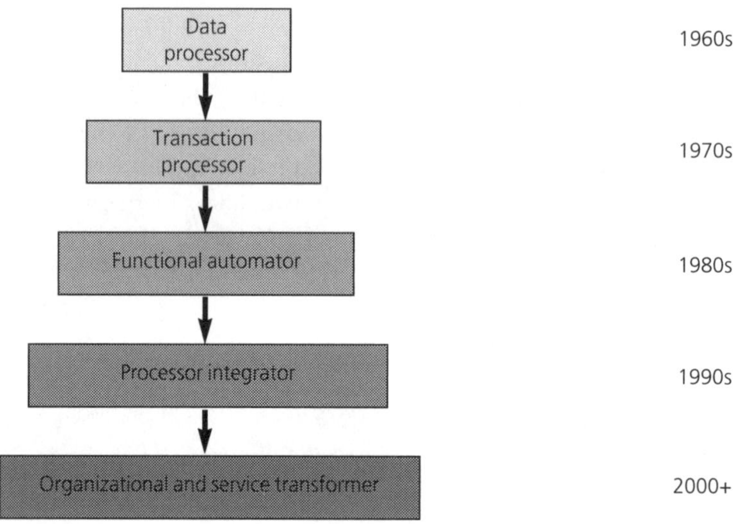

Figure 36 The changing roles of IT in PSOs

Referring to the above diagram, the historic development of IT can be categorized as a series of distinct phases which have occurred largely as a consequence of technological developments:

- **Data processor** – this phase involved the use of computers for the routine analysis of data which was previously done manually. This was particularly important in those organizations concerned with analysing large amounts of data for statistical purposes. In the public sector this involved central government departments concerned with processing large volumes of data.
- **Transaction processor** – in the 1970s many PSOs started to use IT for processing various types of transactions, particularly financial transactions such as payroll and creditor payments. In central government and local authorities, large mainframe computers began to be used, mainly for internal financial management purposes such as payroll, payments and storekeeping. Also, mainframe computers started to be used for the administration of certain aspects of external service delivery such as social security payments and local government welfare benefits. However, during these years computing was still very much in the hands of the technical experts and a typical arrangement was for there to be a remote and physically isolated computer unit to which data input was physically sent and from which data output was received. PSO staff generally submitted the data on paper, which was then encoded onto punch cards, or paper or magnetic tape, by specially-trained operators. The cards or tape were then input into the computer and the output, in the form of cheques, statements and so on was produced by the computer. Thus, usually, the average PSO

employee never saw the computer or had any direct physical contact with it. Given the strong financial emphasis during this era on the use of IT, it was not surprising that the management of the IT operation often became the responsibility of the chief financial officer.

- **Functional automator** – the 1980s saw the introduction of various new technologies such as personal computers (PCs) and various forms of automated data collection such as optical character recognition and bar code readers. Within PSOs, these developments meant that IT could be used to undertake functions which were traditionally done manually. One example of this is the use of optical character recognition and bar code readers as a means of inputting data in preference to manual input. Another example would be the use of computers to manage and control the energy consumption of an organization in place of human controls.
- **Process integrator** – whereas, initially, PCs would have operated in a stand-alone mode within the organization, as years went by it became more common and useful to have several PCs linked together within a local network arrangement, thus facilitating the use of shared databases for example. The development of relational databases enabled data from different sources in the same organization to be stored in the same place and for different sets of data to be related to one another. This meant that the various management processes in the organization which utilized this data could also be cross-related and integrated with one another. Earlier in this chapter the example was quoted of a local authority which is able to closely integrate the processes of council tax receipt and housing benefit payments.

However, as the IT function adapted to each new role described above it still continued to undertake the roles from previous eras. Thus, IT still undertakes the basic tasks of transaction processing even though it has subsequently taken on the roles of functional automator and process integrator. Consequently, the IT function in any medium-sized to large organization such as a PSO comprises a complex and interrelated set of tasks.

It will be noted that the last phase in the diagram is described as 'organizational and service transformer'. This is a phase of development which has already commenced and will continue for the foreseeable future. It will have immense implications for all aspects of PSO activities and is discussed in greater depth in a later section.

AIMS AND OBJECTIVES OF IT INVESTMENT

In this section consideration is given to some of the main aims and objectives of IT investment and the reasons underpinning the level of investment involved. These issues which apply, to a lesser or greater degree to all types of organization, including PSOs, are as follows:

- efficiency improvement
- service effectiveness
- volumes of data storage
- speed of responses
- integration of data and processes
- access to data.

EFFICIENCY IMPROVEMENT

This was, in many ways, one of the earliest reasons for investing in IT and it still has relevance today. In the early days of IT, certain labour-intensive functions such as payroll, billing and so on could be automated using computers, thus reducing the manpower needed to operate these functions. The capital cost of the IT investment could then be recouped through staff savings and would provide a very quick payback. Today, although the technology has changed, the economic principles are the same. Take, for example, the digitization of X-ray images in a hospital. One advantage of this process is that the images are stored in a digitized electronic form and not as physical film images stored in files. This means that the costs of storage are reduced but also, since the images can be retrieved directly by a doctor via the hospital's information networks, the costs of retrieval and transportation are also reduced. It is probably also the case that the digitized images have clinical benefits compared to traditional X-rays, since the equipment involved results in a lower dose of X-rays for the patient and the images produced may be superior.

As discussed in Chapter 5 one of the main failings of this approach is that in practice the cost savings on which the IT investment was predicated are not always achieved. There are many reasons for this including overoptimistic forecasts of costs and cost savings, and/or a failure of management to realize those savings. In any event, this severely limits the benefits of investing in IT.

SERVICE EFFECTIVENESS

IT can make an important contribution to the effectiveness of services delivered by making key information and knowledge easily available to service professionals. For example, in the medical field, modern IT enables doctors to access information worldwide about specific clinical conditions and the efficacy of alternative treatment profiles. Similarly, the development of the electronic patient record (EPR) will enable the doctor to have complete information about a patient prior to making clinical decisions. Prior to the IT revolution such information would either have been completely inaccessible or too difficult to access for practical purposes. The existence of large-scale databases and modern communications such as the Internet means that vital information is now more easily accessible. The role of IT in delivering effective services is a key trend for the future and will be further discussed in a later section.

VOLUMES OF DATA STORAGE

IT developments such as optical character reading, bar code readers and portable data capture units have meant that very large volumes of raw data can be collected quickly, easily and at reasonable cost. Furthermore, the use of computers means that organizations can store these large volumes of data relatively cheaply. In theory, all of this could have been done manually prior to the IT revolution, but the costs involved and the time delays in analysing the data would have been prohibitive. Using jargon, this increase in the volume of data stored and collected is often described as increasing organizational memory. What it means in practice is that the PSO has a much larger and wider database available which can be used to provide valuable management information for the planning and management of its activities, to an extent which was inconceivable prior to the IT revolution. Consider, for example, the case of performance indicators. As discussed in other chapters, many PSOs such as local authorities and NHS Trusts are now required to publish a wide range of indicators of their performance. A moment's reflection will indicate that thirty years ago this would have been an impossible task since PSOs could never have manually collected, stored and analysed the data which underpins the production of these performance indicators.

Thus, the IT revolution means that within PSOs large volumes of data can be stored at reasonable cost, and subsequently converted into information about three main issues:

- **Services** – information about the services undertaken by the organization in terms of volume, type, location, timing and so on. Some examples of this from PSOs might be:
  - number of social security payments issued each day
  - volumes and types of hospital outpatients
  - response times for undertaking repairs to council houses
  - the numbers of nights of respite care provided by local authority social services
  - the numbers of households where waste collection was missed.
- **Clients** – information about the clients or consumers of the organization's services including their age, sex, residence, social class, needs and incomes. Some public sector examples of this are:
  - age profile of hospital inpatients
  - the destinations of students who leave an FE college (for example employment, higher education, additional FE, unemployed)
  - the length of time that claimants of unemployment benefit have been unemployed
  - the geographic distribution of children taken into care.
- **Resources** – information about the resources used by the organization in providing services covering human resources, physical resources and finance. Some public sector examples would include:
  - number of teaching hours devoted to various FE college courses
  - costs of treating individual patients or disease groups
  - utilization of university teaching buildings by different departments and courses
  - costs of repairing different sections of roads
  - age profile of the organization's employees.

SPEED OF RESPONSE

The computerization of data storage has meant that response times to queries has dramatically improved. Consider the following:

- a supplier making an enquiry to an organization about payment of an invoice
- an enquiry to a hospital about the location of a patient
- an enquiry to a local authority about the progress of a grant application.

Prior to the IT revolution such queries would have necessitated staff accessing manual records and thus the response time to the query could have varied between several hours and several days depending on the efficiency of the organization involved. The IT revolution has meant that details on all of these issues can now be stored on a computer or a network of computers and can be accessed in a matter of seconds.

INTEGRATION OF DATA

Traditionally in PSOs, data about the same individual was held on several separate databases within the same organization. An example of this might have been that of the local authority which held data about individuals on its council tax system, its housing benefits system, its creditor payments system and its social services systems. Similarly, data about an individual could be held on the separate databases of several central government departments and agencies (Benefits Agency, Inland Revenue, Job Centres and so on). The IT revolution and the development of large-scale databases means that data about an individual can be centralized in one database in the organization. Thus it becomes possible to link together and relate the data which was originally held on separate databases.

ACCESS TO DATA

Prior to the introduction of IT, access to data was by reference to paper records. In the early days of IT the main route for obtaining data held on computers was by means of paper printouts. Access to data was limited to the recipients of those printouts and constrained by the frequency and timing of printout production. Modern developments in IT have drastically increased the access to data in terms of its range and timing. Some examples of this are as follows:

- Using locally networked PCs, users can quickly access, at any time, data held on their own computer or on any other computers in the local network. Thus, for example, managers can access data on the expenditure incurred by their department.
- Wider area networks enable users to access data from databases held in computers in other locations. In the commercial world this is commonplace and, using retail chain stores as an example, data on customers and products of the firm can be obtained from any store in the country via established networks. In the NHS, doctors might ultimately be able to access data about bed availability in hospitals across the country.
- Using PCs and mobile phones users can access data held on computerized databases from remote locations.

Clearly, the Internet is the extreme example of this, whereby users can access data from millions of web-sites throughout the world.

POLICY DRIVERS OF IT DEVELOPMENT IN THE PUBLIC SECTOR

In the light of the above general reasons for investing in IT, it is important to consider what are the main public policy drivers for PSOs undertaking such investment. There is probably something of a symbiosis here, since not only have these factors driven the development of IT in PSOs but also, in the absence of modern IT, many of these policy developments probably could not have taken place. There are five factors to consider:

- market mechanisms
- managerial delegation
- cost pressures
- quality and consumer satisfaction pressures
- the requirements for central control.

MARKET MECHANISMS

As already noted, over the last twenty years, the use of market mechanisms has become extremely prevalent in the public sector. This has taken the form of real market mechanisms applied through market testing exercises such as those in local and central government, but also through the use of quasi-markets and contractual relationships as has been the case with executive agencies and the NHS internal market. In either case, the use of these market mechanisms has meant that larger and more varied amounts of data have needed to be collected, stored and analysed. It is probably true to say that in the absence of modern IT it would not have been possible for many such market-based developments to have taken place. However, the situation has been far from perfect and policy developments such as the NHS internal market struggled because of the absence of adequate flows of data.

MANAGERIAL DELEGATION

In Chapter 3 it was mentioned that one of the major organizational trends in PSOs has been the delegation of managerial authority to lower levels in the organization. Such delegation has encompassed both the delivery of services and the use of physical, financial and human resources. For such delegated arrangements to operate *effectively* it is necessary that a large number of middle- and lower-level managers in the organization are provided with information about the activities they have undertaken and the resources they have used. Take, for example, the matter of budgetary control. A delegated system of budgets requires that each month a large number of managers are provided, promptly, with information about the income and expenditure of their departments. In turn, this requires the collection, storage and analysis of large amounts of data about the expenditure and income transactions of the organization. In practice, the only way this can be done is by the use of computers to store and analyse the data, and for managers to have access to that information via organizational networks.

COST PRESSURES

The pressures on PSOs to improve their revenue efficiency have existed for many years and in Chapter 10 it is noted that such pressures are set to continue in the future and to be extended to other parts of the public sector. It has been mentioned frequently throughout this chapter that capital investment may facilitate reductions in running costs, largely through reductions in manpower. Investment in IT is one means of improving revenue efficiency and not surprisingly, therefore, many PSOs have often invested heavily in IT. There are many examples of this, including automated telephone switchboards in place of manual switchboards, computerized data storage in place of paper storage and the use, by managers, of word-processing facilities in place of secretaries. Ongoing technical developments in IT will mean that PSOs will continue to invest in IT for the purposes of cost reduction. One example of this would be the use of Internet procurement processes in place of traditional paper processes.

QUALITY AND CONSUMER SATISFACTION PRESSURES

Pressures to improve the effectiveness of service delivery (coupled with pressures to reduce costs) have often been met by investment in IT. Thus, investment is seen in:

- computerized medical technology and medico-legal documentation to improve services in hospitals
- computerized communication equipment to improve emergency services
- computerized learning facilities in schools and colleges
- computerized data bases to improve crime detection in police services
- computerized systems to improve the speed and accuracy of benefit payments in the Benefits Agency and so on.

CENTRAL CONTROL

The continually increasing trend towards centralized control of PSO activities has been noted throughout this book. Ten or twenty years ago, prior to the IT revolution, such centralized control might have been difficult or even impossible to achieve, since PSOs would not have been able to provide central government with the information required for monitoring and control purposes. The availability of the technology coupled with the political trend for increased central control have thus generated an imperative for PSOs to invest in the necessary systems.

MAIN PROBLEMS OF PUBLIC SECTOR IT DEVELOPMENT

Over the years there have been many, sometimes well publicized, cases of serious problems and failures with IT developments in the public sector. However, these failures often disguise the fact that many thousands of IT implementations have been undertaken in the public sector with little or no problems. Nevertheless, there are some clear patterns that can be observed with regard to public sector IT developments and these should act as a warning and a guide to the future. The main patterns identified here are as follows.

RUNAWAY SYSTEMS

These are usually large-scale systems developments where a number of factors cause the project to go seriously wrong in one or both of the following ways:

- the implementation timetable has been substantially exceeded
- the implementation budget is significantly exceeded, possibly by several hundred per cent.

Examination of runaway systems suggests that the main reason for these problems occurring is basically a lack of adequate project management procedures and skills in the organization undertaking the implementation.

FUNCTIONAL FAILURE

With these types of IT development the implementation may well be completed on time and within budget but once operational, it is found that the system does not have the degree of functionality expected or needed by systems users. In some cases this may involve relatively small problems which can either be dealt with or ignored, but in other cases the problems may be so great that a major redesign has to be undertaken and the original system may even have to be scrapped.

Probably, with few exceptions, it is the case that these functional failures are the result of poor systems planning rather than there being any substantial operational changes in the organization which have made the system outmoded or inadequate. Factors often found include failures to adequately estimate volumes of data or a failure to obtain the views of operational staff about how the system should operate.

FAILURE TO UNDERTAKE PROCESS REVIEW

Quite often it is the case that public sector IT investments have involved adding a technological dimension to existing operational processes and procedures in the organization. Thus, for example, a computerized invoicing system may be introduced to automate the existing centralized invoicing process of a finance department, while keeping the processes largely unchanged.

Experience has shown that such an approach can substantially reduce the potential benefits of IT investment. A greater level of benefits can be obtained by first reviewing the appropriateness of the processes in the organization and then seeing how IT investment can support a revised set of processes. Thus, in the invoicing example a better approach might be to first consider the benefits of decentralizing the invoicing function from the finance department to individual departments and then building the systems needed to support such a revised approach. This is very much the province of business process re-engineering which was discussed in Chapter 6.

FAILURE TO MANAGE SUPPLIERS EFFECTIVELY

PSOs use suppliers of IT services in a wide variety of ways including hardware supply, software development, implementation and the outsourcing of the whole IT function. It is sometimes the case that IT failures in the public sector occur because of a failure to manage such suppliers effectively. This can include a variety of faults such as poor contract specification or ineffective monitoring and supervision. Where the majority of the IT function has been outsourced then such failures to manage the supplier contract effectively can have significant repercussions.

Although these IT failures in the public sector cannot be excused, it would be extremely naïve to think that such failures do not occur in the private sector. The implementation, some years ago, of a new system for the stock exchange is a well publicized example of this. The difference is that in the public sector major IT failures are difficult to hide and often become the subject of NAO investigations and Public Accounts Committee enquiries.

THE FUTURE ROLE OF IT IN PSOs: TRANSFORMING THE ORGANIZATION

Earlier in this chapter, consideration was given to the historical development of IT in the public sector. The final developmental stage in the diagram was termed 'organizational and service transformer'. This term is no exaggeration since in most PSOs in the next few years, IT can be expected to transform radically the organizational arrangements, the methods of working and the means of service delivery. The effects of such changes cannot be overstated and all PSO managers need to understand the nature of this change and the challenges it will bring.

If one looks at specific aspects of this transformation process the potential future impact of IT in a number of different aspects of PSO activities can be seen, and these are outlined below:

- **Procurement** – it is well known that massive increases in the procurement of goods and services via the Internet are anticipated both in the case of business-to-business procurement and in terms of procurement by individual consumers from supplier organizations. So it must be the case that in the public sector, in future years, there will be substantial increases in procurement by PSOs and from PSOs via the Internet. This will largely replace traditional paper-based methods of procurement and will have major implications for the organization and staffing of PSOs.
- **Consumer information and marketing** – PSOs can make use of Internet web-sites to provide information to consumers and other organizations about their activities and, where appropriate, to market those activities. A substantial expansion in this area of activity can be envisaged. Some examples of this might include:
  - the provision of information on waiting times and bed availability in hospitals across the country
  - the provision of information by universities on the availability of places on courses
  - the provision of information by local authorities on the availability of local leisure facilities (and other types of local authority service).
- **Service delivery** – there are a number of examples where modern IT developments can actually become the means for delivering the service provided by the PSO. Consider the following:

- In the commercial sector the Internet is used, with increasing frequency, as the actual means of distributing products to consumers. Some examples of this include the distribution of computer software, music, information and written material. Where appropriate, there is no reason why PSOs cannot use the Internet as a means of distributing their products, and some examples of this might include the distribution of education materials, the provision of information and written materials, and the provision of consumer advice (for example health advice).
- Using video-teaching technologies, educational institutions can deliver classroom teaching to large groups of students located at various sites remote from the teacher or lecturer. In such a situation the teacher can be in another room, another town or even another country from the students.

- **Service improvement** – there are many examples which can be quoted of where IT developments can facilitate improvements in the quality of service through knowledge improvement at the point of service delivery. Some examples of this are:

  - The use within the NHS of the electronic patient record (EPR). Once available this will enable any doctor in the country to have immediate access to the medical records of a patient, irrespective of their place of residence or the location of previous treatment episodes. This should improve the accuracy and speed of diagnosis and improve the chances of the correct therapy being selected.
  - The availability to social workers of a wide variety of information, from various sources, about their clients. This will facilitate better decision making regarding the structure of service plans for those clients.

- **Joined-up government** – improved working between PSOs (in the same sector or from different sectors) is a key plank of government policy for improving the delivery of public services. This is referred to as 'joined-up government' and is discussed further in Chapter 10 under the heading of 'Modernizing Government'. IT can contribute towards joined-up government by facilitating the sharing and transfer of knowledge and information between PSOs.

  Obviously, for this use of IT to be successful there will need to be some co-ordination of activity at a technical level in terms of such matters as data definition, data transfer routines and so on. Where PSOs are within the same sector then it is easy to see how such co-ordination might be achieved (for example the NHS Information Authority and the NHS Executive would have this role in relation to co-ordination between NHS Trusts). However, for PSOs within different sectors it is more difficult to see how such co-ordination might be facilitated. Consider, for example, the task of co-ordinating the IT activities of several social services authorities and several NHS Trusts within a single urban conurbation.
- **Communications** – traditionally, devices such as telephones and fax machines have been a major means of communication both within organizations and between the organization and various external parties. However, various IT developments have revolutionized the means of communication in terms of mode, volume and speed of communication. Some examples of these developments include:

  - electronic mail
  - mobile phones
  - voice-mail
  - video-conferencing.

- **Organizational management** – the historical development of IT as described earlier in this chapter highlighted the role that IT had played in various aspects of organizational management. This can be expected to continue in the future, and IT will be the means of providing management information about the activities and resources of the organization. However, it can be expected that IT developments will make this an increasingly sophisticated process.

It must be emphasized that many PSOs have already gone down this road, and are already making use of modern IT in at least some of the areas discussed above. However, the reality is that other PSOs have barely scratched the surface of such developments and thus have tremendous scope for change in future years. Undoubtedly, the messages contained in the White Paper entitled 'Modernizing Government' (see Chapter 10) emphasize this strong role for IT in transforming the methods of service delivery in PSOs.

The extent to which PSOs have the scope to extend their use of IT in any of the above areas should radically impact on their IT strategy and their management of the IT resource.

IT STRATEGY

In Chapter 4 the importance for PSOs of developing strategic and business plans was discussed. The discussion in the previous section about the future pivotal role of IT in PSOs should indicate that because IT is a key resource in any organization, an IT strategy should be an integral part of the strategy of the organization and should not be developed independently.

The main factors to be considered when developing IT strategies are illustrated in Figure 37.

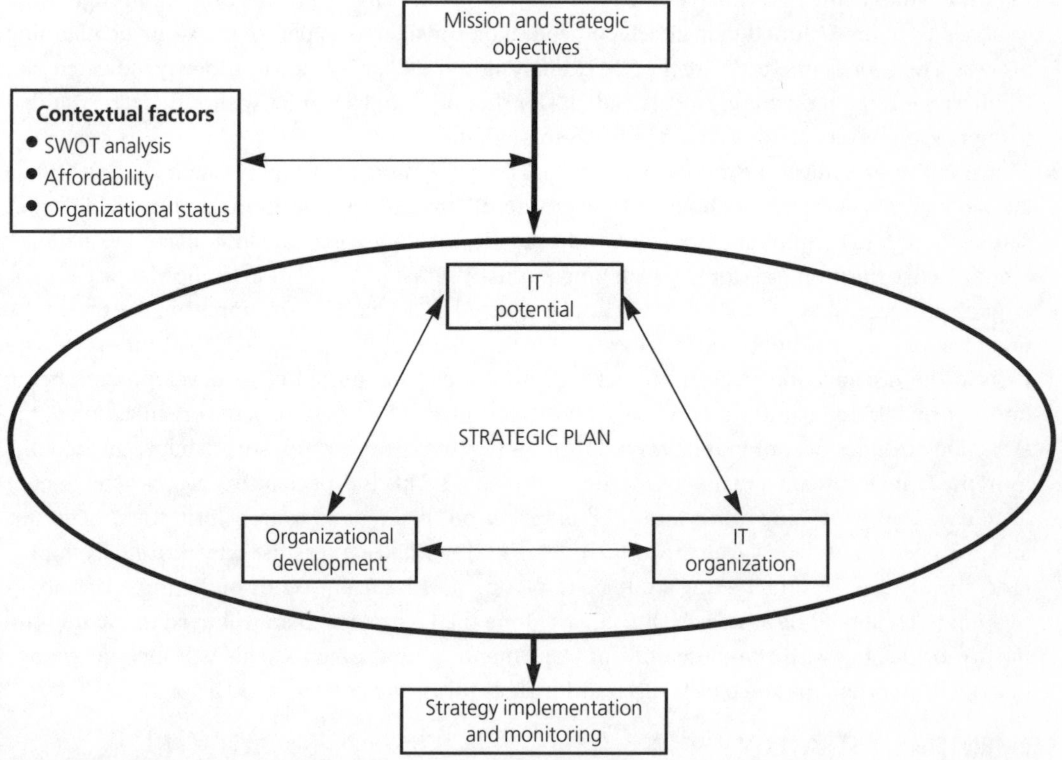

Figure 37 Developing and implementing IT strategy

MISSION AND STRATEGIC OBJECTIVES

In developing the strategy for IT, the focus must be on the overall mission and strategic objectives of the organization, and the contribution IT can make to achieving those objectives. The strategic objectives of the organization might be concerned with:

- improved service effectiveness
- improved service configuration and service delivery
- increased access to services
- prompter response to service requests
- improved resource efficiency
- increased consumer satisfaction.

It may seem self-evident that IT strategy should be related to and derived from strategic objectives, but this is not always the case and many examples can be quoted of IT strategy being developed in virtual isolation from broader strategic objectives.

CONTEXTUAL ISSUES

There are three main contextual issues which will impact on the IT strategy:

- **SWOT analysis** – there are many approaches towards identifying the potential application of IT in an organization, and one such approach involves referring to the results of the SWOT analysis since this will indicate the potential, strengths, weaknesses, opportunities and threats in the service provision activities of the PSO which IT can help address. It will also indicate the existing strengths and weaknesses of the IT function itself which need to be considered as part of the strategic planning process. Thus, for example, where the SWOT analysis undertaken by a local authority indicated that it had a poor reputation among local residents for the speed and accuracy with which it responded to queries, then IT investment could improve this situation.
- **Affordability** – whatever the merits of particular IT developments, the reality is that all PSOs will be limited in terms of the affordability of IT investment. This can apply in terms of the availability of capital funds for IT equipment or revenue affordability in relation to IT outsourcing or PFI arrangements. Hence the proposals for IT development must be assessed in relation to affordability.
- **Organizational status** – since IT should not be allowed to develop in isolation from the rest of the organization, consideration needs to be given to the existing culture, knowledge, attitudes and skill base in the organization in relation to IT. Examples can be quoted of IT developments being imposed on PSOs with little or no consideration being taken of the culture of the organization or the skills and attitudes of staff in relation to IT. In these circumstances, not surprisingly, the benefits from the IT investment were much less than anticipated. This is especially the case when IT is not just an add-on to existing procedures and practices but is intended to transform the procedures and practices themselves. Given the future roles of IT described earlier this is clearly a vitally important issue. Hence, in undertaking strategic IT planning, the current status of the organization, in relation to IT, should be assessed. Once this is done the IT strategic plan will need to incorporate means for dealing with the difficulties of implementing new systems. This will include change management programs and basic skills training. This will be further discussed below.

ELEMENTS OF IT STRATEGY

The IT strategy of the organization should comprise three main elements as discussed below:

- **IT potential** – IT strategic planning must consider the areas where IT development and application can facilitate achievement of the PSOs strategic objectives and generate significant benefits to the organization. As already discussed above, this IT development may be in a number of areas including:

  - procurement
  - provision of information and marketing
  - service delivery
  - service improvement
  - communication
  - facilitation of joined-up government
  - organizational management.

  In particular, emphasis must be placed in PSOs on the potential for IT developments to improve service configuration and the methods of service delivery. For example, in the NHS, IT will make a substantial contribution in future to improvements in the delivery of NHS services at the actual point of care, through developments such as EPR and telemedicine.

  The way in which this stage in IT strategy development is undertaken will vary from place to place, but it seems clear that such a process *must* involve a combination of line managers to provide the wider organizational perspective and IT specialists to provide the technical perspective. It must be emphasized that for strategic planning to be successful it has to be recognized as a creative task which requires the right combination of creative people operating in a disciplined but unconstrained environment.

  The comments made above should make it clear to the reader that in developing IT strategy it is vital to think radically about the future potential of IT in the PSO. IT must not just be thought of in terms of its applicability in the current organizational arrangements, but also in terms of its potential to radically alter the current organization and methods of service delivery. This point cannot be emphasized too strongly. Hence it is inevitable that IT strategy will be inextricably linked to that of organizational development and change and this is discussed in the next section.

- **Organizational development** – the future role of IT in PSOs has frequently been described as organizational transforming. Thus it cannot be emphasized too strongly that IT developments in the public sector have the potential to transform the working methods, structures, skill requirements and cultures of PSOs in all sectors. To implement these sorts of IT developments successfully it is vital that the organization also implements a robust organizational development plan alongside to deal with the sorts of organizational changes that are required. This will need to cover a range of issues including basic skills training, change management and IT awareness. It cannot be emphasized too strongly that in implementing such plans the impetus must come from the top of the organization, where an example must be set. Too often in PSOs it is the case that change management programmes in relation to IT are undertaken for the bulk of staff while the chief executive and other senior staff manage to remain insulated from the impact of that IT investment.
- **IT organization** – later in this chapter the various aspects of IT organization will be discussed at some length, and an outline given of the various options available. It will suffice to say, at this stage, that one of the key strategic themes in relation to IT is identification of the most appropriate organization for the IT function covering:

  - IT roles
  - balance between insourcing and outsourcing of IT

- location of facilities
- internal organization of the IT function.

The organization of the IT function should be determined not by tradition, fashion or prejudice, but according to the best means of enabling the successful implementation of the IT strategy. This may imply changes in the IT function, and with all organizational changes there will be discomfort and resistance. Hence, the usual approaches to change management will need to be applied. Thus it will be seen that change management may be needed throughout the organization, as a consequence of implementing IT developments, and within the IT function itself.

STRATEGIC IMPLEMENTATION AND MONITORING

As discussed in Chapter 4, in any organization a strategy does not implement itself, and IT strategy is no exception to this rule. Hence there will be a need for a programme of strategic implementation and for the monitoring of the implementation of that strategy. In particular, the implementation of an IT strategic plan will raise severe concerns about resistance to organizational change in relation to IT and these issues must be addressed as part of a process of strategy implementation.

MANAGING THE IT FUNCTION

As IT comes more and more to shape the organization and working methods of the PSO, it is increasingly important that all PSO managers have a broad understanding of the key aspects of IT management. Thus, the remainder of this chapter is concerned with those key IT management tasks where all managers and service professionals need to have (or will need to have) a minimal level of understanding and involvement. The IT management tasks discussed below are:

- organization of the IT function
- procuring IT
- risk and the management of IT security
- assessing the benefits of IT investment.

ORGANIZING THE IT FUNCTION

In the private sector there exists a large number of small companies whose sole IT capability might be just a few stand-alone personal computers. Compared to the majority of organizations in the private sector, most PSOs are medium to very large in size and tend to have a multiplicity of activities. Hence it is usually the case that their IT requirements are of a reasonably substantial size and complexity. Thus, one of the key management issues concerning IT in PSOs is the most appropriate organization for IT in the PSO. In a newly-formed organization one is starting with a clean sheet of paper and one can devise and implement the most appropriate IT organization. However, in existing organizations there will already be established IT arrangements, but these may not be the most appropriate arrangements for the future. Therefore, it is important that managers constantly keep this IT organization under review in the light of changing circumstances.

There are four main issues to consider under this heading:

- IT roles
- insourcing or outsourcing of IT
- IT location
- internal IT arrangements.

IT ROLES

Before considering issues of IT organization it is first useful to say a few brief words about the activities of the IT function and the roles it undertakes. There are a number of ways of describing and classifying IT activities but the following is suggested as being fairly comprehensive:

- IT strategic planning
- systems development and implementation
- systems architecture management
- systems procurement
- systems operation and maintenance
- database management
- systems information, advice and consultancy to end-users
- management and co-ordination of distributed computing.

Simplifying this classification means that IT roles can be considered as being primarily one or a combination of:

- a support service role (for example payroll or management information)
- a service delivery role (for example marketing or service distribution).

The configuration of the IT function adopted in the PSO should be influenced quite strongly by the sorts of roles that IT is expected to fulfil and, particularly, the balance between the support role and the service delivery role. In particular, the balance between these two roles will influence a number of IT activities including the following:

- **Operations** – the types of roles adopted by IT in the organization will impact on the structure and management of the IT infrastructure and its operations.
- **Development** – the roles undertaken by IT in the organization will impact on the composition and resourcing of the IT development activity. If the organization requires leading-edge IT solutions then it may need to invest in sufficient IT development.
- **End-user computing** – the amount of end-user computing undertaken in the organization will impact on the roles to be undertaken by the IT function. In turn this will have a knock-on effect on the IT function in terms of provision of advice and consultancy services to end-users.

In considering the roles of IT, and the balance between support and service delivery, the important issue is not the current role, but that which will be required in the future. Research evidence from the private sector suggests that even in those organizations where IT currently occupies mainly a support role the expectation is that, in a matter of a few years, it will occupy a mainly strategic role in terms of product or service delivery. In PSOs, the trend in general terms is bound to be an increasing role for IT in service delivery, and as already noted this is backed up by the policies of the government set out in 'Modernizing Government' which envisages an increasing role for IT in this area. Some examples of this increasing role for IT in service delivery in PSOs include:

- the increased use of telemedicine in the NHS
- the development of computer-aided learning and video-teaching in universities and colleges
- the provision of 24-hour advisory services in many areas of activity
- the use of call centre technology (for example for dealing with queries in the Inland Revenue and Customs and Excise)
- improved efficiency and accuracy (for example in the payment of benefits and tax credits).

Thus, the key message for PSO general managers is that prior to reviewing the configuration of the IT function and making any changes it is first important to consider the future roles envisaged for IT in the organization.

INSOURCING OR OUTSOURCING OF IT SERVICES

Traditionally, most PSOs have had an in-house IT department and thus insourced most, although not all, IT services. However, in recent years there has been a strong shift in both private and public sectors towards outsourcing some or all of the provision of IT services to one or more external suppliers. In future, given the expanding role of IT, PSOs may opt to have the provision of systems, communications or knowledge provision and so on outsourced to a private provider rather than be provided in-house. In practice, there will be many different patterns of outsourcing IT activities but usually these can be described under three main headings:

- **time-share vendors** – the purchase of on-line data processing capability
- **service bureau** – the purchase of specific IT-related services such as application processing (for example payroll), software development and IT training
- **facilities management (FM)** – the externalization of the provision and/or management of IT services to a private contractor. The physical IT facilities (although owned by the private contractor) may be located on the client's site or on the contractor's site.

In many private sector organizations the outsourcing option may have been taken because the organization has been substantially downsized and needs a lower cost base for IT, or because management wishes to concentrate on its core business activities and therefore wishes to divest itself of the task of managing IT resources. In the public sector these issues of lower cost and concentration on core activities may also apply, but there are other considerations including difficulties in retaining specialist IT staff and lack of access to capital funds for IT equipment. However, any outsourcing decision must be considered carefully since research shows that there can be some severe downsides to outsourcing, including:

- excessive dependence on the FM company
- lack of control of IT
- lack of flexibility in response to changed needs
- loss of security
- loss of in-house expertise.

In practice, the strategic outsourcing decision is not likely to be a case of 'all or nothing' and PSOs will have to consider which IT activities to outsource and which to retain in-house. However, whatever the objective merits of outsourcing, and these will vary from situation to situation, a trend towards increased outsourcing of IT in PSOs can be expected to continue and, probably, to accelerate. Firstly, the increasing range and complexity in the use of IT within PSOs means that few PSOs will be large enough to be able to acquire and afford the range of equipment, and afford the specialist staff, needed to maintain an in-house IT function. Secondly, the lack of public investment funds (essential to invest in new technologies) and the increasing emphasis placed on the PFI as a means of acquiring capital assets, will also promote increased IT outsourcing in the public sector. Thus, it seems probable that the outsourcing of IT activities is the way forward for most PSOs in the future. However, there may still be a need to retain a certain 'client-side' IT capability in-house in relation to the development and maintenance of an IT strategy for the organization.

IT LOCATION

This section concerns the physical location of the IT facilities. Whether IT is insourced or outsourced, the issue of where IT should be physically located will still be relevant and, if outsourced, will need to be specified in the outsourcing contract. Outlined below are the main approaches which can be adopted but, of course, there will be many different variations from these main approaches. Having described the main approaches, the factors which need to be examined when deciding on IT location are discussed.

- **Centralized IT** – in the early days of IT it was usual for the function to be centralized and for services to be provided to users from a central location. Over a period of years many aspects of IT became decentralized. Thus, a centralized IT location might come about as a continuation of previous practices or as a firm decision to recentralize what has already been decentralized. In general terms, some of the potential advantages and disadvantages of centralized IT are as shown in Table 16.

Table 16 Centralization of IT: advantages and disadvantages

Advantages	*Disadvantages*
Greater control over the use of IT resources	Lack of appreciation and understanding of the needs of front-line staff
Easier to recruit and retain high-calibre IT staff	Communication costs between the centre and the periphery can be substantial
Improved capability to develop sophisticated support tools	Access to systems may be difficult at certain times
Improved standardization and integration of systems	
Improved IT security	
Facilitates cross-department process re-engineering	
Potential economies of scale	

- **Non-centralized IT** – the term non-centralized IT is used to describe two distinct approaches, neither of which is centralized. These are:
  - **Decentralized IT** – this involves the physical location of IT facilities (for example data centres) being decentralized to multiple locations in the organization, while the management and control of IT resources is still retained centrally. Under this arrangement IT users have only limited authority and control over the use of IT services provided.
  - **Devolved IT** – as well as physical decentralization this involves considerable delegation of authority and control for the use of IT resources to end-users of IT.

  Clearly, this distinction is not precise and ultimately is concerned with the degree of dispersion of authority and control to end-users. In addition, it is possible to maintain a centralized operation while devolving the management and control of IT. However, caution is needed: a scenario of too much decentralization coupled with too little delegation can provide the worst of both worlds since it can lose the benefits of centralization, in terms of cost savings, while failing to gain the advantages of having the IT user intimately involved in decisions about IT provision.

In general terms, the advantages and disadvantages of a non-centralized approach to IT provision are summarised in Table 17.

Table 17 Non-centralized IT: advantages and disadvantages

Advantages	*Disadvantages*
Greater potential to achieve compatibility of IT with the needs of the organization (if delegation takes place)	Potential loss of control over the use of IT resources
Increased ownership of IT among front-line staff (if delegation takes place)	Higher aggregate costs due loss of economies of scale
Lower communication costs between the centre and the periphery	Risk of future systems incompatibilities unless there is an established strategic framework
More effective targeting of IT resources	More difficult to recruit and retain high calibre IT staff
	Reduced capability to develop sophisticated support tools
	Potential loss of IT security
	Difficulty in facilitating cross-department process re-engineering

When considering issues of location it is often assumed that non-centralization of IT is the correct approach in all circumstances and centralization should be avoided. This is not necessarily true, and each case should be argued on its merits since there are often good reasons for continuing with a centralized arrangement or even undertaking some degree of recentralization. In general terms, centralized IT is probably most appropriate where IT resources are relatively very expensive and their use is relatively limited, while devolved IT is most appropriate where IT resources are relatively less expensive and their usage is very high. However, this is very much a simplification and it is vital to examine matters more closely. Some specific factors which indicate a preference for centralization or non-centralization of IT facilities are summarized in Table 18.

INTERNAL IT ARRANGEMENTS

Whatever form the IT function takes, an important issue is the internal arrangements of the IT function. This has changed radically over the last forty years, reflecting changes in technology and the use of IT in the organization. The traditional mode of the 1960s was for there to be a central department, with one section comprising operational staff who actually loaded data and operated the early computers, and another section comprising analysts and programmers responsible for systems development. Times and technology changed and the IT function changed too, as illustrated by the following points:

- data input and output became decentralized and was undertaken directly by users via live terminals
- data input became automated via the use of bar code readers and so on
- there were very large increases in the storage capacity and processing speed of computers
- software became more sophisticated and there was an increasing reliance on packaged software rather than bespoke developments

Table 18 Centralized or non-centralized IT location: key factors

Factor	*Favours centralized IT*	*Favours non-centralized IT*	*Either*
Senior managers utilize executive information systems	√		
Senior managers do *not* utilize executive information systems			√
IT service requirements are largely common across departments	√		
Individual departments have unique IT requirements		√	
Fast and responsive IT services are *critical* to the effective and efficient working of departments		√	
Fast and responsive services are *not critical* to the effective and efficient working of departments			√
The integration of different data sources is a vital factor for the organization	√		
The integration of different data sources is not a vital factor for the organization			√
Individual units within the organization are of small size and would struggle to obtain IT support	√		
Individual units within the organization are of large size and would be able to justify their own IT support		√	
Efficient and low-cost IT provision is paramount	√		
IT is a key component in service delivery activities and thus effective IT provision is paramount		√	

- the PC revolution drastically increased the scope and scale volume of end-user computing
- networks and communications software linked many computers together and permitted communication between them.

The internal arrangement of the IT function also altered radically in response to these and other changes. A number of points can be emphasized:

- the demise of the traditional operations section, since computers virtually ran themselves and data input and output was undertaken by users
- systems development staff became less generic and more focused through being organized in project teams
- given the expansion of end-user computing there was a need for the IT function to provide an advice and consultancy service to users
- the need for effective management of communication networks in the organization
- the increasing need for strategic planning of the IT function.

The key issue for PSOs today is to determine the most appropriate form of IT arrangement in future years given the increasing involvement of IT in service provision. There are two main factors to consider and these are illustrated in Table 19.

Table 19 Options for IT management

Structure	*Management style*
Functional	Mechanistic
Activity	Flexible
Matrix	

- **Structure** – the IT function may be arranged on the basis of IT functions (for example systems analysts, programmers and network specialists) or on the basis of the activities or projects being undertaken within the organization (for example a benefit payments project or council tax project). Also, some form of matrix structure may be appropriate, which comprises the functional and the activity groupings.
- **Management style** – this may be mechanistic in nature, involving detailed control and limited staff discretion, or it may be more flexible, involving less control and greater staff discretion.

For the IT function of the future, each of the above factors may be combined in different combinations. This is not a uniform process nor even a random process since different combinations will suit different IT activities more closely. Some possible examples of this are illustrated in Table 20, but it must be emphasized that this is purely hypothetical and it is for each organization to establish its own arrangements.

Table 20 Options for applying IT arrangements

IT function	*Structure*	*Management style*
Strategy	Activity	Flexible
Systems planning	Matrix	Flexible
Systems development	Matrix	Mechanistic
Systems implementation	Matrix	Mechanistic
End-user advice	Functional	Flexible
Operations	Functional	Mechanistic
Administration	Functional	Mechanistic

This approach does not make for 'clean' arrangements as traditionally found in PSOs, but it must be recognized that the pace of technological development and the increasing importance of IT in the public sector requires an increased degree of fluidity in such arrangements.

APPROPRIATENESS OF THE IT ORGANIZATION

To complete the discussion in this section, some comments need to be made about the appropriateness of the IT organization and the symptoms of a failing situation. The following symptoms *might* be caused, in part or in full, by an inappropriate IT organization:

- **complaints about IT** – the existence of poor relations between the IT function and other staff in the organization and continual complaints about IT services
- **lack of IT awareness** – a general lack of awareness or lack of interest among non-IT staff in the organization's existing systems and the future potential of IT in service provision
- **lack of IT skills** – a serious lack of IT skills throughout the organization
- **IT staff turnover** – a high turnover among staff in the IT department
- **development failures** – a consistent pattern of IT development failures in terms of inappropriate systems developments and/or poor implementations
- **systems redundancies and gaps** – where there is a significant incidence of systems being developed which are of limited use in the organization and/or clear organizational needs for systems which have not been met.

In such circumstances some remedial action regarding IT organization may be needed, although it must be remembered that every situation is unique and whole range of other factors could be at work.

PROCURING IT

It is through the procurement of IT, in its various forms that the IT strategy begins to be put into effect. IT procurement can be undertaken in two main ways, as illustrated in Figure 38.

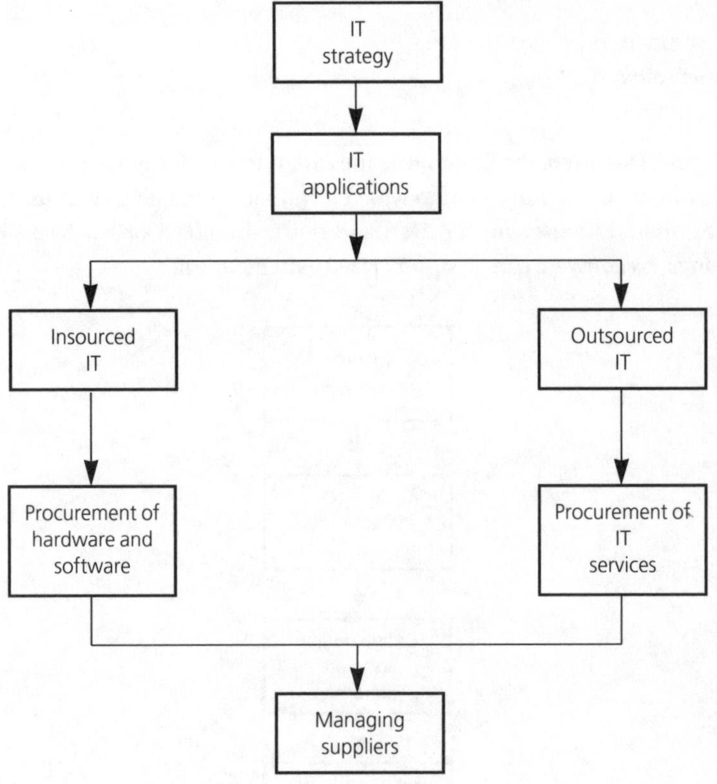

Figure 38 Procuring IT

PROCURING IT SOFTWARE AND HARDWARE

OVERALL APPROACH

Where IT is largely insourced, it is nearly always the case that the procurement process should be software-driven rather than hardware-driven. This overall process is illustrated in Figure 39.

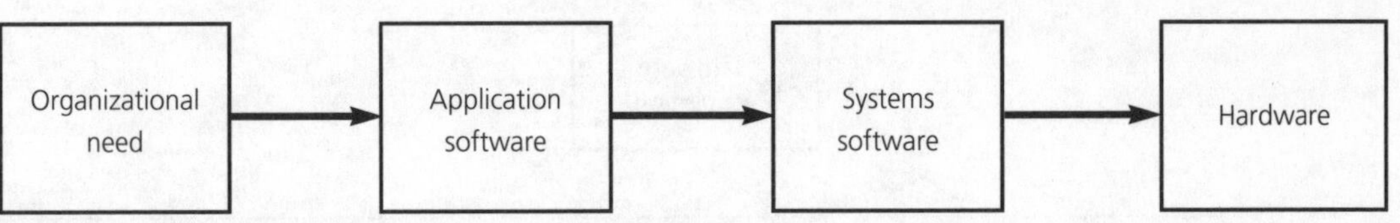

Figure 39 Systems development pathway

SOFTWARE ACQUISITION

The need for new software can take a variety of forms and it does not always imply a completely new development. Quite often all that is needed is some modification or enhancement to the existing software. Basically, software can be developed in three main ways:

- acquisition of standard package software
- tailored package software
- bespoke development.

Whichever approach is adopted, the key issue is the extent to which the software acquired will do the job for which it is intended and the extent to which it will meet the needs of its users. In other words, software planning should be user-need driven and not technology- or hardware-driven. Thus, the process of planning new software can be summarized as in Figure 40.

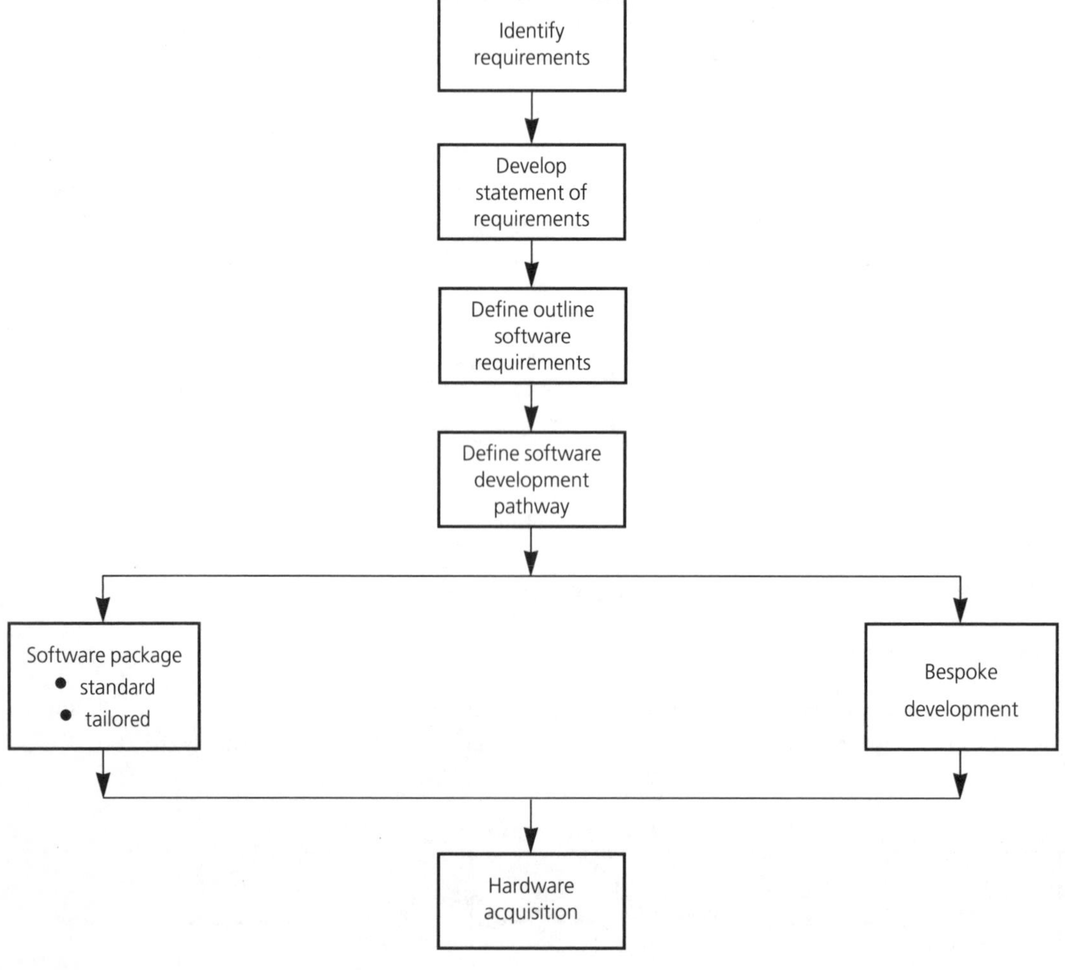

Figure 40 Software development pathway

The elements of the pathway are discussed below:

- **Identify organizational requirements** – this is a key issue. Software design must be driven by the requirements of the organization and its users, and not the views of the IT function. Hence, it is important to devise methods of establishing the requirements from the new software. In saying this, users should not have a completely free hand in deciding what the new software should do. In assessing organizational requirements, consideration has to be given to the strategic objectives of the organization and the organizational processes which are to be supported by the use of IT as a means of achieving those objectives. Various approaches may be employed to assess such requirements, such as questionnaires, interviews and group discussions.
- **Develop a statement of organizational requirements** – this should evolve from the process described immediately above. It should be a non-technical statement of the requirements of the organization, covering such matters as:

  - organizational processes to be supported
  - key functions
  - types of information to be produced
  - frequency of availability
  - timescales for obtaining information
  - ease of access required.

- **Define outline software requirements** – based on the statement of users' requirements a technical definition of the proposed software needs to be developed. This will cover a wide range of matters including:

  - data input methods
  - data output methods
  - data handling processes
  - data storage
  - system response times
  - transaction volumes
  - audit trails.

  At this point it may also be appropriate to attach some degree of priority to the various features to be built into the system. Thus, at its simplest, the various features of the proposed system could be classified as being mandatory or desirable.
- **Decide software development pathway** – at this point in time a decision must be made about how the proposed new software is to be developed from among the various approaches shown above. At this point the decision about which pathway to take may be influenced by a number of factors including the following:

  - Some PSOs may have established IT development sections and may traditionally undertake much of their systems development in-house to make use of available resources.
  - In some PSOs it may be thought that the proposed system is too sensitive to have development work undertaken by an external organization. Hence in-house development is preferred.
  - In other PSOs the in-house IT development sections may be required to compete with external providers to undertake the systems development work.

- **Software package** – in the early years of IT, all software tended to be bespoke developments. Gradually, the idea of the 'off the shelf' software package evolved, for a number of reasons. The purchase of an existing software package usually has the advantage of lower cost, quicker implementation and less chance of problems since it is tried and tested. Against that it has the disadvantages of being, by definition, a compromise solution and the organization may at some future date be forced to undertake an upgrade if the supplier stops supporting an earlier version of the package.

  If after consideration of the options a PSO concludes that the preferred pathway for system development is that of acquiring a basic software package, then an appropriate selection process is needed and this should have the following features:

  - a clear definition of system requirements identifying essential and desirable features
  - a formal and systematic method of evaluating different packages against the requirements
  - the provision of both technical and user input into the selection process
  - site visits to see the packages in operation
  - effective negotiation
  - a clear statement of contractual commitments from the supplier as to matters such as support, training and implementation advice .

  An alternative to purchasing a basic software package is to tailor an existing software package to meet the needs of the organization. This might be thought to be a compromise between a basic package and a bespoke development. The tailoring of the package could be done by the supplier or by an in-house team under license. In either case there will be additional costs of development and delay in implementation. Furthermore, if there are faults in the conversion process this may lead to operational problems at a later date. Nevertheless, this may be an appropriate approach for an organization to take.
- **Bespoke software development** – a bespoke development could be undertaken by an in-house team or by an external software house. In either case a bespoke software development should have the advantage of fully meeting the system requirements and being capable of easy modification. Against that it usually has the disadvantages of higher cost, slower implementation and a greater chance of problems since it is not tried and tested. If the bespoke development is undertaken externally then there needs to be a clear contractual commitment incorporating quality standards and timescales as well as an agreed fee. In addition, there needs to be effective control on the modifications made to the original specification since these can substantially add to the development costs. If the bespoke development is undertaken by an in-house team, then if a customer-client relationship operates in the organization there will need to be a clear contractual commitment between the user and the IT department regarding quality standards and timescales, as well as an agreed fee. Within the IT department, the comments made earlier about runaway systems point to the need for effective project management.

HARDWARE ACQUISITION

Earlier in this section the point was made that systems developments should be software-driven and not hardware-driven. Hence, unless there are good reasons to the contrary the process of hardware acquisition will follow that of software acquisition. In some cases the existing hardware will be adequate to run the new software but in other cases this will not be the case and additional and/or enhanced hardware will be needed. Aside from ensuring that the hardware platforms acquired can effectively support the chosen software, there are two strategic issues to consider:

- **sizing and architecture** – right-sizing is the term given to choosing the most appropriate hardware platform for a given application. It is important when procuring a particular piece of hardware to ensure that it will align with any proposed changes in the organization's overall systems architecture.
- **procurement source channels** – hardware can be purchased from a number of different sources and the choice of procurement channel should take account of not just the immediate purchase but also the longer-term hardware needs of the organization and the potential for obtaining effective procurement and good value for money.

IMPLEMENTATION PLANNING

The other aspect of IT project planning concerns implementation. Clearly, poor implementation of a new development can result in delays in the system becoming operational and in increased costs. One of the keys to a successful implementation is a comprehensive and feasible implementation plan. Such a plan should comprise the following features:

- main tasks to be undertaken
- timescales for completion of tasks
- individual responsibilities for completion of tasks
- monitoring arrangements.

PROCURING IT SERVICES

The procurement of IT services involves three main issues:

- deciding what IT services should be outsourced and what should be retained in-house
- arranging to enter into contractual relationships with an appropriate IT supplier
- managing the supplier relationship.

OUTSOURCING DECISION

It was noted earlier in this chapter that outsourcing decisions are rarely all-or-nothing decisions and a PSO needs to decide what services it wishes to outsource and what are to be retained in-house. A general rule is that an organization should think carefully about outsourcing those IT applications which are seen as strategically important, or where there are overwhelming concerns about data confidentiality. Beyond that, PSOs must consider outsourcing options on their merits. However, as already noted, the pressure for PFI solutions means that PSOs may be forced to adopt IT outsourcing more than may be warranted by its merits.

CONTRACTUAL ARRANGEMENTS

Having decided to outsource a particular IT service the PSO needs to take steps to enter into contractual arrangements for the provision of those services. This can be a complex process with several stages to be followed:

- **Tendering** – in the public sector, the scale of IT provision means that much of the tendering for IT services will be governed by EU procurement rules for public sector purchasing. PSOs must be aware of these rules and must comply with them. Having identified organizational needs and developed a statement of requirements, the PSO will need to place appropriate advertisements requesting details from potential suppliers as to ways in which they might meet those needs and inviting them to tender for the provision of services. Respondents to the advertisements will be provided with details of what is required, and it is suggested that the following should be included:

- introduction (purpose, contact names, dates for submission)
- organizational background of the PSO
- requirements (emphasizing the service outputs and not inputs)
- format of the tender submission
- preliminary contract terms
- tender evaluation criteria.

In the light of the above, potential suppliers of IT services will submit their tenders.

- **Evaluation and choice** – the PSO needs to apply a formal evaluation process against which potential suppliers should be judged. This process will use certain criteria and tenders should be judged against those criteria. Some possible criteria might be:

  - experience of the supplier organization
  - financial stability of the supplier organization
  - extent to which supplier meets the essential features of the service specification
  - extent to which supplier meets the desirable features of the service specification
  - cost.

  At this point the PSO might choose a preferred supplier or may reduce the list of suppliers to a shortlist and then ask for further information before making a decision about a preferred supplier.
- **Negotiation** – the purchaser need not feel bound by the tender details submitted by suppliers, and having identified a preferred supplier the PSO may wish to enter into further negotiations with that supplier. It is important that the PSO has a 'hard-nosed' attitude to such negotiations since it is inevitably the case that the supplier wishes to sell more than the purchaser wishes to buy. Also, the purchaser should apply the well-known tools of effective negotiation, such as only dealing with the supplier representative who has negotiating authority and, if necessary, halting negotiations to allow the suppliers to reconsider their position.
- **Contract** – it is important that at the end of the procurement process an effective contract is formed between supplier and purchaser. Some points for the purchaser to ensure are that:

  - standard supplier contracts are to be avoided
  - legal and commercial advice is taken where appropriate
  - the contract adequately specifies the services to be delivered
  - the contract specifies the penalties for contract failure and the arbitration procedures in the event of a dispute
  - the supplier is required to provide accurate and timely statistics on the delivery of service.

MANAGING THE RELATIONSHIP

Experience suggests that there are two broad ways in which the relationship with an IT service contractor can be managed:

- **Supplier relationship** – where the contractor is seen as a supplier of services then management of the relationship will focus on the monitoring of contract compliance and the application of penalty clauses where necessary.

- **Partner relationship** – where the contractor is seen as more of a partner then management of the relationship will focus on informal communication and flexibility. For this approach to work it is important to have a good degree of cultural fit between the PSO client and the contractor.

In all probability these positions are two extreme ends of a spectrum and the actual position is somewhere in between. However, it is vital to be aware of which situation exists, and which management approach is being applied and why. Application by a PSO of the partner relationship to a contractor only concerned with delivering minimum contract requirements could prove disastrous.

PSOs should always be aware of contractors emphasizing, for marketing reasons, the use of the term 'partnership' while, in reality, not acting as a partner. In many situations it is probably difficult for a PSO to find a private contractor with good cultural fit and so the partnership model of contract management may be difficult to apply.

RISK AND THE MANAGEMENT OF IT SECURITY

All elements of the IT configuration in an organization face various risks of failure and such failure can affect the configuration in three main ways:

- service or application availability
- the integrity of data held
- the confidentiality of data held.

The high level of dependency placed by organizations on IT means that failure of systems, for even a short time, can place the whole organization in jeopardy. For example, it has been estimated that in the commercial world the percentage of organizations able to operate following a loss of their IT capability is as shown in Table 21.

Table 21 Impact of loss of IT capability

Days lapsed after loss of IT capability	*% of organizations able to continue operating*
1	84
3	56
5	28
10	9

Clearly, what the table shows is a very general picture, and the situation will vary substantially from industry to industry. For example, it is probably the case that a financial services organization or a travel agent would lose operational capability in a much shorter period of time than most manufacturing companies.

Many PSOs would also face similar degrees of difficulty when placed in similar circumstances although, again, the situation will vary substantially from sector to sector. Thus, for example, it is probably the case that PSOs such as the Benefits Agency would lose operational capability in a shorter period than, say, a school. Moreover, the increasing reliance likely to be placed by PSOs on the use of IT (see Chapter 10) means that the risks of organizational failure will continue to increase. In these circumstances it should be obvious that adequate approaches to the management of IT risk are essential, and it would be a serious concern if there were PSOs which did not have fully developed approaches for dealing with this issue.

The management of IT risk requires the application of a comprehensive, structured and rigorous risk management methodology and probably the best-known methodology in the public sector is that entitled the CCTA Risk Analysis and Management Methodology (CRAMM) which was developed by the Central Communications and Technology Agency (CCTA). This methodology comprises various checklists, questionnaires and computer software designed to assist PSOs in pursuing a systematic pattern of risk identification, analysis and the development of appropriate counter-measures. Other similar types of methodology are also available but it is beyond the scope of this book to describe them in any detail.

Whatever methodology is adopted, effective risk management of IT comprises four main activities as outlined in Figure 41.

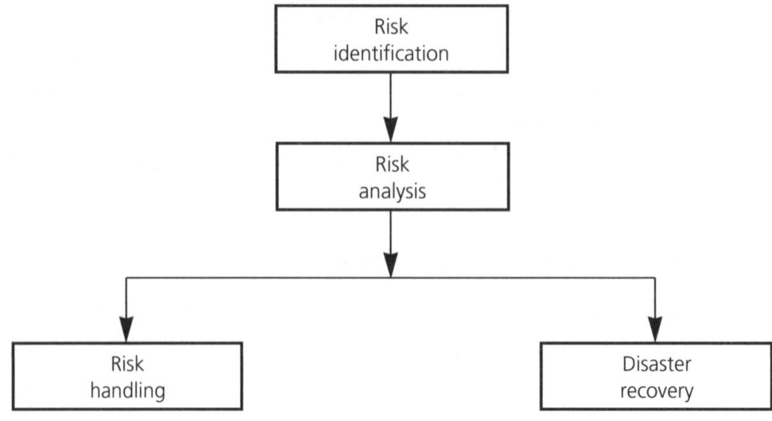

Figure 41 IT risk management process

Although a risk management methodology is an important or even vital tool it must not be allowed to be a substitute for clear thinking about the issue. In the author's experience, one of the problems with risk management (in IT or any other area) is that some managers fail to think through the risk potential of various factors and just assume that there will be no problems. Too often, managers take an overoptimistic view of the situation rather than a realistic view and this can cause problems. Each of these elements of the risk management process will now be discussed below.

RISK IDENTIFICATION

This requires firstly a thorough knowledge of the way in which IT is used within the organization, and secondly a technical understanding of likely areas of vulnerability. The first aspect of this must be done by employees of the organization while the second aspect can be done by employees (providing they are competent to do so) or external consultants. Risk identification needs to bring together two main themes:

- **Potential sources of risk** – risks can come from a variety of different sources and these need to be identified. One approach suggested is to separately identify those threats which create sources of risk for the organization as follows:
  - **Deliberate** – some threats could result from deliberate harmful intent either by employees of the organization or external parties such as hackers.
  - **Non-deliberate** – this includes those threats which derive from non-deliberate actions. This could include real accidents such as power failures or floods, but the author is of the view that in practice, there are few real accidents deriving from natural disasters and most so-called accidents derive from negligence in one form or another (for example failure to service a machine or failure to follow standard operating procedures). Thus, risk identification must incorporate those threats to IT which could result from both natural accidents and potential negligence.

- **IT entities potentially affected** – this must cover the type and geographic location of the various parts of the organization's IT framework which might be affected by any of the threats described above. This could cover:
  - physical items such as hardware and communications infrastructure
  - non-physical items such as operating systems, application software or databases.

These two themes need to be combined, and again it must be emphasized that this process needs to be conducted thoroughly and systematically using appropriate checklists. Figure 42 shows some examples of the various threats which may be identified for each combination of sources of risk and entities affected.

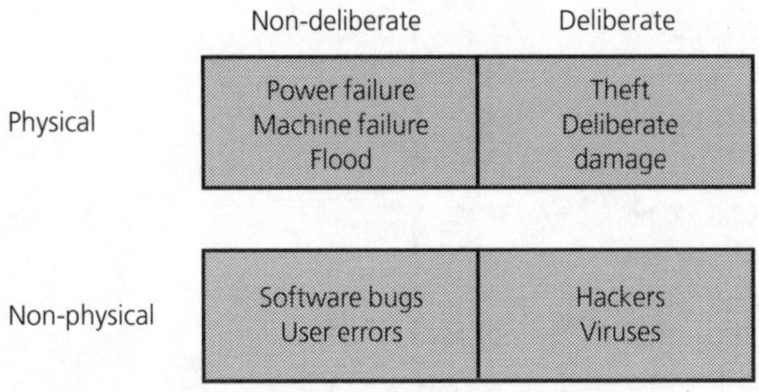

Figure 42 IT risk identification matrix

RISK ANALYSIS

Having identified the possible threats to the IT configuration of the organization, the next stage is to analyse those risks in a systematic and objective manner. There are two main issues to consider:

- **Organizational impacts** – what impacts will a particular IT failure have on the activities and processes of the organization?
- **Implications** – what will be the likely implications of these impacts resulting from the occurrence of an IT failure in the organization? In a commercial organization (or a commercial activity in a PSO) it is sometimes possible to estimate a financial 'bottom line' associated with different threats by the use of expected values derived from application of the following formula:

> **Expected value of loss =**
> probability of threat occurring × potential loss × probability of loss occurring

The results of such an approach are illustrated in the simple example shown overleaf.

This table shows the likely magnitude of each threat, expressed as an expected value of each threat. However, it must be recognized that construction of such a table is easy in theory but may be difficult in practice. For example, there may be some implications of an IT security breach (such as loss of client confidence) which may be difficult to quantify in monetary terms but are nevertheless important.

In PSOs it is probably not possible in most situations to evaluate the impact of the various threats in such a direct quantifiable way, since the nature of service provision means that IT failures do not

Threat	*Probability of threat*	*Potential loss and probability of occurrence*		*Expected value of loss (£000)*	*Expected value of threat (£000)*
1	*2*	*3*	*4*	*5 (= sum (3x4))*	*6 (=2x5)*
Hacking	1%	£3.0 million	5%	980	10
		£2.5 million	10%		
		£1.5 million	12%		
		£1.0 million	20%		
		£0.5 million	40%		
Power failure	20%	£0.4 million	2%	83	16
		£0.3 million	5%		
		£0.2 million	15%		
		£0.1 million	25%		
		£0.05 million	90%		
Virus	5%	£3.0 million	3%	975	49
		£2.0 million	8%		
		£1.5 million	15%		
		£1.0 million	25%		
		£0.5 million	50%		

manifest themselves in terms of a financial loss. For example, how does one quantify, in terms of a financial bottom line, the impact of an IT failure in a health authority, the Benefits Agency or the education department of a local authority? In these situations the losses associated with an IT failure are more likely to involve shortfalls in service provision rather than financial loss. Thus, it is necessary to assess risks in a more qualitative and more subjective manner. This could involve completing the following matrix:-

Threat	*Probability of threat occurring (H,M,L)*	*Probability of threat succeeding occurring (H,M,L)*	*Likely impact on the organization (H,M,L)*	*Overall score*
Hacking	Low	Low	Low	LLL
Power failure	High	High	Low	HHL
Virus	Medium	High	Medium	MHM

In this situation the PSO's managers must make a subjective judgement about the various risks facing its IT configuration. However, any risk assessment, however subjective, is infinitely preferable to no risk assessment.

In both private and public sectors, when considering the potential magnitude of losses it should be recognized that there is both a primary and a secondary loss to consider. Primary losses are the direct result of an IT breach, while secondary losses are a consequence of the primary loss. For a PSO this situation is illustrated in Figure 43.

Following the conduct of the risk analysis stage there are then two other stages that need to be undertaken in a co-ordinated manner. Having identified and analysed the various risks and threats to

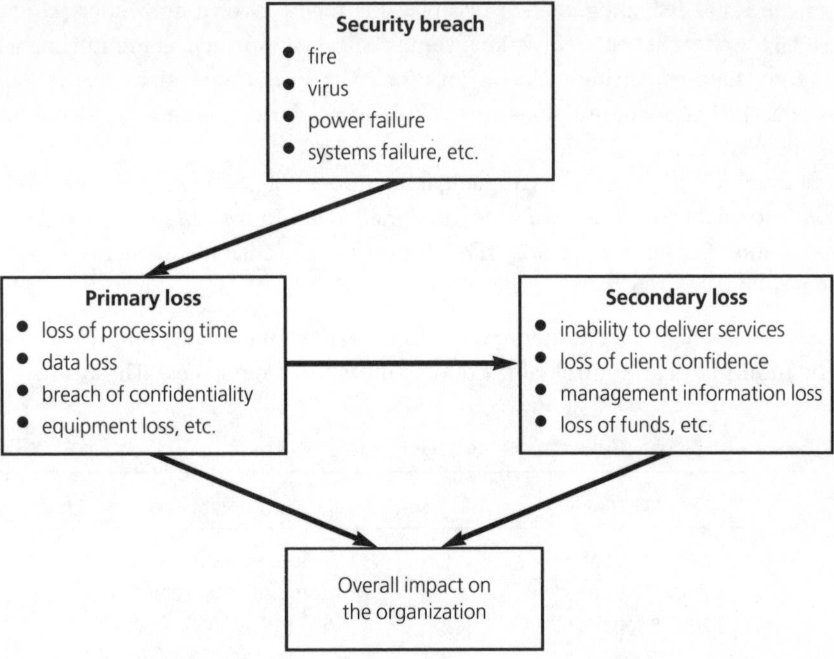

Figure 43 Structure of losses from IT failures

the IT resources of the organization, the next step is to develop and implement an appropriate strategy of counter-measures. Two key things need to be recognized at this point:

- security strategies cost money to implement and hence divert organizational resources from other activities
- there is no perfect set of security measures to defend against threats.

Hence, there will always be some elements of risk which either cannot be mitigated or which it is not appropriate (in cost–benefit terms) to try and mitigate. Therefore, as well as having a strategy of counter-measures the organization will also need a disaster recovery plan in case one of the threats which have (or have not) been identified occurs.

RISK HANDLING

IT is no different from any other aspect of life and risk handling can be broken down into four different approaches:

- **Risk transfer** – with this approach the implications of certain risks are transferred to a third party in return for payment. Examples of this in the IT field include maintenance contracts, standby arrangements and insurance cover. The terms of the agreement will specify the nature of the risk that is being transferred. Any residual risk will have to be dealt with by other means.
- **Risk acceptance** – in certain cases, after analysing a particular IT risk fully, the organization may just decide to 'take its chances' and accept the risk. This might be done where the consequences of the risk are quite small, irrespective of the likelihood of the risk recurring.
- **Risk avoidance** – where a particular IT risk is unacceptably high then the organization may take

action to avoid that risk altogether. If feasible, this might involve not undertaking a particular activity at all, or alternatively undertaking some radical action such as minimizing access to few people or siting hardware in highly secure locations. However, even with radical action there is still some residual risk and so these actions are really concerned with minimizing risk rather than avoiding it completely, and it is to risk minimization that we now turn.

- **Risk minimization** – in practice it is difficult, if not impossible, to avoid risk completely and so the alternative is to undertake courses of action designed to minimize that risk. Risk reduction involves the introduction of counter-measures and controls to minimize the incidence of risks occurring and of consequent losses.

Risk minimization strategies are numerous, and as with risks themselves comprise a combination of physical and non-physical control and counter-measure approaches. These are illustrated in Table 22.

Table 22 IT controls and counter-measures

Non-physical	*Physical*
Anti-virus software	Security controls on IT suite
IT operating standards	Fire prevention and detection devices
Network security controls	Anti-theft devices
Data encryption	Segregation of duties
Passwords – general	Data file back-ups
Passwords – application-specific	

Two points need to be made about the above measures:

- It is pointless introducing such measures if they are then not applied. For example, passwords may be shared among staff or never changed (which inhibits their effectiveness) or anti-virus software may not be applied before opening data files. Hence, in support of these measures clear instructions to staff must be issued and compliance with these instructions monitored.
- The portfolio of measures must be based on the needs of the organization and must consider the costs and benefits involved. For example, the costs of data encryption may not be worthwhile if the data involved is non-sensitive in nature.

DISASTER RECOVERY PLAN

It is inevitable that risk can never be avoided or eliminated completely and hence there is always the possibility of something going wrong. In most cases this will probably not cause too large a problem and the organization can easily take remedial action. However, some untoward events will be very serious and hence the organization will need to have an established disaster recovery plan to deal with such events. Examples of such disasters could include:

- destruction of buildings or equipment through fire, flood or earthquake
- large-scale loss of IT staff (for example a syndicated national lottery win)
- complete loss of data
- major systems or communications failure.

It is important that a written disaster recovery plan is prepared and communicated throughout the organization. Equally, it is important that this plan is not prepared by IT specialists working in isolation but is prepared jointly in collaboration with line managers. The reason for this is that the document must represent a plan for the stabilization and recovery of the organization and its activities (lost as a consequence of an IT failure) and not just a document covering technical IT matters. For example, the plan for a hospital should outline what actions are to be taken with regard to patient admissions in the event of a major failure in the patient administration system. The disaster recovery plan of the organization will need to address two main issues:

- **Containment** – the steps to be taken to ensure safety and minimize damage following discovery of the disaster.
- **Recovery** – the steps to be taken to recover the situation. Three matters need to be covered in this part of the plan:
  - **downtime** – actions to be taken while IT functionality is lost
  - **fallback** – actions to be taken to restore at least some degree of IT functionality to the organization
  - **reinstatement** – actions that need to be taken to reinstate normal capability.

Specific components of an IT recovery plan could include the following items:

- provision for off-site data and software storage
- provision for using standby hardware facilities
- maintenance contracts
- approaches to accessing contract IT staff
- alternative procedures to be applied (for example manual or semi-manual)
- personnel procedures to be applied in the event of an IT disaster
- press and public relations responses.

ASSESSING THE VALUE FOR MONEY OF IT INVESTMENT

Each year public and private sector organizations undertake large amounts of investment in IT, in terms of both capital costs and running costs. Consequently, it is not surprising that organizations and their managers wish to be assured that they are getting value for money (VFM) from that investment. Unfortunately, surveys of managerial opinion in the private sector suggest that many managers in many organizations are not convinced that they are actually getting VFM from that IT investment and in fact are very negative about the benefits of IT investment. Interestingly, however, evidence suggests that IT professionals take a different view and believe that IT investment does give value for money. It seems quite likely that this negative perception among managers also exists in the public sector as well. There are three possible phenomena at work here:

- PSOs are genuinely not getting value for money from IT investment.
- PSOs are getting value for money from IT investment but their managers do not perceive this and do not have the tools to make an assessment of the value for money of IT investment.
- PSOs do have the tools to make a VFM assessment but insufficient time has yet to elapse for the benefits from IT investment to have been obtained. It has been suggested that new IT can take up to three years to achieve a steady-state position and for the planned benefits to be obtained.

This points strongly to a need for all PSOs to undertake some formal approach to the assessment of VFM of IT investment. This is a notoriously difficult area but it is important that some attempt is made, however difficult or imperfect that might be. Furthermore, there are two aspects of this assessment process, the ex-ante and the ex-post:

- **Ex-ante** – implies the assessment of likely value for money from IT investment prior to that investment being made. In other words, it informs the decision about whether to make that investment. This emphasizes the need for a good business case that is clear about the benefits realization of the investment and the organizational development plan.
- **Ex-post** – implies the assessment of actual value for money obtained from IT investment (both in absolute terms and in comparison with the ex-ante assessment) some time after the investment has been made and the systems involved have been up and running. The results of such an appraisal can also inform future decisions about IT investment.

As will be seen later, there are substantial problems in undertaking an ex-post assessment, particularly in relation to the issue of benefits realization. This problem is compounded with the ex-ante assessment because of the need to predict future consequences in terms of both costs and benefits.

In simple terms the assessment of VFM in IT requires the assessment of two main factors:

- costs of IT investment
- benefits of IT investment.

ASSESSING THE COSTS OF IT INVESTMENT

There needs to be a thorough assessment of all costs associated with an IT investment. The following is suggested as being a comprehensive list of IT costs which should be incorporated into any assessment:

- **Hardware costs** – including computers, printers and accessories .
- **Software costs** – the cost of package solutions and/or the cost of in-house developments.
- **Installation costs** – the costs associated with physically installing the equipment. These may or may not have already been included in the hardware and software costs.
- **Security costs** – the costs of any measures undertaken to provide security against deliberate or non-deliberate threats to the physical or non-physical parts of the systems.
- **Running costs** – including power costs, communication costs and subscription costs.
- **Maintenance costs** – including planned maintenance and breakdown maintenance. These costs must include the costs of maintenance contracts plus the cost of any in-house maintenance.
- **Network costs** – with some types of IT investments, networking capability might be required. Thus, where appropriate, the costs of hardware, software and other costs associated with the provision of networks should be included over and above the costs associated with the applications. However, where the networks are already established in the organization then only part of the costs need to be included.
- **Implementation costs** – the cost of implementing and testing the systems prior to live running.
- **Training costs** – the costs of formal and informal training of both IT staff and end-users need to be included. Care is required, since these costs are often underestimated.
- **Other costs** – care needs to be taken to include any other costs not identified above. Some possible examples could include:
  - costs of management time associated with the project
  - legal costs

- insurance costs
- health and safety costs
- non-IT equipment costs (for example furniture)
- change management costs.

One other point which should be considered when assessing the costs of IT investment is that of cost compounding. The reality is that many IT investments generate additional costs which are automatic and become non-discretionary. The classic example of this is the cost of upgrading operating systems software which cannot be avoided because otherwise new application software becomes inoperable.

In relation to an ex-post assessment it should be possible to get reasonably accurate figures for each of the above costs. However, one word of warning is required. In Chapter 5 of this book the section on costing differentiated between full costs and marginal costs. Since the cost information on IT investments will be used to undertake an economic evaluation of those investments, it is important that the costs included are the total costs and not just the marginal costs. Thus, for example, in the case of an in-house software development the marginal costs involved would be close to zero since the various analysts and programmers would be paid in any event, although the total costs would be substantial, in terms of the opportunity cost of staff time.

With the ex-ante assessment, although the categories of cost will be the same some caution is required. Since the assessment is being undertaken in advance of the systems being designed and implemented there is sure to be a considerable degree of uncertainty about the costs involved. This uncertainty will be exacerbated by a number of factors, including the current stage of development of the proposed project and the past experience of the organization in undertaking such projects. Hence, as well as preparing estimated costs as accurately as possible, it is suggested that the following actions also be taken:

- contingency sums are included to cover potential hidden costs
- an independent audit of the cost estimates is undertaken, possibly by internal audit
- the cost estimates are periodically reviewed in the light of more up-to-date information.

ASSESSING THE BENEFITS OF IT INVESTMENT

Whatever the problems of identifying the costs of IT investment, these can pale into insignificance compared to the problems of identifying the benefits. The reality is that although some forms of IT investment may be made with some tangible and measurable benefits in mind (for example staff savings) a much greater proportion of IT investment is undertaken with a large element of intangible benefits in mind.

There are a myriad of reasons why organizations might invest in IT, but it is important to have some sort of classification of these reasons in order to provide a framework for the evaluation of the investment. It is suggested that IT investment in the public sector could be made for the following main reasons:

- **Short-term financial return** – the investment in IT will provide a demonstrable short-term financial gain to the organization. This could be, for example, through the achievement of staff reductions consequent on the new systems being implemented.
- **Strategic match** – the IT investment is made in direct support of the strategic objectives of the organization concerning service provision. For a PSO this could mean such things as better quality services, faster response times or improved resource efficiency.

- **Management information support** – the investment in IT is made to enable an improved range and/or quality of information about critical aspects of the organization. This could involve systems such as budgetary control systems or estates management systems.
- **Improvements in IT architecture** – investment in basic IT architecture to enable new applications to be used.

Much theory has been written about approaches to assessing the benefits of IT investment but unfortunately much of it is impractical or beyond the scope of many PSOs to undertake. Hence what is needed is some practical guidance as to methods of assessing IT benefits. It seems logical that the approach to assessment of the benefits of IT investment should be related to the purpose and objectives of that investment, and this is illustrated in Table 23 and discussed below.

Table 23 Assessing IT benefits

Investment objective →	*Benefits appraisal approach*
Financial return	Financial appraisal
Strategic match	Strategic objectives
Management information support	Information valuation
Improvements in architecture	Cost enhancement

- **Financial appraisal** – this approach requires little explanation and reference should be made to the sections on costing and investment appraisal in Chapter 5. Basically, the benefits being derived from the IT investment (for example staff savings) should be estimated and quantified in financial terms. Using the technique of DCF the benefits generated can be compared with the costs incurred over the life of the project.
- **Strategic objectives** – if IT investment was undertaken for the reason that it supported the strategic objectives of the organization, the benefits should be assessed in relation to its contribution to the achievement of those strategic objectives. Hence, an estimate has to be made of:

  - the extent of achievement of strategic objectives of the organization over a period of time (for example faster response rates to queries, improved consumer satisfaction and improved resource efficiency)
  - the extent to which achievement of these strategic objectives can be attributed to the IT investment undertaken.

  It should be relatively easy to measure the improvements in strategic outcomes and such strategic monitoring should, in any case, be a key component of the strategic planning process of the organization (see Chapter 4). The problem is that since such improvements could be due to any number of factors (for example new staff, training or new procedures) as well as IT, it is difficult to assess the extent to which the improvements can be attributed to IT investment. There is no simple answer to this and a number of possible approaches might be applied such as:

  - undertaking opinion surveys among staff who use the new systems, about the impact they have had on service effectiveness and efficiency
  - undertaking surveys among consumers, who receive services, about their perceptions of the impact of the new systems
  - where there are several divisions or departments providing the same or similar services in different parts of the country, comparative studies could be undertaken of the impact on

strategic outcomes of those divisions or departments using the new systems compared to those who do not.

The outcome of the above exercises would be an assessment in non-monetary terms, of the benefits of the new systems, expressed in terms of the impact on strategic outcomes. These benefits can be compared against the costs of the investment. It will be recalled that in Chapter 5, cost–benefit analysis (CBA) was described as a tool of economic evaluation. CBA could be used to evaluate IT investments, but might require the expression of the IT benefits in monetary terms for comparison against the costs. Such an approach would probably involve spurious accuracy in expressing such strategic benefits in monetary terms, and some form of judgmental evaluation of benefits versus costs is probably preferable.

- **Information valuation** – this form of IT investment is concerned with improving the range and quality of information available to managers and service professionals in the organization. Thus, to undertake an evaluation of the investment some value must be imputed to the new information generated. A number of approaches could be applied:

  – **Usage data** – measurements could be made of the extent to which new information is actually used by service professionals and managers in the organization. Research-based case studies have highlighted examples, in the past, of where new management information has been used very little within organizations.
  – **Staff surveys** – undertaking opinion surveys among staff and managers who use the new systems, about the usefulness of the information being generated compared to any previous systems.
  – **Case studies** – retrospective case studies could be undertaken of particular decisions in the organization and the way in which those decisions were made and the information used. Consideration could then be given to how those decisions might have been made in the absence of the new systems and the possible implications.

  In the same way as described immediately above, the outcome of the above exercises would be an assessment in non-monetary terms of the benefits of the new systems, expressed in terms of the value of the information generated, which can be compared against the costs of the investment. Again, the limitations of traditional CBA suggest that some form of judgemental evaluation of benefits versus costs is probably preferable.

- **Cost enhancement** – by definition this form of IT investment is made without there being any immediate benefit to the organization, but rather on the basis that it will enable future IT applications to be used within the organization. Thus, it is suggested that the costs of this type of investment be treated as an enhancement to the costs of those new applications when they come to be evaluated.

In concluding this section, recognition is given to the difficulties associated with benefits assessments of IT investment. However, it must also be re-emphasized that the existence of these difficulties is not a reason for undertaking no evaluation whatsoever of IT investment. At the end of the day some evaluation, with whatever limitations, is better than no evaluation. It is worth noting that in some parts of the public sector the use of pilot projects in just a few PSOs (for example a few NHS Trusts in the NHS) can give valuable insights into the potential benefits of IT investment prior to making a decision about a comprehensive development for the sector as a whole.

ACHIEVING AN EFFECTIVE AND EFFICIENT IT FUNCTION

In the competitive global market-place it is often argued that the survival of many private business organizations will depend, to a very large extent, on their ability to adapt and make maximum use of existing and emergent technological developments in IT. While these issues of organizational survival are probably not as critical in the public sector, it is the case that maximizing the effectiveness and efficiency of IT resources is important in providing effective and efficient services. Hence, to finish this chapter, some consideration is given to the key factors that all PSO managers should consider as a means of providing for an effective and efficient IT function. The key factors identified are as follows:

STRATEGIC FIT

For many years, in both public and private sectors, one of the major criticisms of the IT function has been the tendency for it to pursue its own agenda separate from that of the organization it supports. This has frequently resulted in the phenomenon of systems which were technologically advanced, but were inappropriate to user needs or were incapable of being used by end-users. Hence it is vitally important to achieve a strong degree of strategic fit between the strategic directions of the organization and that of the IT function. This point has already been emphasized in the sections on IT planning and configuration, and therefore PSO managers must concentrate on putting in place strategic planning systems which facilitate this strategic fit.

EFFECTIVE RELATIONSHIPS WITH LINE MANAGEMENT

Following on from the above, a key factor is the relationships between IT staff and line managers in the organization. Good relationships and a degree of understanding of different perspectives will facilitate good strategic fit as well as good operational working. For this to happen, however, there are two basic requirements:

- Line managers who have a reasonable knowledge of IT activities and the perspectives of IT staff. Too often, line managers treat IT staff as 'boffins' and make no attempt to understand what they actually do.
- IT staff who understand the organization and the nature and complexity of its activities. This is especially true in many PSOs such as hospitals, police stations and universities where the needs of service users are very specific and complex. Without this understanding there is a strong possibility that IT will not maximize its contribution to organizational effectiveness and efficiency.

Clearly, these matters have major implications for training and development in the organization.

APPROPRIATE IT ORGANIZATION

The decision about matters such as location, organization and staffing of IT must take account of the perceived current and future roles for IT in the organization. Given that PSOs in the same sector (for example FE colleges in the FE sector) might be pursuing a similar range of organizational objectives and activities, it might be thought appropriate that they will have broadly similar aspirations for using IT and for IT configuration. However, even in the same sector, PSOs may be very different in terms of size, diversity, objectives, organizational structure and staff skills. Hence, although one might expect some degree of similarity, at the detailed level there is no one IT configuration which will suit all organizations. It is therefore important that each PSO establishes an IT configuration that best meets its needs.

ADEQUATE IT INFRASTRUCTURE

Clearly, infrastructure is a crucial component of IT and an organization will struggle if it does not have an adequate infrastructure of hardware, communications and operating systems. The pace of IT development means that much of the organization's infrastructure can become technologically obsolescent within a few years. While this does not mean the infrastructure of a PSO is no longer operational, it may mean that the PSO is not making use of the best technology available to maximize the effectiveness and efficiency of service provision. As noted earlier, one of the problems in the public sector is the scarce availability of capital resources, and such resources may be needed to acquire the most up-to-date infrastructure. Hence, it is likely to be increasingly the case that PSOs will turn to outsourcing and PFI arrangements to maintain infrastructure capability.

RELEVANT SYSTEMS

An effective and efficient IT function is one which makes available to end-users systems which are relevant to their needs. However, it is frequently the case that this does not always happen because there is:

- inadequate understanding by IT staff of business needs
- failure by end-users to conceptualize and communicate their needs
- poor systems planning
- poor systems design
- poor systems selection procedures
- poor implementation planning
- lack of resources
- inadequate training, and so on.

Although the above points can apply in most organizations, there are some which are endemic to those PSOs who need very specialized systems which require bespoke developments rather than package solutions. Thus, action must be taken to deal with these and other points, to maximize systems utility in an organization.

HIGH PERFORMANCE STANDARDS

This comment applies to all functions within the PSO as well as to the IT function. For IT to contribute to maximizing service effectiveness and efficiency, it is important that it works to high performance standards in a range of areas including:

- timescales for data processing
- user satisfaction
- minimizing system downtimes
- systems development timetables.

It is desirable for PSOs to benchmark their IT performance against other organizations. However, as has been mentioned elsewhere in this book, since IT is largely a generic function utilized in all organizations, the benchmarking should not be restricted to the PSO's own sector. With suitable caveats and in appropriate areas, there is no reason why benchmarking should not be undertaken against other parts of the public sector and the private sector.

SUPPLIER RELATIONSHIPS

In a PSO, there are important differences between purchasing IT and purchasing stationery, uniforms or furniture. Although it is important with all forms of purchasing to take account of the needs of the organization and its users, IT represents such an important, substantial and complex purchase that it must be treated in an appropriate manner. Without being naïve and recognizing that IT suppliers work under commercial pressures, it is important to establish good relationships with those suppliers so that there can be mutual understanding about the needs of the organization and what the supplier is capable of delivering. This may involve changes in the traditional purchasing arrangements in PSOs of competitive tendering for each new purchase, towards one of establishing long-term strategic relationships with a small number of suppliers. However, in saying this it is recognized that for purchases over a certain limit, PSOs are constrained by EU procurement rules.

Clearly, outsourcing and the PFI have further implications for these supplier relationships. In such situations it will be important to develop contractual arrangements whereby the supplier is paid on the basis of outputs (or performance) achieved, in terms of IT service delivery and not on the inputs they provide. Thus, the contract will need to specify the service outputs, the performance standards to be achieved and the link between these factors and supplier remuneration.

IT SKILL-BASE

Last but not least, the organization needs employees who are skilled and competent at maximizing the use of the IT facilities available. This applies to both specialist IT staff and end-user staff in the PSO, covering both administrative staff and service professionals. This is not always going to be easy to achieve since many PSOs will have a significant proportion of staff at all levels in the organization who are technophobes, and who are very resistant to making use of the new technology available. Clearly, adequate training and development in the use of IT is vital but may not be sufficient to overcome the problem. If IT is so important to the future of the organization then more radical measures may be needed including:

- Incorporation of IT competencies into the job specification of new employees. This could apply both to administrative and support staff and to service professionals such as teachers and social workers.
- Undertaking a programme of staff replacement whereby existing employees who are resistant to the use of IT are encouraged to leave, and are replaced by newer employees who are more adaptable.

As an initial and subjective assessment of their organizational effectiveness and efficiency in relation to the IT function, PSO managers may try and complete the questionnaire shown in Table 24 by indicating their degree of agreement with the statements made.

Clearly, the higher the extent of agreement with these statements then the more likely the organization is to have an effective and efficient IT function.

Table 24 Assessing IT effectiveness and efficiency

	Agree strongly	*Agree*	*Disagree*	*Disagree strongly*	*Don't know*
We have clear strategic objectives for the organization					
Our corporate plan indicates how IT will help us achieve those objectives					
Our IT strategic plan indicates how IT will contribute to corporate objectives					
Our IT staff and line managers have good working relationships					
Our IT staff and line managers understand each other's perspectives					
Our current IT configuration meets the current needs of the organization					
Our current IT configuration meets the future needs of the organization					
Investment in our IT infrastructure could improve service efficiency and effectiveness					
We have access to capital funds and we intend to make new IT investment					
Our existing systems fully meet the needs of end-users					
We achieve high performance standards for our IT function					
We have benchmarked our IT performance against a wide range of organizations					
We have good working relationships with our IT suppliers					
Our IT suppliers understand our organization and our specific needs					
Our whole workforce is adequately skilled and competent in the use of IT					
Our T&D plans incorporate IT skills development					
We have comprehensive strategies to improve the IT skills base of staff					

PART III

Public Sector Management in the Future

CHAPTER TEN

Shaping the Public Sector into the Future

In Chapter 3 the historical development of the UK public sector during the twentieth century was discussed, and following that, consideration was given at some length to the various changes that took place during the eighteen years coinciding with the governments of Margaret Thatcher and John Major. Part II of the book then analysed how these policy and structural changes in the public sector had impacted on managerial practice within PSOs.

This part of the book is now concerned with looking forward towards the future. There are some reasons to suggest that the last few years may represent a turning point (or series of turning points) for the UK public sector which may or may not continue into the future. In turn, these changes may impact on the practice of public sector management. Some of these reasons are as follows:

- the election of a Labour government in the UK following eighteen years of Conservative government
- constitutional reform in the UK incorporating regional devolution and the proposed reform of the House of Lords
- the election of ostensibly socialist governments in other parts of Europe following two decades of conservative hegemony
- the continued development of a globally-based economy with a decline in the power of national and even transnational institutions
- the virtual political consensus on approaches to economic management with the emphasis, for better or worse, on privatization and tight control of public expenditure
- the continued integration of Europe, both in terms of width through the membership of a number of East European countries, and in depth through policies such as monetary union and the extension of EU involvement in public policy
- global informational and IT developments.

On the other hand, the various policy statements of the current government may be regarded as largely rhetorical and the substance of government policies, as they affect PSOs, may remain largely unchanged from the previous government. Take, for example, the NHS internal market. The government claims that it has abolished the internal market in health but many independent health policy analysts would suggest that merely a change in the use of words has taken place.

This chapter of the book aims to try and elucidate the sorts of pressures on the public sector which might be expected to impact on PSOs over the next 5–10 years. Chapter 11 will then look at the possible impact of such policies on public sector management practices and the likely skills needed by public sector managers in the future. However, since these changes in policy are still largely speculative, then the likely trends in public sector management practices must also be viewed with caution.

This chapter will consider likely future pressures impacting on the UK public sector in two main categories, as illustrated in Figure 44.

Clearly, this division is somewhat artificial since it is the case that forces external to government

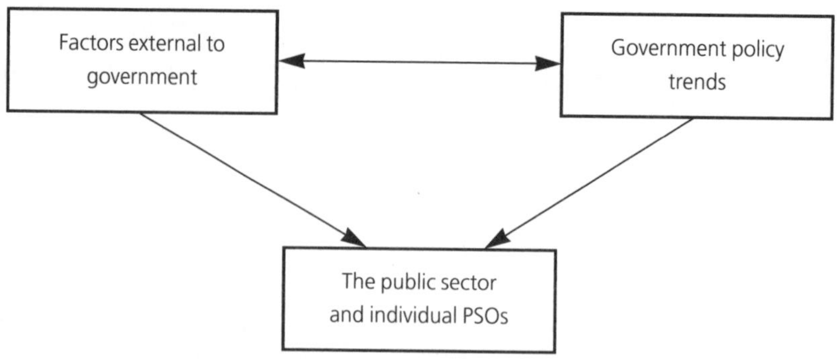

Figure 44 Pressures shaping the public sector

will have a significant impact on domestic government policies. Nevertheless, it is a useful categorization and the interdependencies between the two categories will be highlighted where appropriate.

FACTORS EXTERNAL TO GOVERNMENT

These are the factors outside the province of UK government policy and, largely, beyond its direct control. The following will be discussed under this heading:

- social and demographic trends
- European Monetary Union and Maastricht convergence criteria
- involvement of the European Union in public policy
- global economic trends
- technological developments.

SOCIAL AND DEMOGRAPHIC TRENDS

It is obvious that public services are provided for the benefit of the general public. Some services (for example health services) are provided for all ages and social groups in the population while other services (for example primary education) are provided for a specific part of the population. Thus, one of the key factors which will influence service provision, and hence the organization and practices of PSOs, are the trends that will occur within the population at large. A number of factors are important:

- overall size of the population
- population structure in terms of age, sex and social class
- family size and household structure
- employment levels and types
- population lifestyles, and so on.

An examination of trends forecast to take place over the next 10–20 years suggests the following trends will occur.

ELDERLY IN THE POPULATION

More than 9 million people in the UK are currently aged over 65 – half as many again as in 1961. In the next ten years this figure is expected to rise slowly before beginning to increase sharply, reaching 12 million people by 2021 and peaking at over 15 million in the 2030s.

This trend is accompanied by an anticipated decline, over the next two decades, in the birth rate for the UK, as compared to the European Union as a whole.

As a result of the above factors it is now estimated that the number of people past the state retirement age of 65 will outnumber those below 16 by 2008 – eight years earlier than previously thought. Linked to this there will also be a substantial growth in the numbers of very elderly (over 80) in the population. These trends have major implications for future planning of services such as health and social services, and especially when it comes to planning the future provision of the state pension.

FAMILY SIZE AND STRUCTURE

For many years in the UK, the concept of the nuclear family consisting of two parents and two children was seen as the norm and the ideal model. In recent years, certain trends have, however, contributed towards the demise of this nuclear family:

- the high numbers of children being born to single mothers
- the high levels of divorce leading to family break-up
- the reduction in the numbers of children being born per family
- the reduction in the numbers of extended family units (comprising grandparents, parents and children).

These trends in family size and structure have had significant implications for the public sector, in particular:

- the need for a greater number of housing units of various sizes
- the need for increased nursery education provision to allow single mothers to enter the job market
- implications for school demand.

Looking to the future, it is very difficult to predict future trends in family size and structure. However, there seems little to suggest any likelihood of a reversal of the historical social trends described above and, indeed, these trends may even continue.

EMPLOYMENT

There are a number of trends in employment which are having, and will continue to have, a significant impact on the structure of the workforce:

- Increasing evidence of fixed-term contracts, as well as part-time and casual work, is testimony to the move by employers to much more flexible working arrangements. It is a trend which is producing significant changes in employment patterns with, for example, the number of men working part-time more than doubling over the last fifteen years to around 1.3 million. Over the same period, the number of women (who are still much more likely to work part-time) employed on a part-time basis rose from 4.4 million to 5.4 million.
- The increasing use of flexitime amongst clerical and secretarial occupations, where 10 per cent of employees now use this mode of working.
- A continually increasing use by employers of temporary workers. Recent years have seen a

marked rise in the number of people employed on fixed-term contracts as well as in casual and seasonal occupations. The effect of this shift was first felt by the male workforce in 1990 when the proportion employed on a temporary basis began to rise sharply. In 1997 it stood at 6.6 per cent of the total. For women, this change did not begin until 1993, since when the number employed on a temporary basis has risen to 8.5 per cent. Shift working has also increased over the last few years. In 1992, 12 per cent of UK employees usually worked some form of shift work – by 1998 this had risen to 14 per cent, with the largest increase (11 per cent) being found within sales occupations.

- A large shift away from industrial employment over the last 20 years. Since 1978, the proportion of both sexes working in manufacturing industries has fallen sharply from 35 per cent of men and 22 per cent of women to 26 per cent and 10 per cent respectively.
- Although some occupations are still associated with women, such as clerical and secretarial work, the proportion of women working in traditionally male roles such as administration and management continues to rise. In 1997 almost 33 per cent of employed women worked in professional, associated professional and technical, or managerial and administrative positions, compared with 29 per cent in 1991.

EUROPEAN MONETARY UNION AND MAASTRICHT CONVERGENCE CRITERIA

The policy of monetary union in Europe is well known and does not need to be repeated here. Those countries which joined the EMU after 1 January 1999 were required to meet a series of economic convergence criteria which are as follows:

- **Price stability** – the average rate of price inflation over the previous year is no more than 1.5 per cent above that of, at most, the three best-performing member states.
- **Sustainable government financial position** – there are two criteria relating to this matter:
  - the ratio of the general government annual deficit to GDP is no greater than 3 per cent unless it has declined substantially and continually and comes close to 3 per cent, or the excess is only exceptional and temporary and the ratio remains close to 3 per cent
  - the ratio of the total stock of government debt to GDP is no greater than 60 per cent, unless it is sufficiently diminishing and approaching 60 per cent at a satisfactory rate.
- **Convergence of interest rates** – the average nominal long-term interest rate, over the past year, is no more than 2 per cent above that of, at most, the three best-performing member states.
- **Exchange rate stability** – participation in the exchange rate mechanism of the EMS, respecting the normal margins of fluctuation, for at least two years without devaluation, is required.

Furthermore, to ensure that EMU participants, once qualified, do not run an excessive budget deficit and endanger the price stability of EMU, the Stability Pact was agreed at the Amsterdam Summit in June 1997. Countries will face sanctions, including fines as a non-interest bearing deposit, within ten months if they exceed a deficit of 3 per cent of GDP, unless the country takes immediate corrective action, or unless it faces exceptional circumstances.

Although the timing of UK entry into the EMU is still in doubt, and is a very sensitive political issue, it does seem inevitable the UK will join the EMU at some point in the future. Before this can be done the UK will first have to meet these convergence criteria, and at the time of writing it only meets the criteria relating to long-term interest rates and government debt. Furthermore, once the UK is a participant in the EMU then the constraints of the Stability Pact will apply.

Coupling these constraints on fiscal deficits and government borrowing with the reluctance of modern governments to introduce substantial increases in taxes, then it can be seen that the potential for overall increases in public expenditure will be seriously constrained in years to come. This does not mean that there will be no overall growth in expenditure, but that any growth will be closely controlled and that downward pressure will continue to be exerted on certain areas of public expenditure such as welfare spending.

INVOLVEMENT OF THE EUROPEAN UNION IN PUBLIC POLICY

As a full member of the European Union the UK participates in various aspects of European public policy and is subject to most of the directives issued by the EU. Without wishing to enter into what is a very controversial political area, it is beyond doubt that the involvement of the EU in matters of public policy goes well beyond what was originally envisaged. Take, for example, environment policy. When the Rome Treaty was written in 1956–57, its authors saw no need to provide for a common policy on the environment because they did not perceive any common threat. It was not until October 1972 that a conference of heads of state or government insisted that a common policy was needed, and since then more than 200 items of Union legislation on the environment have been enacted. These are the products of action programmes which the Council of Ministers has been endorsing since 1973. Environment policy was built into the Treaty by the Single European Act of 1987 and its scope was extended by the Treaty on European Union of 1992. This allowed the use of majority voting on environmental legislation, and introduced as a principle of treaty law the concept of sustainable growth which respects the environment. While leaving plenty of scope for national action and allowing member states to take even tougher protection measures than those agreed at Union level, the treaty says that Union policy should contribute to the pursuit of:

- preserving, protecting and improving the quality of the environment
- protecting human health
- ensuring a prudent and rational utilization of natural resources
- promoting measures at the international level to deal with regional or worldwide environmental problems.

This shows the extent to which the EU now influences (some might say controls) environment policy in the EU member countries, but other examples can be quoted from other areas:

- **Education policy** – the EU is active in matters concerning education, training and youth. Although the shape and detail of education policies are defined in the member states and implemented by them, articles 126 and 127 of the Treaty on European Union created a supportive role for the EU. The former allows it to contribute 'to the development of quality education by encouraging co-operation between the Member States and, if necessary, by supporting and supplementing their action'. Article 127 says that the EU will 'implement a vocational training policy which shall support and supplement the action of the Member States'. The main programmes for the period 1995–99 were as follows:
  - **'Leonardo Da Vinci'** focuses on vocational training. It aims to improve the quality of training policy and practice by encouraging new approaches in initial and continuing vocational training policies and practices. Lifelong learning is a central idea of the 'Leonardo Da Vinci' programme which is seeking to establish the concept that training is a continuous, ongoing process for developing the individual and equipping him or her to deal with the rapid changes in the way we

live and work. The programme provides for three types of measures: transnational pilot projects, transitional placement and exchange programmes, and in-depth studies and analyses of vocational training needs and practices. The programme has a total budget of 620 million ECUs for the 1995–99 period.
- **'Socrates'** aims at furthering transnational co-operation in the education field. The programme is a framework for European co-operation not only between schools and higher education systems, but also in such areas as language learning, teacher training, adult education and open and distance learning. In practice it is linked with the 'Leonardo' programme as well as with various equal opportunities programmes and some components of the Fourth Research and Development Framework Programme. Most of the actions sponsored by 'Socrates' are transnational projects or are networks, partnerships or associations. They will develop curricula and teaching materials, encourage student exchanges and mobility, and offer transnational training courses and exchange opportunities for trainers. They may also be information-gathering and analytical exercises, studying the efficacy of education and training initiatives and disseminating conclusions.

- **Transport policy** – though Article 74 of the Treaty of Rome provided for a common transport policy, progress was slow until 1985 when the Court of Justice partially upheld an action brought against the Council of Ministers by the European Parliament. The court ruled that the council had infringed the treaty's rules on the freedom to provide international transport services. The court's ruling, coupled with the Community's commitment to the goal of a single market by the end of 1992, finally established a political momentum which delivered progress across a broad front including:

  - the liberalization of international road transport of goods with full freedom to operate services in other member states
  - the setting of safety standards and speed limits for lorries and coaches and limiting the risks involved in the carriage of dangerous goods
  - the creation of plans for an integrated trans-European transport network.

  In the field of transport policy, the EU's main instruments of policy are fourfold:

  - the use of directives and regulations (which have the force of law) aimed at the harmonization of fiscal, technical and social provisions in member states which affect competition between companies in the transport sector
  - the issue of guidance about the 'missing link', in cross-border projects needed to achieve the trans-European transport network, by joining up national infrastructures for road, rail, air, sea and inland waterway transport
  - major programmes of research and development focusing on applying new digital information technologies to road, rail, air and sea traffic management in order to make travel safer, easier and less environmentally polluting
  - the use of money: around ECU 15 billion has been earmarked for transport projects via the European Regional Development Fund.

- **Competition policy** – there would be little point in a Single European Market if competition between companies from different member states could be limited by cartels and restrictive agreements. These would be bound to deny the consumer the full benefits of healthy, competitive markets, which are generally a wider choice of goods and services available at the lowest possible prices. Competition encourages suppliers to be concerned about quality, innovation and consumers' needs. While member states have their own authorities to enforce national competition laws, it is the Commission which polices the single market to make sure its benefits reach the ordinary citizen. It has very extensive powers to investigate possible breaches of the competition laws and since 1989 has also been authorized to scrutinize and block large-scale mergers. These requirements on competition apply to the public sector as well, and PSOs are not allowed to favour national firms for the supply of goods and services. The EC Directive 92/50/EC of 18 June 1992 relating to the co-ordination of procedures for the award of public service contracts is well known to PSO managers, particularly those involved in public procurement. Further regulation by the EU is likely to be implemented to prevent PSOs finding ways to avoid the competition requirements of this directive.

The purpose of describing the above examples of EU policy is to show that the EU already has a very wide involvement in matters of public policy. It should be noted, however, that EU policy in some areas is 'hard', using directives and regulations, while in other areas it is 'soft', and involves funded projects designed to encourage member states to co-operate on various issues. The future role of the EU in matters of public policy is an extremely sensitive political issue in the UK. However, with the likelihood that the UK will eventually join the EMU and thus remain 'locked into' the EU, its involvement in public policy seems likely to get both broader (in terms of policy area) and deeper (in terms of the extent of EU involvement).

Two examples will illustrate why EU involvement in domestic public policy seems likely to increase. Firstly, in the field of public health the European Parliament has already debated proposals for the harmonization of drink driving laws across the Union and a draft directive has been issued but not yet implemented. Secondly, it seems inevitable the continuing integration of EU economies, and the increasing dependence of those economies on education and training, must mean that the EU will become yet more active in this policy area.

GLOBAL ECONOMIC TRENDS

Trends in the UK economy are bound to impact on the public sector but increasingly the UK economy, along with other economies, is strongly influenced by global trends. It is beyond the scope of this book to discuss, in any detail, trends in global economic policy and it will suffice to outline a few of the factors which now dictate economic policy in the UK and other developed countries:

- free movement of capital between countries
- vulnerability of national currencies to speculation
- substantial inward investment
- low tariff barriers to imports
- outsourcing of much manufacturing capacity to low wage-rate countries.

A feature of such a global market-place is instability. Multinational companies have virtual freedom to move research and manufacturing capacity (particularly manufacturing capacity) to some other part of the world with the consequent impact on unemployment levels in the UK. Such instability seems likely to continue into the future.

As far as the public sector is concerned, one of the key aspects of this global economy is the emphasis that must be placed on education. In countries such as the UK, competitiveness will not be achieved through a low cost base since a developed country such as the UK can never compete with the cost base of developing countries. Hence, the UK must obtain competitiveness through the skills of its working population, and this means an emphasis on improving educational standards.

Certain industries such as, for example, information technology are undergoing a technological shift which involves introducing new products and new production technologies. These new technologies are more expensive than the old technologies and require a higher skill base to operate them. Hence, developed countries such as the UK need to ensure that their educational system is producing the right numbers of skilled people in the right areas to meet the needs of these new technologies. Unfortunately, there are some real concerns that this is not happening, and that many IT companies will relocate to other parts of the world. The challenge is therefore to reshape the educational system to remedy this problem.

TECHNOLOGICAL DEVELOPMENTS

Clearly, scientific and technological developments are one of the most significant factors affecting modern life and there can hardly be a human activity anywhere in the world which has remained untouched by technological developments. As such technological developments are ongoing, then it is reasonable to assume that they will continue to impact on PSOs and their employees in a significant way. Nor should it be thought that technological developments will impact merely on the administrative functions of PSOs, since there will also be substantial impacts on methods of service delivery and the work of service professionals. In a book such as this it is not possible to review the whole gamut of technological developments and their impact on PSOs. Hence a few random examples must suffice:

- **Internet** – the Internet will impact on many aspects of public sector service provision but one example which might be quoted is that of higher education. More and more higher education organizations, worldwide, are using the Net as a means of delivering higher education programmes on a distance learning basis. This will be a clear challenge to traditional attendance-based methods of service delivery, particularly in the light of the abolition of student maintenance grants and the imposition of student fees. The key point for UK higher education institutions to grasp is that, in future years, they may no longer be competing for students with other UK institutions, but could be competing with prestigious institutions worldwide.
- **Robotics** – although the use of robotics has become fairly commonplace in manufacturing industry, there has been little development in the public sector. This might change in years to come. One example which has been discussed is the use of robotic devices to assist surgeons with certain kinds of operation. Studies have shown that for certain specific procedures, robots can undertake the procedure more quickly and more accurately than the human hand.
- **Communications** – modern communication methods (for example mobile phones, electronic mail and hand-held computers) have, to some extent, been limited to use by managers in PSOs. In future, as the cost of these communication methods reduces, they are likely to proliferate within PSOs and become used more and more by service professionals in the delivery of service. For example, electronic mail could be developed in schools to communicate with teachers and health visitors and community nurses could make increased use of mobile phones.

GOVERNMENT POLICIES

Following his defeat in the 1979 general election, the then Prime Minister James Callaghan commented that he thought his defeat reflected a sea change in government policy. Callaghan was very perspicacious. He recognized that UK politics (and the politics of many countries) had, since the end of the Second World War, rested on a broad bipartisan consensus of Keynsian economic management and the development of a caring and comprehensive welfare state. He also foresaw (perhaps not in detail) that the election of a Conservative government led by Margaret Thatcher represented a clear break with the policies of the previous thirty-five years. Clearly, this was the case, and the policies of the new Conservative government represented a break from the past in terms of:

- economic management, where they emphasized the role of monetarism over Keynesianism
- public sector policy where the emphasis was on privatization, competition and performance improvement.

These sorts of policies were to dominate political thought in Britain during the Thatcher and Major era and also were exported abroad, most notably in Eastern Europe and South America but not, interestingly enough, in Western Europe where traditional welfare approaches tended to continue, for example in France and Germany.

On 1 May 1997, a Labour government was elected to power in the UK for the first time in eighteen years. It might have been thought that this would herald a return to the policies that existed prior to 1979. But the Labour Party had substantially changed. No longer was it the party of nationalization, economic protectionism, employee protectionism and so on. Many commentators glibly stated that the policies of the new Labour government were virtually indistinguishable from those of the previous Conservative administrations. Clearly, many of the policies of the current government towards the public sector are identical to those of the previous government. However, it is possible to glimpse changes in policy which might represent a clear break from what took place in the previous twenty years. The difficulty is that at this point in time it is difficult to decide whether these policy changes represent real changes or are just exercises in rhetoric.

In the sections outlined below are some of the policy trends towards the public sector which have been adopted by the current Labour government. These are categorized as follows:

- governmental structures
- taxation policy
- public expenditure planning and control
- public–private partnerships and the role of the PFI
- 'Modernizing Government'
- enhanced collaboration
- partnership and cross-sectoral working
- enhanced performance improvement
- enhancement of service professionals
- public consultation.

GOVERNMENTAL STRUCTURES

Following its election in 1997, the present government embarked on a wide-ranging set of reforms concerning the organization of governmental structures in the UK. At the time of writing, some of the policies have been put into effect but others are still speculative in nature. The main themes of this reform programme are summarized below.

SECOND PARLIAMENTARY CHAMBER

The government has announced its intention to reform the second chamber of Parliament (the House of Lords). At the time of writing the abolition of the voting rights of hereditary peers has taken place but beyond that the government has given no firm indication about the future role of the second chamber and reform of the second chamber could involve any of the following:

- outright abolition of a second chamber
- retention of a second chamber
    - with direct elections to the second chamber
    - some form of nominated membership.

Clearly, the retention of voting rights for hereditary peers is indefensible in a modern state but there are many arguments both for and against the different reform models for a second chamber. Whichever policy is adopted by the government, one outcome seems certain to be greater control of the second chamber by political parties. If some form of directly-elected second chamber is introduced, majority control might rest with the government of the day, in which case legislation is likely to have a smoother passage than with the present arrangements. Alternatively, the second chamber might be controlled by an opposition party, in which case the progress of legislation might be more difficult. Supporters of a second chamber also argue that outright abolition or the introduction of a directly-elected second chamber might mean that the second chamber will not have the level of specialist expertise that it currently claims to have. In this case, they argue, legislation is more likely to contain flaws which may need clarification by the courts.

REGIONAL DEVOLUTION

One of the key policies of government has been devolution to Scotland and Wales. Following earlier referenda in 1999 an elected Scottish Parliament, with tax-raising powers, was formed in Edinburgh and an elected Welsh Assembly formed in Cardiff. There is also an elected regional assembly in Northern Ireland but the specific political problems of Northern Ireland put this Assembly in a different context to Scotland and Wales. Hence the discussion is restricted to regional devolution in Scotland and Wales.

These developments do not represent real constitutional change (since the UK does not have a written constitution) involving the creation of a truly federal system of government as in the USA, Germany or Brazil. Hence the creation of these regional bodies leaves a number of issues unclear:

- **Roles** – the Parliament and Assembly took over the functions of the Secretaries of State for Scotland and Wales, respectively, with regard to the allocation of resources to public expenditure programmes. However, the posts of Secretary of State for Scotland and for Wales still exist within the UK Cabinet and it is difficult to see in the longer term how Cabinet-level posts can be justified in this context. Hence, in the longer term it seems likely that these posts will be downgraded to non-Cabinet ministerial posts and the responsibilities for Wales and Scotland might be combined into a single post.
- **Audit** – within Wales and Scotland there will be separate Audit Offices accountable to the Assembly and Scottish Parliament respectively. However, the NAO will still exist and will be accountable to the Westminster Parliament. Since all of the funds of the Welsh Assembly and most of the funds of the Scottish Parliament will be voted by the Westminster Parliament it seems unlikely that Westminster will be content for the NAO to have no involvement in Welsh and Scottish spending. Hence there could be confusion between the role of the NAO and the two other Audit Offices.
- **Impact on PSOs** – a large number of PSOs, including local authorities, health authorities and NHS Trusts, and QUANGOS, will become directly accountable to the Assembly and Parliament instead

of the Secretary of State as at present. It is not clear what will be the impact on those PSOs and, in particular, whether they will lose any powers to the Assembly and Parliament. However, there are concerns within PSOs that the level of supervision and interference in detailed operational issues will be greater under the Assembly and Parliament arrangements than was traditionally the case.

To some the creation of the Assembly and Parliament represents an end point in regional devolution, after which there will be a period of stability. However, others see an ongoing power struggle between Westminster and the Assembly and Parliament which have received their own democratic mandate. This could be exacerbated should there be different political parties in place in Westminster, Cardiff and Edinburgh.

Another issue of concern is parliamentary representation for Wales and Scotland (known as the West Lothian issue). Responsibility for a large range of domestic policy issues in Scotland and Wales now rests with the Assembly and the Scottish Parliament. It is difficult to see what long-term justification can be given to the involvement of Scottish and Welsh MPs in English matters, while English MPs have no say in Welsh and Scottish matters since these are now the province of the Assembly and the Scottish Parliament. In the longer term some reform of these arrangements seems inevitable.

At the end of the day Scotland, Wales and Northern Ireland combined represent just over 25 per cent of the population of the UK. Hence the vast majority of the population of the UK are not directly involved or affected by elected regional government. Equally, the vast majority of PSOs in the UK (local authorities, health authorities, universities and so on) will not be affected by the introduction of regional devolution since this is basically a Celtic issue. Within England, the government has created a series of regional development agencies (RDA) which have key roles in the economic development and regeneration of the regions of England. These RDAs will have close working relationships with other PSOs such as Regional Government Offices and local authorities. However, these RDAs will still be unelected QUANGOS and will not have the local democratic mandate of the Assembly and Parliament. The government's plans for the introduction of some form of elected regional bodies in English regions seems unclear at the time of writing.

LOCAL GOVERNMENT REFORMS

There are a number of prospective policies in relation to local government. Although, as promised, the requirements for compulsory competitive tendering have been removed, local authorities now face an arguably stricter Best Value process coupled with a tough inspection regime.

In addition, a number of other structural changes loom on the horizon of local government:

- the requirement for directly elected mayors and/or Cabinet models of government
- the threat, and in some cases the actuality, of transferring local education authority responsibilities to the private sector
- the publication of additional indicators of local government performance
- the creation of RDAs which, to some extent, usurp one of the traditional local authority roles.

Overall, the present government's policies seem to imply a considerable degree of dissatisfaction with the performance of local government in the UK, and local government can expect a continuing degree of interference and pressure to improve performance.

OVERALL IMPACT

Thus, overall, it can be seen that a significant number of changes to UK government structures have been initiated in the last few years and there are still more changes to come. However, the key point is that the impact of the changes already implemented has yet to be felt. It could take many years (perhaps even as much as a decade) for the effect of these major changes to show their full effect and it is probably impossible, at the present time, to forecast what those effects might be. However, if one was to speculate on the possible impacts of these changes on public policy and PSOs themselves, the following might be possibilities:

- greater divergences between England and the Celtic nations in public policy and the organization of the public sector
- increased amounts of 'flawed' legislation caused by inadequate examination of bills by a second parliamentary chamber leading to greater involvement by the courts
- increased involvement of the EU in public policy and the organization of the public sector (as described earlier)
- reductions in the powers and functions of local government, particularly in the Celtic nations.

TAXATION POLICY

Whatever the underlying merits, the Maastricht convergence criteria referred to earlier inhibit the opportunity for the government to increase overall public spending by increased borrowing. Thus, an alternative approach to financing increased public expenditure would be to increase tax revenues. A consideration of the likely tax policies of the government might be illuminating.

At the 1997 general election one of the most controversial issues was taxation and the impact of the previous government's taxation policies. Prior to the election, the Institute for Fiscal Studies published a comprehensive report on the impact of government policies between 1992 and 1997. This was a complex report but probably three of its conclusions should be highlighted:

- The report listed nineteen tax and benefit changes which took place between 1992 and 1997. It concluded that the effects of these changes was an average loss of 2.6 per cent of income, although the percentage loss varied between income groups.
- Notional rates of income tax had been reduced over the period.
- The period 1992–97, and earlier periods of Conservative government, saw substantial increases in gross earnings and net income after tax. However, these increases varied between different classes of taxpayers. Also, these increases in net income could be attributed to increases in earnings rather than reductions in tax or increases in benefits.

Thus, in simple terms, the conclusion could be drawn that people were broadly better off in income terms during the period of office of the last government but that the average tax burden had increased. The conundrum is that whereas the effects of tax and benefit changes can be directly attributable to the government, economic performance and growth in earnings can be attributable to a variety of causes, some within and some outwith government control.

Taxation policy is complicated and involves a lot of detailed changes. However, consideration of the tax polices of the present government, based on two years in office, suggests the following points should be noticed:

- there have been tax increases in certain selected areas either through the introduction of new taxes (for example pension funds) or real-terms increases in the levels of tax (for example road fuel duty)
- there have been tax reductions in selected areas (for example VAT on fuel)

- there is strong reluctance to increase basic rates of income tax and there have been some reductions in basic rates of tax on some income bands
- the overall tax burden has increased by an amount *equivalent* to an increase of 4.2 pence in the basic rate of income tax.

The overall conclusion that must be drawn about public expenditure and tax policy is that the future scope for increasing the overall level of public spending will be limited by the Maastricht criteria and the wish of governments to avoid raising the basic rates of direct taxation. Thus any real-terms increases in public spending will be largely dependent on the economic performance of the country and the growth in GDP, and the government's ability to raise taxes by 'back-door' means.

PUBLIC EXPENDITURE PLANNING AND CONTROL

The present government has initiated a series of changes in the planning and control of public expenditure which have long-term implications. Following its election in May 1997 the government announced its intention to undertake a comprehensive review of public spending. This Comprehensive Spending Review (CSR) took just over a year to complete and its main policy themes are discussed below. However, it should be noted that the government's policy is now for a CSR to be undertaken every three years and this arrangement will replace the traditional annual public spending review. There are a number of important aspects to this change which have significant implications for the future planning of public expenditure, and thus for the public sector itself:

- Once a CSR is completed, government spending departments will be tied to spending levels for a three-year period until the time of the next CSR. Hence, those departments will no longer be able to make annual bids for additional funding as they have traditionally done. This alters the whole culture of public expenditure planning.
- HM Treasury, which is the government department responsible for the planning and control of public expenditure, has itself gone through a series of reforms. For example, it has lost responsibility for interest rate management (to the Bank of England) and for government debt management (to the Debt Management Office). Freed of these responsibilities the Treasury is likely to be more proactive in its attitude towards public policy and public expenditure and will more strongly challenge bids for additional public spending from government departments. This is likely to be reinforced by the three-year gap between CSRs, thus giving more time for new spending plans to be developed and evaluated.
- A key issue in the CSR is the concept of public service agreements (PSA). These require government departments to sign such agreements with the Treasury in return for their allocation of funds. Each PSA contains a variety of targets and objectives which departments are required to meet. Undoubtedly, PSAs will evolve over time and will become more sophisticated and probably more detailed. Again, this will alter the whole culture of public expenditure planning.

The expenditure plans contained in the first CSR were based on a number of conditioning factors and it seems reasonable to assume that later CSRs will also be based on these factors:

- **prudence** – the expenditure plans were to be prudent and in line with the government's two strict fiscal rules:
  - **the golden rule** – over the economic cycle, the government will borrow only to invest and not to fund current spending

- **the sustainable investment rule** – public debt as a proportion of national income will be held constant over the economic cycle at a stable and prudent level.

The above two rules need to be viewed in the context of the Maastricht convergence criteria and government taxation policies discussed above.

- **stability** – as already noted, three-year plans have been set with firm departmental expenditure limits, enabling departments to prioritize resources and plan ahead
- **capital investment** – separate capital and current budgets to help ensure that worthwhile capital investment is not squeezed out
- **public–private mix** – flexible choice between public or private investment to be determined by what works best.

The first CSR identified four main policy themes for public expenditure and these are summarized below:

- **Investing for sustainable growth and employment** – The public expenditure plans derived from the CSR were to support the government's economic policy objectives relating to economic growth and macro-economic stability. Some examples of this policy were:

  - education and training reforms aimed at improving the quality, flexibility and employability of the workforce
  - a new integrated transport strategy, new integrated transport schemes in towns and cities, and improvements to the condition of key national roads, to ease congestion and reduce delays
  - investment in science to modernize the UK's capability.

  As will be discussed later, the CSR had ambitious plans for increasing public expenditure in certain areas. Since the forecast rates of growth will be linked to UK economic performance they will, to some extent, be linked to success in this area. However, it does seem likely that overall global economic trends will be a more influential factor in this than domestic economic policy.
- **Investing in reform for fairness and opportunity** – The spending plans developed as a result of the CSR aimed to promote fairness and opportunity by ensuring universal access to high-quality public services and providing targeted help to tackle poverty and social exclusion. Some examples of these policies included:

  - additional investment in health services with the aim of reducing health inequalities
  - a new criminal justice strategy coupled with investment in tackling the underlying causes of crime through an evidence-based crime reduction strategy
  - investment in opportunities for the youngest children, particularly the disadvantaged, to ensure they are ready to learn as soon as they get to school
  - additional housing investment in council-owned homes and the creation of a Housing Inspectorate, to modernize and improve council housing management
  - investment in the New Deal for Communities to tackle the problems of the most deprived neighbourhoods and a refocused Single Regeneration Budget.

  If these objectives are to be achieved it does seem to be essential that public funds are more closely targeted to particular activities and outcomes than has been the case in the past. Coupling this with the PSAs referred to above, it seems that the overall level of discretion for PSOs to determine the use of funds may be reduced substantially.

- **Investment in priority services** – The government's public expenditure plans incorporated in the CSR anticipated substantial increases in the resources devoted to its two priority services – health and education. The plans incorporated the following resource forecasts:

  - **education** – an average real increase of 5.1 per cent per annum between 1998/99 and 2001/02
  - **health** – an average real increase of 4.7 per cent per annum between 1998/99 and 2001/02.

  It should be noted that these forecast increases in resources are in real terms, in other words over and above the rate of inflation. By comparison, other public expenditure programmes are forecast to increase by an average of 1.8 per cent per annum in real terms, although within that figure there will be variations between different programmes.

  Although there may be some scepticism about the full achievement of these rates of growth, since they must surely be dependent on the overall performance of the UK economy over the next few years, it does seem certain that education and health will have relatively greater levels of growth than other public expenditure programmes.
- **Investing in reform for efficient public services** – The investment in public services in the new spending plans is matched by reforms to make public services more efficient and effective. Some examples of developments quoted in the CSR documents are:

  - cross-departmental budgets aimed at delivering the government's overarching objectives: targeted support for pre-school children and their families, and those living in the most deprived neighbourhoods
  - the development of new quality standards for all government departments: for example, new departmental investment strategies to ensure that the best possible return is obtained on each pound invested in capital projects
  - better procurement of goods and services to secure cost savings: for example, savings in defence procurement and support services will release money to invest in front-line forces.

  Clearly, it is the intention of the government that there be a continuation of the drive for performance improvement initiated by the last government. However, in future, government departments will have to provide greater justification for funds than they have done in the past and new funding will be conditional on achievement of objectives and performance improvement.

PUBLIC–PRIVATE PARTNERSHIPS AND THE ROLE OF THE PFI

As already discussed in Chapter 3, the PFI was first created in 1994 and developed into a key plank of the previous government's financial policy towards the public sector. Thus by the time the Labour government took office in 1997, the PFI was well established as a means of funding capital developments in the public sector, even though few PFI contracts had been signed at that date. In spite of assurances given it was not certain at the time of the last general election what would be the incoming government's attitude towards the PFI. The first two years of the new government's tenure have shown that it has embraced the PFI philosophy wholeheartedly and has even extended the scope of public–private partnerships into other areas.

Soon after the 1997 election the Paymaster General appointed Malcolm Bates, Chairman of the Pearl Group and of Premier Farnell, to conduct a speedy review of the PFI process. The Bates report made a number of recommendations to improve the PFI process which were largely implemented by the government. The importance of the PFI to the present government's public finance strategy is illustrated by the fact that:

- during the first two years of the government's tenure, 140 deals worth £4.7 billion were signed by the government
- it is forecast that during the three years of the current Comprehensive Spending Review 30 per cent of net publicly sponsored or financed investment (equating to £11 billion) will be undertaken through the PFI mechanism.

Nor is the government's enthusiasm restricted to the PFI. Indeed, PFI is seen as but one type of public–private partnership (PPP) and the term 'wider markets PPPs' is used to describe any other form of private–public sector partnership such as that involving the use by the private sector of underutilized public sector assets. In March 1999, Sir Malcolm Bates produced, at the behest of the government, a second report on the PFI which made a series of recommendations for developing the role of PPPs/PFI. Most of the recommendations of this report were accepted by the government but perhaps the key development is the proposed creation of a new private–public sector-led organization entitled Partnerships UK. Although this organization will not be a full bank (as recommended by Bates) which might fund PFI deals, it will have a pivotal role in facilitating the development of the PFI. Thus, it will be able to provide pump-priming funds to get PFI projects off the ground and will provide a range of advice and services to PSOs who wish to enter into public–private partnerships, including PFI.

There are a number of serious financial and economic objections to the PFI approach. As outlined in Chapter 5, for any PFI project to go ahead it is necessary to show that a privately-financed version of the project is superior to a publicly-financed version according to two main criteria, as well as being affordable to the organization involved. The two criteria for judging PFI deals are:

- **value for money** – the PFI approach should give better value for money in the use of public funds than a publicly-financed approach
- **risk transfer** – the PFI approach should enable a substantial proportion of project risk to be transferred to the private sector.

It is difficult to see how PFI projects can really give better value for money than a publicly-financed project, given that the price charged by a private contractor probably has to incorporate a rate of return of say 15–20 per cent which is something a PSO does not have to do. Indeed some concerns have been expressed by the National Audit Office and others about the (lack of) value-for-money aspects of those PFI projects which have already been undertaken.

Nevertheless, in spite of these concerns about the PFI, the extension of the policy is now such a political priority that it seems they will be ignored. The size of planned PFI deals over the next three years, coupled with the creation of an organization whose only role is to promote private–public partnerships, means that this is certain to be a key plank of government policy into the foreseeable future. Indeed, it is possible that the PFI will be extended to other areas not presently covered. In most cases PFI schemes exclude the provision of what are termed core services. Core services could mean:

- teaching in a schools PFI scheme
- medical and nursing services in a hospital PFI scheme
- many policing duties in a police PFI scheme
- fire-fighting in a fire service PFI scheme.

Since it could be argued that these are the services most constrained by professional restrictive practices, then they are the areas most likely to generate the new efficiency savings needed by the public sector. Whether these efficiency savings will result in lower costs to the public sector or will contribute to higher profits for the private sector is a debatable point, but it does seem possible that the extension of the PFI into the area of core services might be a significant future policy development. Furthermore, once there is a strong involvement of the private sector in the provision of these cores services (via the PFI) then it seems but a short step to the full privatization of service provision in these areas, although the funding of these services would continue to be publicly provided.

'MODERNIZING GOVERNMENT'

Modernization has been something of a mantra of the present government, which has been applied to many areas of activity. The process of government itself has proved no exception to this and in March 1999 the government published a White Paper entitled 'Modernizing Government'. This White Paper sets out a long-term programme of improvement in the process of government in this country and has five main themes as shown in Table 25.

Table 25 'Modernizing Government': key commitments

Area of commitment	*Intention*
Policy formulation	Government policy making should be made: • more strategic in nature and less open to short-term pressures • more co-ordinated or 'joined-up' in nature and less oriented towards individual departments or programme areas.
Responsive public services	Public services should be made more responsive to consumers by delivering: • the services people actually need • at a convenient time and location.
Quality public services	With regard to service provision, government should aim: • to deliver efficient and high quality public services • to avoid settling for mediocrity.
Information-age government	The use of new technology is a major theme of the White Paper. In delivering public services government should aim: • to make the best use of modern technology developments • to avoid being left behind by technological developments.
Value public services	Public services should be: • valued and supported • not denigrated.

Clearly with such a long-term programme of development it is inevitable that much of the detailed aspects of the programme will be developed and implemented over a period of years. Some specific changes have already been implemented, and the White Paper really just restates these, while other specific developments have been proposed for implementation in the near future. An analysis of the various changes, actual and proposed, suggests the following key themes:

- **Structural changes** – various structural changes have taken place, or are due to take place, as a means of promoting the achievement of the above commitments. Some examples of these are:
  - the creation of a Social Exclusion Unit and a Performance Improvement Unit based in the Prime Minister's Office as a means of promoting joined-up government and improved public services

- the creation of a public sector employment forum to bring together and develop key players in the public sector.

- **Training and Development** – several proposals have been made to improve the process of policy making and service delivery. These include:
  - the creation of a Centre for Management and Policy Studies
  - joint training for ministers and civil servants
  - recruiting and promoting staff from other sectors into key government posts as a means of introducing fresh thinking and methods of working.
- **IT development** – clearly the development and extension of IT in the delivery of public services is one of the key themes in 'Modernizing Government'. Some specific aspects of this are:
  - the publication of targets for the proportion of dealings with government that can be undertaken by citizens through electronic means (TV, computer and so on). The targets were for 50 per cent of dealings to be capable of being undertaken electronically by 2005 and 100 per cent by 2008
  - the development of a government IT strategy which will facilitate inter-departmental working, that is, joined-up government
  - the appointment of an information age champion in each government department.
- **Accountabilities** – a number of initiatives have been or are being implemented to improve the accountability for the delivery of public services. Two examples of this are:
  - the creation of PSAs with government departments as referred to above
  - getting Permanent Secretaries in government departments to accept personal accountability for the achievement of development targets.
- **Procedures** – there are a whole raft of developments which can be categorized as being procedurally based. These include:
  - undertake peer review of department policy-making procedures
  - the use of the Best Value approach to improve central and local government services
  - mechanisms to assess the regulatory burden likely to be imposed by any new government policy.

The five commitments outlined earlier seem eminently sensible, and few people would argue with what is being proposed. However, there is bound to be some scepticism about the extent to which the White Paper is an exercise in rhetoric rather than in promoting real improvements in government. Specific concerns include the following:

- Will there be greater flexibility at the local level in the use of public funds?
- Will front-line staff really be given freedom to make decisions about service delivery? This goes against the past trends in increased central control described earlier.
- Will it be possible to break down the existing culture of government departments and the boundaries that exist between them?
- Will adequate additional funds be available for development purposes? A mantra of the Thatcher era was that one didn't solve problems by throwing money at them. Perhaps a new mantra should be that some problems can only be solved by throwing money at them?
- Will ministers really be able to resist reacting to short-term political pressures where these go against the longer-term strategy?

- Will the principles and practices of 'Modernizing Government' be applied to the same extent to local government as well as central government?

Only time will tell what the 'Modernizing Government' policy actually achieves, but it is clear that the various proposals and related activities are bound to have a significant impact on a wide range of public sector activities for many years to come.

EMPHASIS ON COLLABORATION

The earlier chapters of this book described in some detail the development, over the last twenty years, of policies which required PSOs to market test certain of their activities. Some examples of such competition-based approaches in the public sector were:

- **Local government** – the requirement, under the Local Government Act 1988, for local authorities to expose certain defined services (for example street cleaning, refuse collection and school meals) to competition from private contractors and other public sector organizations. Later legislation also required local authorities to expose certain 'white-collar' services such as computing, personnel management and financial management to competition from other private or public organizations.
- **National Health Service** – although the NHS did not have the sort of strict legal framework for market testing that existed in local government there was still some element of competition. The purchasers of health services (health authorities) may, in certain circumstances, have required the providers (NHS Trusts) to compete with other NHS Trusts and voluntary and private sector organizations for the contract to provide certain defined services. However, the amount of competition in the NHS market tended to vary from service to service and from geographic area to area. This was for the simple reason that for certain services and in certain areas there may have been little in the way of competitors to the local NHS Trust. In theory, health authorities could have sought bids for patient services from NHS Trusts outside the locality but, in practice, it was rare for this to happen since patients are resistant to travel. Thus, in practice there was a fair degree of market testing and competition for services within Central London where there was a proliferation of providers, but little competition in rural areas.
- **Further education and higher education institutions** – the funding levels of an FE institution is largely determined by numbers of students recruited and retained, predominantly in the local catchment area. In an HE institution funding levels are driven by student numbers recruited from both the local catchment area and nationally, and by the research profile of the institution. Given that the numbers of students are finite, then both FE and HE institutions are effectively competing with one another to recruit students and thus maximize funding levels. Given the nature of the service being provided, the following situation arises:
  - An FE institution competes against other FE and HE institutions, in the same catchment area, for a limited pool of local students who are looking for further education.
  - An HE institution competes against other HE institutions in the country for the limited pool of students who are seeking full-time higher education. An HE institution may also compete against local FE institutions for students who are seeking part-time further education, since many FE institutions also provide higher education services on a franchised basis.

Thus, both FE and HE institutions are competing strongly against each other and must consider what actions they must take to secure a competitive advantage. This could include matters such as teaching standards, student marketing, leisure facilities, student housing and student administrative processes.

- **Central government and executive agencies** – in a similar manner to local authorities, central government departments and executive agencies have also been required to market test certain services.

Clearly, during the 1980s and 1990s, market testing and competition was seen as a key means of achieving greater efficiency in the use of public funds. There are a number of examples of ways in which this policy succeeded. In local government and central government, even if the contract for service provision was retained by the in-house unit, as was frequently the case, the pressure of competition usually meant that the in-house unit had substantially reduced its cost base. In further education, competition partially resulted in reductions in the average level of funding in the FE sector.

However, there were some substantial drawbacks to this policy of competition. Consider the following:

- **Marketing costs** – because of the competitive environment in which they had to operate, many PSOs spent substantial amounts of funds on market research and marketing to sustain their position. Such funds must, by definition, be regarded as funds which had been abstracted from the direct provision of services.
- **Managerial time** – similar to the above, large amounts of managerial time in the organization had to be devoted to fending off the competition rather than trying to run effective and efficient services.
- **Duplicate provision** – the process of competition meant that PSOs had to compete with one another. Often this meant that both PSOs would try to provide an identical service in competition with each other. Sometimes this implied duplication of service provision, underutilization of resources and inefficient use of resources.

The above comments need to be viewed in the context of the market in which most PSOs operate. This market is unlike most commercial markets, where there is the potential for increasing the size of the overall market and any one commercial organization could obtain additional sales of its product without necessarily damaging the sales of a competitor. Most PSOs operate in a quasi-market where the total market size and the funding available is fixed. Take, for example, the NHS internal market. The overall size of the market is effectively constrained by the overall public funding made available to the NHS in any one year. Thus, the only way that one PSO can gain an advantage is at the expense of another PSO. This is in effect a zero-sum game.

It is now clearly the case that a major policy theme of the present government, both now and in the future, is the encouragement of greater collaboration between PSOs and less reliance on competition. Three examples of this policy can be described:

- **Further education** – in the FE sector, the government has given two clear signals. It wishes to see:
  - a reduction in the number of FE colleges through merger of colleges within the same locality
  - greater collaboration between colleges which would fall short of full merger: this could be achieved through actions such as rationalization of course provision and the sharing of services.
- **NHS** – government policy is also to reduce, through merger, the number of NHS Trusts in the country and to promote greater collaboration between those Trusts. It is possible that the total number of Trusts could ultimately be reduced by 30–40 per cent.

- **Schools** – in the schools sector the message is for schools to compete less and to work more closely together. Individual schools are encouraged to take the lead role in the area, in certain aspects of the curriculum such as science, sport and languages.

A number of clear advantages can be identified as arising from enhanced collaboration and/or full merger. In summary these are:

- reduced administrative costs (for example finance, personnel or supplies)
- avoidance of wasted resources on competitive marketing
- avoidance of duplicate provision of services
- potential for rationalization of buildings
- the generation of synergies in service provision: the larger size and enhanced skill base of the merged or collaborative organization often means that additional services can be provided which could not have been provided separately
- protection of services which might have been 'at risk' in the individual organizations.

The increased emphasis on collaboration does not, of course, preclude the use by PSOs of market testing and outsourcing of certain services and activities. Nevertheless, enhanced collaboration between PSOs in the same sector would seem to be a clear policy theme for the foreseeable future.

PARTNERSHIP AND CROSS-SECTORAL WORKING

One of the criticisms of public policy over the years is that it fails to take account of the interdependency between different programmes. Thus, for example, there is a strong interdependence between housing and health, and between education and employment, and these factors have not been adequately recognized in government policy.

The current government has placed great emphasis on partnership and cross-sectoral working as a means of achieving its policy objectives, and the term 'joined-up government' has become something of a buzzword for this approach. A number of examples can be quoted:

- **Health Action Zones (HAZ)** – the concept of Health Action Zones was announced by the Secretary of State for Health in June 1997. They were to be located in areas of high social deprivation and their aim was to overcome barriers between health and local authorities, and between professions in the delivery of services. Forty-one bids for HAZ status were received by the Department of Health from health authorities across the country, and eleven have been selected as pilot HAZs. They commenced operation in April 1998, and will aim to bring together all those in a health authority area or wider, to improve the health of local people. The accent will be on partnership and innovation, finding new ways to tackle health problems and reshape local services. HAZs will aim to remove bureaucratic barriers between primary and secondary health services and local authority services that inhibit the delivery of high-quality services. An early task for each HAZ will be to develop clear targets, agreed with the NHS Executive, for measurable improvements every year.
- **Education Action Zones (EAZ)** – the School Standards and Framework Act provided for the establishment of Education Action Zones consisting of clusters of schools working in a new partnership to raise standards. EAZs will be made up of clusters of schools – usually a mix of not more than twenty primary, secondary and special schools – working in partnership with the local education authority (LEA), local parents, private businesses, TECs and others to encourage innovative approaches to tackling disadvantage. In some cases these partnerships will build on local networks already in place. They may link to health or employment zones and to SRB-funded projects. The

zones are to be established in areas of educational underperfomance – urban and rural – where it is clear that existing systems need to be strengthened by focused and targeted support. However, each EAZ will have different objectives, some concentrating on examination attainment while others will concentrate on the numbers of students going on to FE or HE. Within an EAZ there will be flexibility with regard to teachers' pay and conditions and relaxation of the National Curriculum requirements. Different zones will be run in different ways, with various types of organization taking the lead; but there will always be a range of partners involved. If the LEA takes the lead role in proposing a zone, there should still be a central role for business and for community and voluntary organizations. Government policy is for at least twenty-five EAZs to be set up during this Parliament.

- **Cross-departmental units** – the government has created a number of specialist units which have a cross-departmental remit and have the objective of encouraging better co-ordination between government departments in relation to particular areas of social policy. One such example is the Social Exclusion Unit which has the overall aim of improving policy in relation to the so-called socially excluded members of society.
- **Cross-departmental budgets** – as already noted above, one of the main features of the Comprehensive Spending Review was the creation of cross-departmental budgets aimed at delivering the government's overarching objectives of targeted support for pre-school children and their families, and for those living in the most deprived neighbourhoods.

It is quite clear that this aim of improving the delivery of public services through partnership and cross-sectoral working will be a major theme of government policy for many years to come. Hence, PSOs in various sectors will be required or encouraged to work in partnership with other public and private sector organizations in many different sectors. This may prove something of a culture shock to many PSOs who are more used to organizing and delivering services unilaterally, with a modicum of consultation with others.

ENHANCED PERFORMANCE IMPROVEMENT

The policy of promoting greater efficiency in resource use will, undoubtedly, continue under the present government and the CSR, referred to above, emphasizes the use of efficiency targets for key public services: for example, continuation of efficiency targets for the NHS and a new 2 per cent a year efficiency target for the police to focus resources on the front line fight against crime.

However, in future years it can be anticipated that performance improvement will go beyond issues of efficiency and economy and enter the more difficult area of effectiveness. Some examples of where this is already happening include the following:

- in education, the continued emphasis given to OFSTED inspections of school performance
- in the health sector there is considerable concern that a significant proportion of clinical practice is not effective in diagnosing or treating diseases, hence the government has created a National Institute for Clinical Excellence to promote improved effectiveness
- in the higher education sector, the Quality Assurance Agency has been created to bring together in one organization the functions of quality assurance in higher education
- in local government, the introduction of the 'best value' approach coupled with the role of the Audit Commission in the inspection of service delivery.

Improving effectiveness in public services often cuts across established professional practices and so the implementation of improvements will probably be a more difficult job for managers to undertake than the traditional approach of identifying efficiency and economy improvements.

ENHANCEMENT OF SERVICE PROFESSIONALS

Chapter 3 outlined the tension between service professionals and general managers in PSOs which has resulted in a shift in the balance of power between these two groups. There is already some evidence that government policy aims to shift the power balance away from general management and back towards the service professional. Two examples can be quoted, as outlined below.

HEALTH COMMISSIONING REFORMS

One of the key planks of the current government's NHS policies was the reform of the so-called internal market and the abolition of the general practice fundholder (GPFH) both of which they regarded as wasteful and divisive. One of the key complaints about the internal market was that much of decision making about service provision was undertaken by general managers with little involvement by health care professionals. Nurses, in particular, felt left out of the decision making process. Whatever the truth of these complaints, the government undertook a series of reforms designed to give doctors, nurses and other health professionals a greater say in health service decision making. Of particular note was the creation of hundreds of primary care groups (PCG) which gave health professionals a greater say in commissioning decisions concerning the range of health services to be provided by NHS Trusts.

PROFESSIONAL SUPER-GRADES

As already noted, one of the main complaints among service professionals was that the only way they could gain promotion and earn more money was to leave mainstream service provision and accept managerial posts. This complaint was most often heard from nurses who had to become nurse managers, and teachers who had to take school managerial posts to earn more money.

Hence the government has developed a policy which involves the creation of posts to be filled by exceptional service professionals who can earn substantially more money by remaining within direct service provision. The two examples of this policy which have been declared are:

- **Consultant nurses** – the creation of a number of highly-paid posts for nurses who remain in clinical practice. It is envisaged that such nurses will have waiting lists in the same way as medical consultants and will supervise the treatment regime of patients.
- **Super-teachers** – the creation of highly-paid classroom teacher posts for exceptional classroom teachers who have no wish to enter management.

There appear to be some problems with this particular policy, namely:

- It is not clear how many of these posts are to be created and whether the numbers involved will have any real impact on the perceived problem of lack of career progression.
- Even though it provides for greater remuneration for service professionals it does not resolve the problem of balance of power between managers and service professionals.
- The public sector needs good managers who understand service provision. This policy may be seen to downgrade the importance of management and may inhibit high-quality service professionals from accepting management posts.

- It is not clear how the creation of these posts will affect remuneration structures. For example, in schools, a major problem is the poor remuneration of middle grade teachers.

It is possible to be cynical and suggest that these changes are largely exercises in political rhetoric and will not have a significant overall impact in the various PSOs involved. In that case, the balance of power between service professionals and managers in those PSOs would not really change and many of the traditional tensions would remain and have to be resolved. Only time will tell if this is the case or not.

PUBLIC CONSULTATION

Consultation with the public has been a recurring theme in the public sector for many years. Although public consultation can generate some useful ideas and opinions, and is good for public relations purposes, many service professionals are rightly dubious about the emphasis placed on this issue for a number of reasons:

- In specialist areas such as medicine and education, the majority of the general public just do not have the level of technical expertise and information needed to make judgements about service provision. Some NHS organizations have conducted surveys of public opinion which have had extremely low response rates, unsound proposals and/or conflicting views and opinions.
- PSO managers and service professionals have to work within resource constraints. Consultation with the general public often leads to suggestions and proposals which are completely untenable on resource grounds and often raises public expectations to unreasonable levels.

However, it is not 'politically correct' to be dubious about the idea of public consultation and the current government seems to be as keen on the idea as the last government. Some examples of this include the following:

- The Best Value framework for local government requires local authorities to consult the populace about the types and quality of service provision in their area. Local authorities may make use of opinion polls, citizens' juries and so on to undertake this role.
- A new emphasis on patients' views in shaping the future of the NHS. As well as a national annual survey of patients' experience, NHS authorities will need to consider new ways of involving the public in changes to local health services, and options like opinion surveys and citizens' juries must be more widely used. Consultation documents will also need to be more user-friendly and more widely available.

The overall conclusion must be that consultation with the public will remain a key aspect of public sector management and may even increase in importance in years to come.

CHAPTER ELEVEN

Implications for Public Sector Management

Chapter 3 of this book summarized the various trends which occurred over the period 1979–97 and the chapters in Part II of the book described how these policy trends had impacted on the practice of public sector management. Chapter 10 considered in some depth a wide range of trends impacting on the UK public sector now, and likely to impact in the foreseeable future. These trends covered both government policies and factors external to government. In this chapter consideration is given to the way in which these trends are likely to impact on the public sector and its management practices. It must be emphasized, however, that this is not an exact science and there is a considerable degree of crystal-ball gazing here, and the analysis undertaken must be viewed with a considerable degree of caution. In particular, this analysis covers the impact on:

- public sector configuration
- internal organization and culture of PSOs
- public sector management approaches
- public sector management skills.

PUBLIC SECTOR CONFIGURATION

The first issue under this heading concerns the public–private mix. The present government has plans for further privatizations of PSOs (such as the London Underground). Coupling this with its enthusiasm for extending the PFI and the development of public–private partnerships, it seems likely that the involvement of the private sector in service delivery will continue to increase. Thus, it seems that there will need to be an increasing focus by PSOs on matters of policy, funding and contract monitoring.

The second issue concerns the numbers and sizes of remaining PSOs. The policy of merging NHS Trusts has already been mentioned and there is also a likelihood of merging more health authorities. Hence, in the NHS a substantial reduction in the number of discrete organizations can be anticipated. Similarly, in the further education sector (and possibly the higher education sector) the pressures for merger exist, and once again a substantial reduction in the numbers of FE institutions can be anticipated. The corollary of this is that in both further education and the NHS the individual organizations will be larger than at present. Also, mergers of some quangos are to take place, such as the merger of the Further Education Funding Council and TECs to form the Learning and Skills Councils.

Some other types of merger are a possibility. For example, there could be a reduction in the numbers of police authorities and probation committees through merger. However, government policies seem to be limited to organizational integration rather than service integration. For example, it does not now seem likely that there will be any merger of police, prison and probation services as part of a more integrated criminal justice system.

Finally, there is the issue of government departments. Arguments have been made that in the modern age, and with Britain an integral part of the EU, the current departmental structure of government is outmoded. Some mergers have already taken place, such as the merger of education and employment into one department. However, there are other possibilities. For example, it has been suggested that in this day and age, agriculture no longer deserves to be an individual government department and its functions could be absorbed by, for example, the Department of Trade and Industry. Similarly, there is a case for re-merging the Foreign Office and the Department for International Development. Finally, in the context of devolution, the question of the continued existence of the Wales and Scotland Offices must be questioned.

In Wales and Scotland the existence of the Assembly and the Scottish Parliament give further opportunity for reform. It seems at least possible that in a few years' time the Assembly and Parliament may remove responsibility for strategically-important services such as education and social services from local authorities, and undertake direct provision. This may then fuel another round of local government restructuring.

INTERNAL ORGANIZATION AND CULTURE

There are a number of trends in the internal organization and culture of PSOs which may take place in the years ahead and which are discussed below. To some extent, some of these are just continuations of past trends, while others may represent distinct changes from the past. As such, the degree of organizational resistance which would be associated with the latter group of changes means that there is, at least, some doubt as to whether they will actually occur to any great extent. The following are seen as important:

- delegation of decision making
- enhanced risk taking
- partnership approach
- consumer-orientation.

DELEGATION OF DECISION MAKING

In Chapter 3 the trend of increased managerial delegation in PSOs was noted. Although this process of delegation has been undertaken quite strongly in some types of PSO, in other types it has been much more patchy and thus there is considerable scope for further delegation. Further delegation is probably a strong future trend, but the choice of whether to delegate or not depends on a number of local factors and delegation should not be thought of as being good in all circumstances. Thus, one should always consider the pros and cons of delegation, and the factors that should be identified and evaluated within the organization before extending such delegation still further.

In many situations this process of delegation will involve greater delegation to service professionals as well as to general managers. However, there is an important point here. Although service professionals may be given greater resource autonomy, in terms of deciding how to use available funds and human resources, their professional autonomy may be more constrained than it has been in the past. Thus professional decisions about the delivery of services, over which service professionals, traditionally, had much discretion may, in future, be strongly constrained by a framework of plans and protocols for each particular profession. An example of this is the development of clinical protocols for application in the medical profession concerning the approaches to be applied in relation to various clinical conditions.

ENHANCED RISK TAKING

A commonly-held view about public sector managers is that they tend to play safe and are averse to any form of risk taking. Although the extent to which this is the case may be a caricature, there is evidently some truth in the assertion. There are probably many reasons for this including the following possibilities:

- the recruitment of risk-averse employees
- the existence of a blame culture with little reward for risk taking
- the political environment in which the public sector operates
- the existence of parliamentary scrutiny such as that from the Public Accounts Committee.

It has been argued that following the introduction of policies relating to privatization, competition, managerial delegation and so on, the existence of this risk-averse culture among public sector managers is perhaps the most important barrier to the further improvement of public services. Clearly, the present government sees this as important, and has made a number of policy pronouncements aimed at encouraging greater risk taking in the public sector, including those of external (outside the public sector) recruitment, training and the introduction of incentives.

There must, however, be a considerable degree of scepticism as to whether such policies will be successful, given the context in which they are being applied. Firstly, they have to overcome the existing risk-averse culture which has existed in the public sector for many decades. Secondly, they have to be applied in an environment where PSOs and individual public sector managers are often pilloried out of all proportion by parliamentary and press scrutiny, for failings which have taken place in their organization. For such policies, aimed at improving public sector risk taking, to be effective it is essential for Parliament, the press and the general public to take a balanced view of the public sector and to accept that there will inevitably be some failings (which need to be remedied) but these failings will usually be vastly outweighed by successes obtained elsewhere.

PARTNERSHIP APPROACH

Earlier chapters of this book have outlined developments which require PSOs to work in collaboration with other public and private sector organizations. Some examples of these include:

- the extension of public–private partnerships
- the creation of education and health action zones
- the pressure for 'joined-up government' coming out of the White Paper entitled 'Modernizing Government'.

Furthermore, aside from these central pressures there may be very good economic reasons why PSOs should work collaboratively with other organizations, such as accessing specialist resources and networks or economies of scale. Hence a key trend for the future must be the need for PSOs to work collaboratively and in partnership with other public and private sector organizations. This will pose challenges which are discussed in the next section.

CONSUMER-ORIENTATION

In Chapter 3 the trend towards increased consumer responsiveness from PSOs was discussed, and developments such as the Citizen's Charter mentioned. All the signs from government policy and trends in society suggest that in future years PSOs will need to become even more consumer-oriented than they have been in recent years. This trend is exemplified by the dissemination of the Best Value approach throughout the public sector. The Best Value approach is based around four main themes (the '4C's) with one of these being *consultation* with the general public about the services being provided. This process of consultation may be undertaken in any number of ways, including public opinion surveys, focus groups or consumer panels.

PSO MANAGERIAL APPROACHES

The last two decades have seen substantial change in the structure, organization and method of working in PSOs. As a consequence, the managerial approaches applied in PSOs also changed substantially. If one takes account of definite and possible future trends in policy and external factors, identified in the previous chapter, one can speculate as to the way in which these managerial approaches in PSOs might change in the years ahead.

To a large extent it is a case of more of the same, since it would appear that much of existing managerial practice in PSOs is likely to continue into the future. However, it is equally likely that this existing practice will need to:

- be improved and extended
- be amended in some way.

Also, there are a few cases where there may need to be some specific new developments in managerial practices. However, there seems no likelihood of public sector managerial practice going into reverse and returning to the pattern which existed prior to 1979. Some specific aspects of future managerial practice are discussed below, but it must be emphasized that this is very speculative and no firm conclusions can be drawn at this point in time.

STRATEGIC ORIENTATION

The last twenty years saw strategic planning and strategic development become of increasing importance in PSOs. Consequently, public sector managers have had to become much more strategically-oriented than was previously the case. As noted in Chapter 3, this has come about largely as a consequence of resource pressures coupled with the drive for performance improvement and the delegation of decision making. There is nothing to suggest that strategic planning will become any less important in the future and, if anything, it will be of increasing importance because of the ongoing pressures that PSOs are likely to face. There may, however, be subtle changes of emphasis in public sector strategic planning:

- **Business planning** – the shift from competition to collaboration discussed in Chapter 10 will probably mean some changes in rhetoric and substance in the process of business planning. The decline in the importance of competition will mean a lesser emphasis on looking at the market and competitive activity within the market. Possibly the term 'business planning' will go out of fashion. However, even in the absence of competitive pressures it is vital that the strategic planning process remains outward-looking, with the aim of delivering services that meet public needs and aspirations.
- **Cross-sectoral planning** – the emphasis on several PSOs in the same sector and in different sectors working together to improve services. This implies that in future there will be a need for PSOs to work together to prepare appropriate strategies and to harmonize their own individual strategies.

EFFECTIVE RESOURCE MANAGEMENT

Linked to the above will be the need for more effective management of the resources available to PSOs. This will involve a greater number of managers, and service professionals in issues of resource management particularly in relation to finance and human resources.

With regard to financial management, where this used to be the province of the finance professional the process of delegated decision making has meant that managers and service professionals have had to get involved in various aspects of financial management and develop appropriate skills. Some examples of this include:

- hospital consultants acting as clinical directors having to manage the finances of their particular specialty
- deans of faculty and heads of department having to manage budgets for their faculty or department
- head teachers in grant-maintained schools having to manage the finances of the school
- civil servants in government departments having to manage budgets.

With regard to HRM, the changes taking place in the public sector, and likely to take place in future years, suggest that HRM is perhaps the biggest challenge facing PSOs and their managers and service professionals. There are three main aspects to this which should be emphasized:

- **Performance review** – the need to develop skills in performance assessment to cope with the expansion of performance review processes referred to below.
- **Training and development** – the need to develop programmes of T&D to maintain staff skills and programmes of retraining for those staff whose jobs have been made redundant through technological development. The culture of the public sector suggests that retraining is preferable to mass redundancy.
- **Change management** – the need to design and implement change management programmes to deal with the continuously changing public sector environment referred to below.

In spite of complaints by some service professionals that involvement in resource management issues mean they are getting involved in 'administrative' tasks to the detriment of service provision, there is no going back. The ongoing resource pressures on the public sector mean that service professionals can no longer expect to be able to provide services in a resource vacuum.

DEMONSTRABLE RESULTS

Whereas the traditional image of a public servant was that of a bureaucrat undertaking procedures, strictly, according to some form of rule book, the modern public sector manager is expected to be results-oriented. In recent years we have seen the proliferation throughout the public sector of systems of performance review of individual managers. These required specific objectives to be set for individual PSO managers and for their achievements against those objectives to be reviewed during and at the end of the year. The success or otherwise of managers in achieving those objectives might determine the training requirements of the manager and might impact on their future career progression. In addition, where a PSO had implemented some form of performance related pay, the results achieved by a manager could impact on their remuneration.

It seems likely that this emphasis on results and the application of performance review is likely to develop further in the public sector. Moreover, it is likely to spread further into service professional areas as well as traditional managerial areas.

ENTREPRENEURIAL

To a large extent PSO managers have had to become more entrepreneurial than was traditionally the case twenty years ago. Two factors which have encouraged this entrepreneurialism are:

- **Market testing** – where units of the public sector were subject to market testing the managers of those units had to be entrepreneurial about matters such as searching for new markets, delivering new types of services and identifying different ways of delivering services.
- **Income generation** – many PSOs have undertaken large programmes of external income generation. Usually this income generation activity could be classified into four types of activity:

  - sale of spare capacity in the PSO to external parties (for example spare laundry capacity in a hospital)
  - sale of specialist skills (for example consultancy services provided by an HE or FE college)
  - sponsorship or advertising (for example hospital advertisement boards)
  - sale of surplus land or buildings.

  Although, to some extent, such levels of income generation are to be commended, since they supplement public sources of funding, there are dangers. Too often, PSO managers 'take their eye off the ball' and allow issues of income generation to divert their attention from the main business of delivering public services.

These pressures are likely to continue into the future and there will be a continuing need for PSO managers to be entrepreneurial. The increasing role of the PFI will reinforce this.

IT EMPHASIS

In Chapter 9 the future role of IT in transforming both the organization of PSOs and their service delivery methods was emphasized. As mentioned in Chapter 10, the development of IT was one of the key themes of the White Paper 'Modernizing Government' and thus it is inevitable that the role of IT in PSOs will continue to expand at a very high rate. There are two main implications to this:

- An increasing role for IT in administrative aspects of PSOs, thus requiring the increasing involvement of general managers.
- An increasing role for IT in service delivery and an increasing involvement by service professionals with IT. Some examples of the latter might be:

  - The introduction of computers into the school classroom, providing the classroom teacher with an information source and a tool. Some examples might include the direct input of data on pupil performance and pupil attendance.
  - The use by doctors of computers to display diagnostic information. Instead of having X-ray images sent from the medical records department to the doctor's clinic (with the usual risks of delay and loss), these images will be stored in digital format on a main server and the doctor can summon and display the images on the computer screen. The system will also permit the doctor to undertake some image enhancement, thus assisting the diagnostic task.

The result of this is that, in future, there are very few general managers or service professional staff who can avoid working with IT. However, in many PSOs the IT revolution still has a long way to go and this poses huge challenges for the future.

PARTNERSHIP WORKING

Earlier in this chapter, the trend towards increased partnership working was discussed. Many PSOs have rarely worked in true partnerships with other organizations, since the partnership model applied has often been one of the dominant organization undertaking a limited amount of consultation with other PSOs and private and voluntary organizations but then undertaking the majority of service delivery unilaterally. True partnership means a more equal involvement in the planning and delivery of services by all partners. Hence, PSOs will need to develop new approaches to a number of tasks including the following:

- **joint strategic planning** – the need for greater co-ordination of strategic planning was discussed earlier in this chapter
- **operational co-ordination** – the need for improved co-ordination at the operational level in the planning and delivery of services; historically, this has not always been good
- **accountability arrangements** – the partnership approach can easily diffuse accountability and hence revised accountability mechanisms need to be developed.

EFFECTIVE CHANGE MANAGEMENT

It was noted in Chapter 3 that the public sector has had to undergo a significant period of organizational and cultural change in recent years. It was also commented that many still anticipate a return to organizational stability. However, if one considers some of the trends taking place such as PFI, privatization, merger and partnerships then it is clear that there is nothing to suggest that such stability will be forthcoming. Thus, PSOs will continue to face an environment of organizational change, possibly on a continual basis, and will face the well-known barriers and difficulties that all organizations face when undergoing change. Hence the management of change will, undoubtedly, continue to be a key aspect of public sector management for the future.

PUBLIC FACING

Earlier in this section the emphasis on increased consumer orientation was discussed. Whether in terms of market research, assessment of quality or measurement of consumer satisfaction, consulting the public and the users of services will clearly be a major issue for the future. Hence PSOs will need to become more skilled and sophisticated with regard to techniques of market research, consumer assessment and so on.

Furthermore, effective presentation of policy is one of the key themes of the present government and this will probably be the case with all future governments. The need for communication with the public to be 'on-message' is emphasized almost daily. It can be anticipated that this emphasis will spread throughout the whole of the public sector, and PSOs will need to be increasingly adept at matters of public relations.

COMPETENCY FRAMEWORK FOR PSO MANAGERS

Clearly, the changes which took place in the 1980s and 1990s had a profound effect on public sector managers. New managerial skills were identified and new managerial training approaches were implemented. However, having undergone such changes it would now be folly for public sector managers to think that the situation has now stabilized and that they can rest on their laurels. The changes in the policies of the present government are likely to lead to public sector managers requiring new or additional skills yet again. Thus, they will need to consider and evaluate the skills they will need, their attitudes and their approaches to career development and career planning.

In this section the term 'managerial competencies' has been used to describe the broader range of attributes that PSO managers are likely to require in the years to come. The term 'competencies' embodies more than just managerial knowledge but incorporate other attributes, as illustrated in Figure 45.

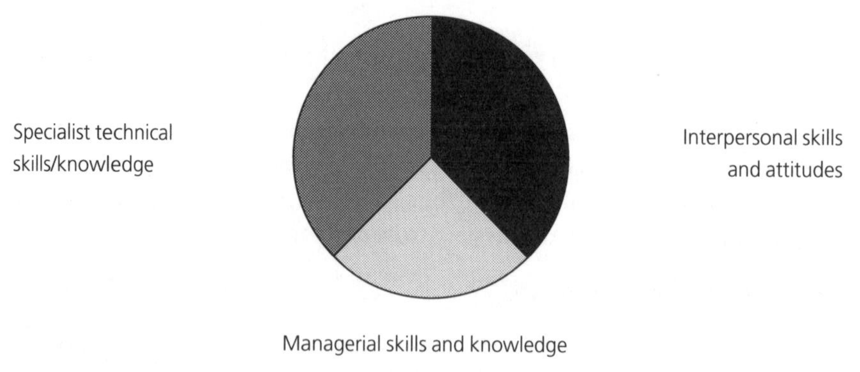

Figure 45 Framework of competencies for PSO managers

SPECIALIST TECHNICAL SKILLS AND KNOWLEDGE

Most employees in the public sector will have some specialist area of expertise. This could be in the area of service delivery (such as teaching or nursing) or some specialist management area such as finance, marketing or IT. Each and every employee will have an individual and professional responsibility to maintain their level of technical skills and knowledge in that specific area.

MANAGERIAL SKILLS AND KNOWLEDGE

Whatever their specific area of expertise, all managers in PSOs , whether they are senior service professionals or they hold posts in administrative support areas, will need a basic knowledge and understanding in the various aspects of management. The preceding sections of this chapter, and previous chapters, indicate that an understanding of the basic principles and application of the following will be of particular importance in future years:

- purpose and techniques of strategic planning
- main techniques of financial management
- main techniques of human resource management
- the scope and application of IT
- main techniques of change management
- main techniques of marketing
- main techniques of public relations
- management of contracted-out services.

Thus, PSO managers and service professionals will need to develop and maintain their skills in these areas.

INTERPERSONAL SKILLS AND ATTITUDES

In addition to specific specialist and managerial skills, PSO managers and professional staff will, in the future, have to exhibit certain interpersonal skills and attitudes. These include:

- effective team working and team leadership, particularly in relation to cross-sectoral working
- knowledge of the contribution to service provision of other agencies
- an entrepreneurial and commercial outlook
- a focus on achieving demonstrable results
- innovation and creativity in relation to methods of service provision
- the motivation of employees
- the ability to foster organizational change
- effective communication to other employees, consumers and the public at large.

In conclusion, therefore, it is important to emphasize the need to develop and maintain skills in relation to management practice, and adequate interpersonal skills and attitudes, and these must be in addition to specific technical skills which will vary from job to job.

Bibliography

In this book no attempt has been made to give large numbers of detailed references. The main reason for this is that the proliferation, in recent years, of academic and professional journals on management issues leaves one with great doubts about the quality of much of the content. In this situation there are dangers in quoting references relating to published research where there is no evidence as to the quality of the research undertaken. Academic publications sometimes have too much of a tendency to quote the work of other authors to support the author's own views, without having any firm information on the robustness of the work referred to.

Consequently, all I have done is to list a relatively small number of books to which the interested reader may turn. These are:

CCTA, *BPR in the Public Sector*, GSO 1994

CCTA, *Managing Contracts for IS/IT Services*, GSO 1994

D. Chapman and D. Cowdell, *New Public Sector Marketing*, FT Management 1996

H.M. Coombs and D.E. Jenkins, *Public Sector Financial Management*, Thomson Business Press 1994

D. Farnham and S. Horton (eds), *Managing the New Public Services*, Macmillan 1996

L. Gaster, *Quality in Public Services*, Open University Press 1995

R. Jones and M. Pendlebury, *Public Sector Accounting*, FT Management 1995

P. Joyce, *Strategic Management in the Public Sector*, Open University Press 1999

J.E. Pynes, *Human Resources Management for Public and Not for Profit Organizations*, Jossey-Bass Inc. 1997

W. Robson, *Strategic Management and Information Systems*, FT Publishing 1997

Index

Best Practice Creativity

Peter Cook

The ability to generate new products and services is emerging as one of the few sources of competitive advantage. There is no shortage of books on personal creativity or collections of creativity techniques. What makes Peter Cook's approach unique is its strategic perspective. He is concerned with ways of developing organizations where creativity is valued and systematically encouraged.

Drawing on both the published literature and the experience of a wide range of organizations, he:

- describes methods of promoting creativity in organizations
- summarizes established concepts and practices on the subject
- examines the role of leadership in organizational creativity
- looks at organizational structure as a source of creativity
- sets out principles for the design of problem-solving processes
- presents a critical guide to creativity techniques.

Throughout the text there are 'activities' to help readers identify and analyse potential improvements in their workplace, and the book concludes with '101 ideas for increasing organizational creativity'.

In a world where turbulence is the norm, 'business as usual' is probably the route to extinction. For any executive or functional manager determined to find 'a better way', Peter Cook's stimulating and practical book will repay careful study.

Gower

The BrainSmart Leader

Tony Buzan, Tony Dottino and Richard Israel

• Why do so many organizations find it difficult to use teamworking?
• Why do change programmes fail so often?
• How can organizations process information more effectively?
• What does a modern manager need to do to ensure success?

These and other important business issues are dealt with in this challenging book by Mind expert Tony Buzan and his American colleagues, Tony Dottino and Richard Israel. To illustrate their ideas they introduce the concept of the BrainSmart Leader - a corporate change agent who has learned how to harness the awesome capacity of the human brain.

The authors' aim is to help you to become a catalyst for productive change. 'We want you to understand,' they say, 'ways of accessing both your own creativity and intelligence and those of others in your organization.'

The book opens with a quiz designed to identify your existing strengths and weaknesses and direct you to the corresponding chapters. It goes on to explore, in turn, the key elements of effective leadership, with the aid of studies of successful BrainSmart Leaders, exercises, quizzes, Mind Maps® and practical guidance for applying the ideas described. Working through the text and the related material will equip you with the mental technology to apply your creativity to maximum effect. The result should be a dramatic improvement in your own performance and that of your organization.

Gower

Bridging the Performance Gap

Trevor J Bentley

Does your organization suffer from 'the performance gap'? The chances are that you have managers and staff who - on paper at least - have all of the competencies and experience to do a really good job. Why is it then that some of them never seem to fulfil their true potential?

The fact is that we all need to be competent to perform but competency is no guarantee of a successful outcome. *Bridging the Performance Gap* is a practical guide to effective performance management that enables you to:

- identify the missing ingredients in an individual's performance
- measure the gap between performance and potential
- develop skills, techniques and systems to: encourage learning; support personal development; review, recognize and reward performance improvement.

Trevor Bentley shows you how to release the latent potential of everyone within your organization through a process of encouragement and support that relies on bringing a human TOUCH (Trust, Openness, Understanding, Consideration, Honesty) to everything that they do. *Bridging the Performance Gap* offers a complete and effective strategy for making this work for the benefit of you, your people, and your organization.

Gower

Ethics at Work

Bob Kelley

Do you buy your raw materials where they're cheapest - even when they are produced by Third-World workers in conditions that would be illegal in your own country?

You're negotiating with a government department in a developing country: to secure the contract that will safeguard your company and your workforce, do you pay the customary 'commission' to the minister responsible?

When recruiting staff in Britain it isn't unlawful to discriminate on the grounds of religion - but is it right?

It's hardly possible to operate in the business world without encountering ethical dilemmas. Yet few companies pause to work out a set of policies and a way to apply them in its day-to-day dealings. In this timely book Bob Kelley identifies some of the underlying questions, explores possible answers and describes recent attempts to control corporate conduct.

Part I discusses ethical behaviour, including the attitudes found in various different cultures, and explains why the subject has risen so high up the current business agenda. Part II looks at the issues from the point of view of each of the five 'stakeholders' involved - owners, employees, customers, suppliers, and the community. Part III examines some of the methods used to regulate business, indicates some of the practical implications and speculates briefly about the future. The book concludes with a set of appendices containing the Nolan recommendations, the Institute of Management's guidelines, and details of relevant organizations.

Bob Kelley's book will be invaluable to every manager seeking guidance in this important and sensitive area.

Gower

The Excellent Manager's Business Library

Philip Holden

Philip Holden's book puts the distilled wisdom of the world's leading business writers at your fingertips. Taking fifteen issues in turn - from corporate culture to personal development - he examines the most important publications, providing for each of them a short biography of the author, a summary of the book, five brief quotations, five 'lessons for managers', a glossary and a critical review. In addition there are summaries of, or references to, related books and articles.

The Excellent Manager's Business Library concludes with a set of indexes designed to make it a multi-purpose tool. For example, if you need a striking phrase to spice up a speech, look at the index to quotations and see what Drucker or Harvey-Jones had to say on the subject. If you're writing a paper on creativity, the subject index will lead you to summaries of the key publications in the field. Or you can consult the author index to track the views of someone like Charles Handy across a range of topics.

For managers, consultants, academics and students, this concise yet comprehensive overview of business writing represents a powerful resource.

Gower

The Excellent Manager's Companion

Philip Holden

This is for every manager who aspires to excellence in everything they do, but wonders how they'll ever find the time ...

With *The Excellent Manager's Companion* in your desk drawer, you'll be equipped with succinct guidance on today's most talked-about business issues. And you'll be able to pepper your conversation with pertinent quotations, and even know which books to turn to when you really do need more detailed guidance on a specific topic.

Twenty-one chapters look at key topics, ranging from corporate culture to customer orientation, and from innovation to influencing people. Each chapter is organized around standard sections, which makes 'dipping' into the book quick, easy, and rewarding.

Sections are:

- questions for self-analysis
- a step-by-step guide to best practice
- the ten 'don'ts'
- pertinent quotations
- summaries of key books and articles
- a case study
- a glossary of terms.

Philip Holden's lively *Companion* combines expertise with entertainment, with a supporting cast that ranges from Walt Disney to Confucius, and from Dilbert to Drucker. This book is guaranteed to appeal to busy managers in all sectors.

The Gower Handbook of Management

Fourth Edition

Edited by Dennis Lock

'If you have only one management book on your shelf, this must be the one.'

Dennis Lock recalls launching the first edition in 1983 with this aim in mind. It has remained the guiding principle behind subsequent editions, and today *The Gower Handbook of Management* is widely regarded as a manager's bible: an authoritative, gimmick-free and practical guide to best practice in management. By covering the broadest possible range of subjects, this *Handbook* replicates in book form a forum in which managers can meet experts from a range of professional disciplines.

The new edition features:

- 65 expert contributors - many of them practising managers and all of them recognized authorities in their field;
- many new contributors: over one-third are new to this edition;
- 72 chapters, of which half are completely new;
- 20 chapters on subjects new to this edition; and
- a brand new design and larger format.

The Gower Handbook of Management has received many plaudits during its distinguished career, summed up in the following review from *Director*:

'... packed with information which can be used either as a reference work on a specific problem or as a guide to an entire operation. In a short review one can touch only lightly on the richness and excellence of this book, which well deserves a place on any executive bookshelf.'

Gower

Gower Handbook of Teamworking

Edited by Roger Stewart

Team-based organizations are now the norm, and interest in how they function continues to grow. There is no shortage of published material on teamworking. Most of it, however, is concerned with one particular aspect, such as organizational structure or behavioural psychology. This *Handbook* covers the entire spectrum in a single volume. Its 30 contributors have been carefully selected to represent a variety of backgrounds and viewpoints. What they have in common is an acknowledged expertise and a practical approach.

The *Gower Handbook of Teamworking* is in four Parts. The first Part looks at teams in an organizational context. It examines the different types of structure, and the problems and benefits associated with each. Part II explores the nature of teams, including team processes, and team and individual behaviour. Part III deals with the design, building and management of teams, including the relevant training. The final Part shows how modern technology can be applied to improve team performance.

The result is a book that will be of immense value to anyone involved in leading, training or studying teams in the workplace.

Gower

Harnessing the Unicorn

How to Create Opportunity and Manage Risk

Pat O'Reilly

Jim Hallam suffers a daily diet of blame and shame for failed targets and missed deadlines; an irritating boss, irrational staff and irate customers; a backlog of jobs, all of which were either emergencies, panics or mad crises. He has no effective solution - hardly surprising, because he is treating opportunities as if they are simply risks with attractive outcomes. With the help and guidance of his colleague, Larry Farlow, Jim begins to understand and implement processes that enable him to break free from his troubles. He learns how to spot, to create and to manage opportunities, be they business or career, and all within his high risk, change-orientated environment.

Harnessing the Unicorn is for any project manager, change agent, team leader, systems and product developer who needs to identify and exploit opportunities and, at the same time, to manage risk and uncertainty. Pat O'Reilly has written a unique book on a subject, opportunity management, which many know is important but few actually seize upon. Written as a novel but incorporating real case studies and helpful checklists, this book is the first to look at opportunity and to differentiate it from risk.

In our fast-paced, ever-changing and demanding world, *Harnessing the Unicorn* offers a refreshing way to break out of our self-imposed box.

Gower

New Leadership for Women and Men

Building an Inclusive Organization

Michael Simmons

What are the key attributes of successful leaders in today's organization? The answer to this question is of course hotly debated. But Michael Simmons' ground-breaking book is the first to place the development of a new leadership for women and men at the heart of the argument. In particular, it is the first to focus on the benefits of helping leaders to overcome the negative effects of gender conditioning on the quality of their leadership.

The author proposes that leaders must transform their organizations by learning how to manage a turbulent environment, increase productivity and quality, and build an 'inclusive organization'. Achieving these aims requires that everyone is involved in planning the future direction of the enterprise and contributes to its continual improvement. But gender conditioning leads many managers to put up barriers to the full involvement of all their people. Transformation means reaching beyond equality to an organization where boundaries and limitations are not placed upon anyone. It needs a new kind of leadership capable of harnessing the intelligence, creativity and initiative of people at all levels, especially those who have traditionally been excluded.

This timely book provides much more than a searching analysis of women and men's leadership. Using real-life examples and case studies, it sets out strategies, programmes and techniques for improving organizational performance, and describes in detail the type of training needed. In short, it is a book designed to inspire not just thought but action.

Profiting from Diversity

Trevor Bentley and Susan Clayton

Trevor Bentley and Susan Clayton offer a refreshing and innovative approach to recognizing and embracing diversity within your organization. Diversity has for too long been confused with, and compromised by, arguments for equal opportunities: this book makes the case for diversity as distinct and separate. It tackles the subject head-on, demonstrating the link between diversity and the bottom line and helping you to develop the systems, attitudes and policies that form the basis of a culture of diversity.

This is an ideas book, which introduces the concepts of 'diversity tolerance', 'unity' and 'appropriate diversity', and encourages the reader to embrace new paradigms. It is also a pragmatic how to book, which provides techniques and guidance for intervening on a one-to-one basis, with small teams or in large systems, to help people throughout the organization understand and adopt new ways of thinking.

Profiting from Diversity provides team leaders, trainers and developers, consultants, and anyone concerned with drawing on and expanding the potential of the workforce, with a compelling blueprint for discovering and developing the diversity that is present in any group of people.

Gower

Superboss 2

The New A-Z of Managing People Successfully

David Freemantle

You too can be a Superboss! David Freemantle will persuade you that every manager can take action today to become a Superboss. In this entertaining book, a revised and updated version of a worldwide bestseller, he describes more than 130 effective ways of managing people.

Amusing, stimulating and often provocative, *Superboss 2* is a treasure trove of practical advice for anyone aspiring to managerial excellence.

Gower